THE ITALIAN JOURNALIST

The Italian Journalist

WILLIAM E. PORTER

ANN ARBOR

The University of Michigan Press

Copyright © by The University of Michigan 1983
All rights reserved
Published in the United States of America by
The University of Michigan Press and simultaneously
in Rexdale, Canada, by John Wiley & Sons Canada, Limited
Manufactured in the United States of America

1986   1985   1984   1983   5   4   3   2   1

Library of Congress Cataloging in Publication Data

Porter, William Earl, 1918–
  The Italian journalist.

  Includes bibliographical references and index.
  1. Journalism—Italy. I. Title.
PN5244.P67   1983   075   82-20146
ISBN 0-472-10028-9

Acknowledgments

A study such as this involves time, effort, and financial support. The last of these, in a way, is the first consideration; therefore I want to thank first the Howard R. Marsh Center for the Study of Journalistic Performance at the University of Michigan, which provided funds for travel and materials; and its administrator at that time, Professor Peter Clarke, then head of the Department of Communication at the university.

Before the establishment of the Marsh Center, this project was supported by a grant from the university's Horace H. Rackham School of Graduate Studies, to which I give my thanks. Before that, there was the award from the Fulbright program for international exchange which started it all. I was a lecturer in journalism at the University of Rome in 1952; it was the beginning of a continuing attachment to Italy and of a lasting friendship with Cipriana Scelba, who has been connected with the administration of the program since its beginning. She has helped with this study in many ways. I thank her warmly.

As the text indicates, much of the substance of the book came from interviews with Italian journalists over the decade. Some are identified in the text, but most are not. There are no attributed quotes in the text that might embarrass the people who made them; that is by design. I do want to identify, however, three Italian professionals who were particularly helpful: Felice La Rocca, Edoardo Magri, and Gianni Fusato.

Three other collaborators in Italy made major contributions. Domenico De Gregorio, a teacher and writer, translated my university lectures that first year and rehearsed me in their presentation. We have remained friends, and he has contributed to several aspects of this book.

Angelo Del Boca, author of a major study of the Italian press, who is now a professor of history at the University of Turin, made contributions throughout. During the decade that work on the project was underway, he was one of two managing editors of *Il Giorno* in Milan; trips to Italy generally began with a visit to Del Boca, and when the manuscript was finished he gave it a painstaking review.

The manuscript was also read by Bruno Scarfi, of the press section of the United States embassy in Rome, whose knowledge of the Italian journalistic establishment, particularly that of the capital, was invaluable.

Three American journalists also provided a great deal of help. When the research process began, the late Allan Jacks was the Associated Press bureau chief in Rome. He was succeeded by Dennis Redmont. Jacks was, and Redmont is, a marvelous negation of the stereotype of the insensitive and unapologetically ignorant foreign correspondent. The late Stan Swinton, vice-president for world services of the Associated Press and once Roman bureau chief himself, opened many doors.

All these Italians and semi-Italians were helpful not only through the information and access that they provided, but as advisers. That makes particularly important the disclaimer that invariably appears in acknowledgments. The judgments and generalizations in the text are entirely mine, and I suspect some of them appear inaccurate to the people with whom I conferred most. The reader who also finds them suspect should in no way hold responsible the people named above.

Among my academic colleagues, Raymond Grew and Charles Eisendrath of the University of Michigan read early drafts and made many helpful suggestions; Sidney Tarrow of Cornell University read the final version and saved me from sin many times. Giovanni Bechelloni, of the Consiglio Italiano di Scienza Sociale, provided useful material.

Two of my students in the communication department also were of great assistance. Jean-Richard Cojuc has shared my interest in Italy and Italian journalism for several years and provided help as well as reinforcement. My translations from Italian were checked, and sometimes touched up, by Lavinia Theodoli.

I also owe thanks to several institutions in addition to the Howard R. Marsh Center. The American Enterprise Institute for Public Policy Research commissioned me to do studies of the media in the Italian election campaigns of 1976 and 1979; some of that material appears here in somewhat different form. The staff of the national office of the Order of Journalists in Rome was generous, friendly—and quick—when I called on them for help; so was the press section of the Italian embassy in Washington, D.C. And I owe the staff of the University of Michigan Press praise for careful editorial work at a time when it seems to be otherwise disappearing from American publishing.

Finally, I thank my wife Lois, who not only is an editor and consultant, but who also understands why I feel so strong a tie to Italy; she feels it, too.

Introduction

This book is intended to provide a picture of the profession of journalist in Italy during the 1970s. It gives particular attention to the movement that attempted to introduce some reforms both within the profession and within the mass communication business, a movement that grew out of the trade union of professional journalists, rising about the beginning of the decade and drifting into quiescence toward its end.

This is not to say the reform accomplished nothing, but rather that the activist spirit went out of it. Some of its objectives were accomplished, and Italian journalism now shows their impress. But the importance of the reform movement goes well beyond its effect upon Italian journalists and journalism. Some issues fundamental to the profession in every country received not only careful intellectual scrutiny, but actual trial in the newsroom: for example, the journalist's role in the making of editorial policy; in the hiring, dismissing, and professional advancement of his or her colleagues; in the relationship between the publication that employs him or her and the government; in the maintenance or disestablishment of the system of licensing journalists; in the business of defining, in operational and contractual terms, the whole concept of professionalism. In dealing concretely with such concerns, Italian journalists in the 1970s were, I would contend, ahead of their time, pathfinders for professionals in countries where confrontation of such issues is eventually certain. What went on in Italian journalism during the decade had significant meaning for journalists in countries, including the United States, whose journalism generally is considered "better" than Italy's.

Since it is necessary to put the reform movement in perspective, this book traces in detail the history of the statutory Order of Journalists in Italy and the *Federazione Nazionale della Stampa Italiana* (FNSI, "National Federation of the Italian Press"), the national trade union that negotiates the labor contract for all members of the profession. It examines the process through which the aspirant attains full professional status; it documents the rise and diminution of the reform movement, and offers some comparisons of the ways British, American, and Italian journalists see their jobs, their futures, and their societal roles.

Incidental to all this it also provides something of a survey of the Italian press during the period, although, since it concentrates upon a few publications that were generally considered the nation's best or were for some other reasons particularly pertinent to the study, the survey is not comprehensive.

Before the discussion can move to something more detailed and systematic, a certain amount of term defining and background explanation seems necessary.

To begin, there is the matter of translation from the Italian. My original intention was to leave such things as job titles in that language, on the predictable academic grounds that, after all, there are no real equivalents. As a matter of fact, with a few exceptions which will be noted below, the terms commonly used in American journalism serve quite well.

The Italian word *direttore,* for example, is flexible within the same general boundaries of meaning as the U.S. *editor.* Some American editors maintain close control of most elements of the paper or the newscasts; others concern themselves largely with policy matters and decisions that subordinates cannot make. The same is true of Italian papers. All editors, in both countries, are the owners' men, but the extent to which they operate independently varies widely.

One special category of direttore, however, has no U.S. equivalent, and is a creation of Italian press law. Government authority of one sort or another has tried to bring pressure on those who issue publications ever since the invention of writing. For centuries, suppression and punishment were directed at printers, not only because most early publishers were printers, but because they had heavy equipment and could not easily escape. Printers continued to be the first targets even if they had no editorial function at all, however, and it was 1848 before the Albertine edict (issued by and named for Carlo Alberto, king of Sardinia) put an end to such harassment by separating the printer from responsibility for content. As a substitute, the edict created the requirement that each publication have a *direttore responsabile*—the designated arrestee and defendant, in effect. Most other European countries have adopted the device, and the United States is uncommon in the lack of it.

The Italian direttore responsabile cannot be a member of Parliament, because deputies and senators have immunity; he also, under the provisions of recent legislation, is required to be a member of the Order of Journalists (also called the Order). A "special list" within the Order permits editors of technical and otherwise arcane journals to hold their jobs without having gone through the process leading to regular membership.

In most cases the actual editor is also the direttore responsabile, but there are exceptions where the appointment is essentially political and the person involved has little to do with the day-to-day operations of the publication. In such cases the informal term *direttore operante* for the actual administrator is sometimes used in shoptalk.

Because there is nothing comparable in American journalism I have simply used the word *responsabile* when it seems necessary to refer to that role.

The Italian *vice-direttore* is quite accurately conveyed, however, by *associate editor,* and, as in the case of the English phrase, the meaning may describe several different roles. *Managing editor* is a narrower, more specific phrase; it refers to the individual actually supervising in detail the putting together of the newspaper or periodical, with no role in the formation of larger policy. The Italian equivalent is *capo-redattore.*

The various departments on most Italian dailies are much like those of an American one; sports, national news, local news, foreign affairs, entertainment, and the like. The individual in charge of each department is called a *caposervizio.* His counterpart in this country is generally referred to as the sports editor, national editor, city editor, and so on. For the Italian word *redattore,* which can refer to either a desk man or a reporter, I have used *journalist.*

There are three institutions in Italian newsrooms, be they newspaper, magazine, or broadcast, which are unknown in U.S. newsrooms. The Italian word *praticante* means simply *apprentice.* It is a precise, legally established term describing the first stage of becoming a licensed professional journalist. This stage can be terminated at the end of eighteen months by passing examinations for professional competence, and the apprenticeship in no event can extend beyond thirty-six months. The activities and compensation of apprentices are carefully laid out in the national journalists' contract, and we shall look at that later.

Every Italian newsroom and magazine editorial office also has a *segretario di redazione* ("secretary of the editorial department"). This always has seemed to me a rational role which American journalism might well adopt. The role might be defined as day-to-day administration of those things that are not directly involved in newshandling. The segretario generally manages the mechanics of hiring and firing, of communication with distant staff members, of managing expense accounts, of handling all kinds of nonprofessional visitors. It is a role that does much to make the newsroom work.

The third of these institutions for which there is nothing comparable in U.S. newsrooms is the *comitato di redazione,* a term that seems to be best translated as "Journalists Committee." The capital letters are to set out its official and unique character; without them the phrase could refer to any group of reporters.

The burgeoning and decline of the role of Journalists Committees is a critical element in the recent history of Italian journalism. Later chapters of this book deal with the history of this institution and its part in the reformist movement in considerable detail, but there are so many references throughout the text that some explanation seems necessary before going further.

Under the law of 1963, which formally established the Order of Journalists in its present form, and the national contracts regularly negotiated by the journalists' trade union, every editorial enterprise is required to have a Journalists Committee. It is a group, generally of three members, elected by the full editorial staff of the newspaper or magazine or, in the case of Radiotelevisione Italiana (RAI), the government broadcasting system, workers in broadcast news operations. It represents the staff on a day-to-day basis in a wide variety of relationships with management. Its formal authority has always been slight, its role essentially consultative, but its real power rests in the fact that the full staff, when convoked formally as the Assembly, has in most cases tended to follow the recommendations of the committee. The intensity, frequency, and range of activity of Journalists Committees varies greatly from one newsroom to another, but the institution has been a major influence in the conduct of Italian journalism since 1970.

It is also worth noting that Journalists Committees have a far wider range of concerns than the shop committees of the Newspaper Guild in the United States. Guild leadership in whatever editorial setting generally has concentrated on classic trade union concerns, and particularly upon better salaries and working conditions. Journalists Committees have also tended to be concerned with matters of political stance, adequacy and balance of coverage, and the importance of professional dignity and status within society.

Published materials consulted for this study are set out in the bibliography; there has been a sizable amount of solid, analytical criticism of the Italian press printed since the late 1960s, as well as a handful of serious histories of the institution. There is, in addition, a good deal more coverage of journalists and journalism in Italian newspapers and magazines than in similar publications in the United States.

Most of the rest of the material was gathered through personal interviews during six trips to Italy in the period 1970–79. There was no attempt at a systematic sample. I have always been most comfortable with the technique Harold Isaacs developed so well, beginning with *Scratches on Our Minds* in 1958.[1] With this method one chooses people who are most likely to have important and useful things to say. Most interviews were conducted in Rome, Milan, and Turin, and the people interviewed for the most part worked on the largest general dailies in the country: *Corriere della Sera* and *Il Giorno* of Milan, *La Stampa* of Turin, and *Il Messaggero* of Rome. I also interviewed two staff members of *Il Tempo* of Rome, several members of the news staff of RAI (the government-controlled broadcasting system), three members of the Associated Press (AP) bureau in Rome, one staff member of a small daily in Verona, one each from United Press International (UPI) and *Agenzia Italia*. All told, about fifty journalists were interviewed; a half-dozen were interviewed repeatedly during the seven years.

All the interviews were comfortably long and relatively unstructured; I tried to make certain I got the answers to some obvious questions, such as the mechanics of the interviewee's job, his professional history, his education, and where he came from. I guessed at ages. I was able to make educated guesses about salaries, but in several cases the figure was volunteered. I sought out opinions about the Order of Journalists and the present state of Italian journalism. Beyond that, the conversations took their own shoptalk directions.

In six cases I was invited to the journalist's home, but most of the interviews were at the office either before or after the peak work period of the day or at a restaurant over a meal. Nobody was paid for being interviewed, and when a meal was involved I was as likely to lose the discreet battle for the check as to win it. Nobody turned me down; the talk was good Italian conversation—open, vigorous, full of personal flair.

The list of those interviewed represents a considerable range of jobs in Italian journalism, from editor to apprentice, a good spread in age (from the late twenties to the mid-sixties), and a wide variety of backgrounds. It tends to be heavy, however, with special correspondents and news administrators, such as assistant managing editors. The political spread ranged from Communists to right-wing monarchists. I made no special effort to seek out neo-Fascists and turned up none.

In addition to omitting representatives of that force in Italian politics, my conversations provided no representation of some other elements. I interviewed no women; women professional journalists are few in Italy.*

---

*The mention of female journalists in Italy always brings to mind, of course, Oriana Fallaci. At the cost of some oversimplification, it might be said that Fallaci is to Italian journalism what Amelia Earhart was to American aviation. She is unique; she represents nothing. She has never been identified primarily with an Italian publication (most of her journalism has been for *Paris Match*). She is admired and respected in Italy; Italian magazines print, or reprint, almost any of her work they can lay hands on, and her books are immensely popular. To put it another way, there is indeed a Fallaci—but there is not, nor has there been, a Sylvia Porter, Gail Sheehy, Flora Lewis, or even Dorothy Kilgallen or Barbara Walters in Italian journalism. There are important critics and commentators on

The weekly newsmagazine *Panorama* reported in the spring of 1977 that there were 7,000 certified male professionals in journalism and 500 women, a little more than 7 percent overall. Of 1,003 professionals at RAI-TV (which includes both radio and television) 65 were women, and most of them were handling shortwave overseas broadcasts. The worst record in the country belonged to *Il Messaggero* of Rome, which at that time hired exactly one female journalist to work alongside 140 men.[2] I interviewed only one staff member of a party paper—*L'Unità*—and none from afternoon papers.

Most of these exclusions were fortuitous, the result of my relatively narrow concern in this project. I was after the best possible understanding of the people who produce the bulk of the important journalism in Italy, who provide the leadership and primary force of the journalists' organizations, and whose outlets are most likely to have influence on Italian affairs, insofar as any publications have such influence. The mass communications system of any country is highly structured, and my interest was in the beams and girders which bear most of the weight. I have not been blindly trapped into studying the Establishment in Italian journalism; the Establishment was precisely what I wanted to study.

All of my interviewees had some university education, a clear indication of superior social status in Italy. Most had a degree, and a few had some graduate work. They were from the classic universities: Rome, Turin, Milan, Florence, Bologna. The field of study most represented was law, the field generally chosen by Italian university students uncertain of their career plans or simply in search of general education; most law students in that country have no intention of practicing. Several more had studied economics, and several political science; beyond that there was considerable variety, ranging from a political writer who studied philosophy with Croce to a factotum in the news department of RAI who had studied chemistry. There are no journalism schools attached to major Italian universities, but several of my respondents had experience on student newspapers and magazines.

Italian journalism has continued to evolve after the period analyzed here, of course. The final chapter of this book provides a summary updating of significant changes since 1979. By the time this volume gets into print the summary will be dated, too, but that is one of the prices paid for the challenge of trying to analyze a living institution rather than one frozen in time.

---

the arts, the best-known of whom in the 1970s probably was Natalia Ginsberg, but they are no more conventional journalists than are Mary McCarthy or Nora Ephron in this country.

Contents

Chapter 1. Elitists, Inattention, and Life in the Open Air............ 1

2. The Context of the Profession...... 24

3. Becoming a Professional.......... 51

4. The Profession and the Union...... 79

5. Newspaper Owners, Politicians, and Purity............ 94

6. The Beginnings of Reform........ 118

7. Reformers at Work.............. 141

8. "The Return to Prudence"........ 169

9. The Profession in Italy and America: Some Comparisons and Speculations................ 187

INTO THE 1980s: AN UPDATE...... 210
NOTES........................ 217
A NOTE ON SOURCES............ 223
INDEX........................ 225

Chapter 1

Elitists, Inattention, and Life in the Open Air

In the spring of 1953, when I first lived in Italy, I made a speech at the Press Club in Naples. Despite the name, this was no ordinary press club, and few working journalists belonged to it. The club was posh and the membership rich. After the speech there was an elegant banquet. Several working journalists had been invited for the occasion, and one of these sat beside me.

It was a great meal and a great party, and at one point my companion excused himself to make a phone call. When he returned he explained, with no self-consciousness at all, that he had called his colleagues at his other job to say that he was having such a splendid time that he didn't want to leave; they would have to do without him. He moonlighted as a fiddler in a trio in a restaurant. He did it to make ends meet.

My first interview with a working journalist in connection with this project was in January, 1970, about seventeen years later. He asked me to come to his home, which was in an apartment house at the top of the first range of hills north of Rome, in an elegant neighborhood not far from the Cavalieri Hilton. We talked in his library across an antique desk. This was at eleven in the morning and, by way of small talk, I said something to the effect that it was a rather early hour for a man who worked on a morning newspaper. Not at all, he said; he went to the office around 4 P.M., and always was home by 9:30, which is the dinner hour in Rome.

He was an intense, well-educated fifty-year-old who was a political writer for a Roman daily. In the course of our discussion of his work he volunteered the amount of his salary, which was about $18,000 a year—a high figure by Italian standards at that time. He had done no writing for several weeks. He disagreed with his editor about his paper's handling of an important story (the investigation of the bloody bombing of a bank in Milan in early December), and he and his editor agreed that he was not to do any writing about politics for a while. He spent his time at the office, participated in a daily story conference, and chatted with his colleagues. The paper was not likely to fire him; under the terms of the national journalists' contract, his severance pay would have been about $37,000—in a lump sum.

During our conversation he spoke with great pride of his profession, and asserted that Italian journalists had better pay, working conditions, and job security than any other journalists in the world, with the possible exception of the Americans. After many more interviews with journalists on other major papers, I was convinced there were no exceptions.

This was not an ordinary reporter, of course; he was the chief political writer for one of the largest papers in the country, had much seniority, and probably was among the ten leading nonadministrators in terms of salary in the news department. He was, at the same time, no special case; he simply was near the top of his profession, and he symbolized dramatically how far that profession had come since the days when a good journalist had to play the violin after hours to make ends meet. If his salary was not as high as that of journalists of comparable stature in the United States, his working conditions, fringe benefits, and job security were much better, and his salary must be seen in context.

He made $1,500 a month at a time when the average senior university professor in Rome made $480 a month (about the same as a skilled industrial worker) and a general in the Italian army, including his special supplements, $720 a month.[1] (It should be remembered that the stated salary for any job in Italy above the blue-collar level frequently does not represent the potential full income, since there are numerous ways, which will be discussed later, in which the discreet and well-connected may improve upon the figure.)

I later came to know this journalist well, but at that time he seemed to me to symbolize the rich irony of the profession of journalist in Italy. He was drawing a fine salary while not working at all, on what would have seemed to an American journalist a specious pretext. Even if he had been working, it would have been for something less than forty hours a week. (His union was then negotiating to get it down to thirty-five.) He had six weeks of fully paid vacation every year, plus eighteen other paid holidays, and the moment work intruded upon any holiday, he benefited from generous overtime rates. Membership in his trade union was tightly controlled with the help of national legislation; there was no real possibility of competition for jobs, no eager young running up the backs of the well-established.

With all that compensation and protection, Italian journalists were turning out the least believed and, with the exception at that point of the newspapers of Portugal, least read newspapers in the Atlantic community. The whole thing seemed to me a remarkably cynical, self-serving performance. Its implications were tragic in light of the need of a troubled country for the strength that a responsible and energetic press can add to democratic government.

It was a neat analysis, an Italian kind of cosmic joke. It did not hold up, however. As I was carrying out that first set of interviews, things were getting more complicated, although only a few of my respondents realized it. I realized it not at all.

In the summer of 1976 I had another interview with that first respondent. This one was at his office. Much had gone on since the conversation of 1970; his newspaper, along with others that had once been money-makers, was now running great deficits, and had been doing so for several years. Concentration of ownership was sweeping the industry; his paper had been sold by the family that had owned it for decades and then resold, ending as a small part of a conglomerate that had already taken in some of the country's best-known dailies. The staff of his paper had become concerned and then militant; he had been among their elected leaders, and there had been a photograph in a news magazine of him and two or three others in shirt-sleeves and rumpled ties, headed across a piazza to see some magistrate or other.

The building occupied by his paper, like those of most other Roman dailies, is an elderly rabbit warren which rather resembles, one suspects, the headquarters of a Balkan civil service. It had been under reconstruction for years, and I worked my way around ladders and plywood and up the back steps to the second floor. The porter who took my card away returned looking impressed.

"The associate editor will be out in just a moment," he said.

Under a contract that had been negotiated between the new owners and the paper's staff, the staff had acquired the right to elect one of the two associate editors, and my old interview subject had been elected. His office was big, but sparsely decorated, with reproductions of front pages on the walls, and everything badly in need of paint.

Nevertheless it became apparent within a few minutes that this was one of the centers from which the assembly of the next issue was being directed. Stories and layouts were brought to him for approval; assignments were discussed. The editor called, and a starchy argument went on for a half hour. The editor was the appointee of the owner, a man whom the associate editor, along with most of the staff, detested. My acquaintance was barely polite during the conversation; he kept explaining things carefully, emphasizing their obviousness in the fashion of someone demonstrating patience with the intellectually slow.

Around these interruptions we talked for an hour and a half. He was full of his job. He recited with pride the record of the Journalists Committee, of which he was a member, in guiding the political line of the paper, and of the extent of broad participation by the staff in the making of decisions about the news. It was not uncommon at that paper, for example, for some staff member to object to a headline after he saw the first edition and to call a meeting of the Journalists Committee to rewrite it. If the issue was really important, in the staff's eyes, the entire establishment, including the pressroom, might be shut down while votes were taken and the issue settled.

He talked earnestly of reform, not just of his newspaper or his profession, but of Italian politics as well. Like most good Italian journalists, he knew the history and internal anatomy of politics in his country thoroughly. He saw his paper and its "democratic newsroom" as a means of doing things that must be done for Italy.

His working conditions, his salary, his perquisites were better than ever. But he is not a cynic, and I now know him well enough that I am convinced he was not self-serving. He was doing his best to produce what he saw as a better newspaper.

Internationally, Italian newspapers have hardly been visible at all. *Corriere della Sera* of Milan sometimes appears on one of those foolish lists of the ten (or five, or twenty) best newspapers in the world, but that is about the end of it.

A closer, more systematic look over recent history and the current product does little to encourage a more elevated opinion. Italian dailies have never been particularly bad, in the sense that the most popular British papers are bad. Nor have most of them been very good, by common standards of quality in news gathering and presentation, and of late there has been an increasing smell of death about them.

Consider some figures. A standard measure for newspaper diffusion is copies per thousand of population. According to United Nations Educational, Scientific, and Cultural Organization (UNESCO) data gathered in 1975, the middle of the period with which this study is concerned, the most devoted readers of newspapers were the Japanese and the Swedes; total daily circulation in those countries came to slightly more than 500 per 1,000 of population. In the United Kingdom the figure was 437; in the United States, which ranked eighth, it was 314.

For years in Italy the figure has been around 100 buyers per 1,000. A survey made in 1965 estimated that 60 percent of the population never read a newspaper. In 1968, according to Angelo Del Boca in his thoughtful *Giornali in crisi*,[2] the percentage was even higher, around 62 percent. Pushing the analysis further, he set aside children under fifteen, illiterates and semiliterates, even the unemployed, and still came up with a hard figure of 19 million people out of a population of 53 million who had the maturity, the means, and the education to read a newspaper and never bothered to do so.

Although the foreign visitor would not notice unless he were told to look for it, there is simpler evidence: newspapers are not much to be seen in Italy. They are seldom seen on the ubiquitous transit buses in the cities, and it is no explanation to point out that the vehicles are so crowded there is no room to read; even a Roman bus is no more crowded than the BMT subway at rush hour, and a newspaper is basic gear to the American subway rider. As customers of the open-air cafés in Paris reappear in memory's eye they are reading the papers; in the sunshine along the Via Veneto, the readers are tourists, and the Italians are watching each other. I remember sitting in Heathrow airport one day shortly after the first edition of the *Daily Express* appeared, suddenly aware that there were dozens of people, seated like me against the wall in a line stretching out on either side, each in approximately the same position, holding the paper at the same angle, as in a self-consciously artistic photograph. Such a scene in Italy is unimaginable.

Even the newspaper component in the country's litter seems sharply down from 1952, when my wife and I first lived in Italy. At that time newspapers were the standard wrapping paper—not second-hand newspapers, reclaimed, but fresh new ones. It was a time of great press overruns, particularly on the part of *L'Unità,* the Communist daily, which simply laid on the grass-roots party apparatus copies representing inflated "sales" quotas. In those days a kilo of green beans often came sheathed in dialectic.

The newspaper in this commendable role has been replaced by the punched-out plastic bag, white and slick to the touch (the sea bed at Ostia is said to be heavily layered with them), and the depressing clutter along Italian roadsides seldom shows the elevating touch of newsprint.

Several explanations have been proposed for Italian disinterest in newspaper reading. One of the most engaging, perhaps because it never can be really tested, was set out a good many years ago by Bernard Voyenne, a French student of the mass media. He contended that the Mediterranean peoples are not readers by nature, that their style of living is out-of-doors and their style of communication face-to-face. There may be reinforcement for that of a reverse sort in reflecting upon life a few hundred miles north. The Scandinavians are prodigious readers, and when I once commented to a Norwegian friend that about one in every three shops in Oslo seemed to be a bookstore, he shrugged and said, "How many things can you do during a Norwegian winter?"

On the other hand, watching television is also a cloistered activity, and the audience research carried out by Italy's broadcasting monopoly, RAI, indicates that its audiences watch just about as intently as those of any other country, especially during prime time. Perhaps the distinction is that television is, and the newspaper is not, attractive enough to pull them in from what Del Boca calls "life in the open air."[3]

The crippling effect upon newspaper circulation of the distribution system is more easily demonstrated. There has never been home delivery of newspapers in Italy. There still are a few street hawkers (called, rather wonderfully, *strilloni*), but these are almost gone. The only outlets of importance are the newsstands, and there are not enough of them (one for each 2,670 people in Italy, compared to, for example, one for each 1,250 French). Permission to open new ones must be granted by a joint commission of publishers and newsstand owners, and the latter, who have a good thing going, refuse to admit competitors. The newsmagazine *Panorama*, in an examination of the problems of the press, found at the beginning of the 1970s that there were three thousand pending applications, and concluded that it was almost impossible to get a permit unless one's father was in the business.[4]

Nevertheless there seem to be a great many newsstands to the American visitor, and some, such as the famous pair at the top and bottom of the Veneto in Rome, are splendid indeed, piled high and bunkered with books and magazines in half a dozen languages. Italian newspapers are not conspicuous, however; most are kept behind the counter, apparently on the assumption that only the addicted will want them, and that they will ask. Newspapers are a minor item on most newsstands in the country.

In addition, this tightly controlled little industry takes 35 percent of the copy price of newspapers, compared to about 20 percent in the United States, and thus has helped the Italian daily to the edge of pricing itself out of the market. Until 1977 newspaper prices were set by a government committee that also set the price of books. Government involvement is everywhere in Italian journalism, in complex and sometimes tenuous ways, and government's interest in newspaper prices grew out of the fact that the newspaper has been one of the items on the cost of living index to which most Italian labor contracts are pegged by escalator clauses. A 10-lire increase was thus reflected throughout the economy. Since the 1950s newspaper publishers had complained that the permitted increases were not sufficient to cover increased costs, and many still contend that the catastrophic losses of the 1970s (see chap. 8) were due in great part to the artificial ceiling. That lifted, prices soared to 300 lire in 1979 (the equivalent of twenty-two cents) and 400 by 1980 (even in the inflated lire of that year, equivalent to about 33 cents).

Even problems in coinage and currency may have had at least some minor effect on newspaper sales. For decades the country was chronically short of small change. Any transaction involving a figure smaller or less round than 500 lire was likely to be complicated, and its consummation to involve discussion and improvisation. Fifty- and 100-lira coins, useful in buying small necessities and essential for vending machines and other coin-operated apparatus, were for most of the 1970s rare as gold florins. During one of our stays in Rome the operator of a wine shop down the street tipped me off to the fact that he generally had some on Mondays, because that was the one day of the week he could get them from the bank on the corner.

There were paper 50- and 100-lira bills, but they, too, were in short supply. In 1977 scrip appeared—bits of paper issued by banks, generally for 100 lire. Dozens of banks printed them, generally on cheap paper and in monocolor. One kind looked suspiciously as if it had been mimeographed. They quickly became part of the monetary system.

More imagination was shown during a brief period beginning in 1971 when the newspaper was priced at ninety lire. A remarkable number of substitutes for the necessary ten-lire change developed; the most common was a piece of hard candy. Protests and charges of profiteering arose immediately, since the candy was worth only a couple of lire. Sometimes a stamp was offered, and I once got back a couple of rubber bands. A Roman entrepreneur invented a four-page publication consisting entirely of advertising, priced it at ten lire, and instead of change the newspaper buyer received an advertising supplement.

As the end of the decade approached, the government finally met the problem through massive new coinage, including a handsome new 200-lira piece. For years, however, the distribution of newspapers was affected not only by their price and some difficulty in finding them, but also by an irritating inconvenience in paying for them.

At a given moment between 1970 and 1980 there were between eighty and ninety daily newspapers in Italy. The number changed frequently. Despite the neglect of newspapers by the general population, the country's political movers and shakers still believe in the medium, and among the first of the symbolic behaviors of a new political faction has generally been the founding of a daily paper. When the political tempo quickens, the number of new papers goes up. In the single month of January, 1979, for example, there were announced (1) the first issue, on January 21, of a daily called *Ottobre* (October), a publication of the "Marxist-Leninist Party of Italy"; (2) the first issue, on February 1, of *La Sinistra* (The Left), publication of the Workers Movement for Socialism; (3) the first issue, on May 1, of *Quotidiano Donna* (Woman's Daily), published by leftist Roman feminists. All these, of course, reflected the discontent on the

Italian left with the essentially cooperative stance toward the Andreotti government taken by the regular Communist party at that time. All suspended publication within a few weeks.

Some of these may have been designed from the beginning to be short-lived, published only through the next election, rumors of which already were in the air at the beginning of 1979. In any case, such publications have almost no prospect of permanence; the traditional party papers have been in deep financial trouble since the early 1970s, even with the substantial resources of a major party behind them. The ferment speaks not of the vigor of Italian journalism, but of its persistent equation with politics.

The traditional success of another group of dailies says more about that country's journalism, perhaps. In the 1970s Italy had four daily newspapers devoted exclusively to sports.[5] All were among the twenty newspapers of highest circulation in the country. For many years all were money-makers, although finally, long after the rest of Italy's papers had slipped into financial crisis, they began to run losses. Their remarkable stability, long history—two were founded in the 1920s, the others immediately after the Second World War—and overall success have been the more remarkable in the face of elaborate sports coverage by the conventional newspapers. Italians seem to have no prejudice against newspapers as a medium, but only against what is in most of them.

Most Italian dailies are classified as *giornali d'informazione,* the best translation of which might be *"news* newspapers," complete with the emphasis to distinguish them from journals of opinion, political party publications, and those with specialized content such as sports. Many journalists pull an ironic face when they use the phrase, and it is standard small talk to say that Italy in fact has no such newspapers. Regardless of the accuracy of the term, the four best-known papers in the country during most of the 1970s were classified in that group. They were:

Corriere della Sera (Evening Courier) of Milan;
La Stampa (The Press) of Turin;
Il Messaggero (The Messenger) of Rome;
Il Giorno (The Day) of Milan.*

---

*There is a place somewhere for an essay about the wondrous improbability of some Italian newspaper names. *Corriere della Sera* is a morning paper. A respected daily in Genoa is called *Il Secolo XIX* (The Nineteenth Century). A Naples paper is called *Roma,* and in Bologna there is a fine newspaper called *Il Resto del Carlino,* which means "the change from a carlino," which was a small coin circulating in Emilia in 1885. The whole story involves a Savoyard king and the price of a cheap cigar.

All had circulations above 250,000; *Corriere della Sera,* at the top, claimed around 700,000 during most of the decade. One party paper had circulation above a quarter million; the Communist *L'Unità* (Unity) published separate editions in Rome and Milan which totaled, according to the party, around 450,000.

All four of the top general newspapers had national distribution. The pattern of concentration in urban areas common in all countries goes to extremes in Italy, where most of the circulation is in an industrialized belt across the north part of the country and in Rome. In 1979 there were seven major cities with populations of more than 100,000 that did not have a local newspaper. The entire province of Umbria, one of the wellsprings of the Renaissance with cities such as Perugia, Assisi, and Spoleto, with a total population of 800,000 had not a single masthead.

For a good many years the major dailies have been, in physical appearance, a good deal alike and within a familiar pattern. During the week, around twenty-four pages is standard for major papers. Sunday editions are commonly around thirty-two. Traditionally, front pages are a bit "heavy," with headlines in boldface type of relatively small size, narrow columns (the nine-column page has been standard), and small body type. These characteristics tend to make a page uninviting; another old Italian practice makes it difficult to read. Much of the front page material is commonly set in italics, sometimes as much as 50 percent. Experts in such matters agree that more than two or three lines of italics makes heavy going for the reader, but the testimony of experts is hardly necessary for one who has had to live with such a problem.

In recent years some of the papers have undertaken moves to improve appearance and readability. *Il Giorno* of Milan was innovative from its founding in 1956, most visibly in the use of color, an eight-column front page, and the generous use of white space. Color in news sections was later dropped, but continued in various supplements. *Corriere della Sera* reduced the amount of italic and generally lightened the first page in the mid-1970s, but was drifting back to its traditional appearance as the decade ended.

The same basic front page layout has been common to almost all general newspapers in Italy. Column one, at the left margin of the page, contains an *articolo di fondo,* literally an "article in depth," but more likely to be described by an American as an editorial or by a Briton as a "leader." Its content invariably is political.

The most striking characteristic of Italian daily journalism is a preoccupation with politics. A good deal of the average front page—generally around one third—traditionally has been given over to discussions of party affairs, Byzantine in detail and requiring of its readers not only special knowledge, but particular status.

That kind of journalism, and the journalist who produces it, was described years ago in an article that is still famous. Enzo Forcella wrote it for the magazine *Tempo Presente* in 1959. It is called "1,500 Readers—Confessions of a Political Journalist," and begins:

> A political journalist in our country can count on around 1,500 readers: the ministers and undersecretaries (all of them), the members of Parliament (some of them), the leaders of the political parties, trade union officials, high prelates, and some industrialists who want to appear informed. The rest do not count, even though the paper sells 300,000 copies. First of all, it has not been established that ordinary readers read the first page of their papers, and in any case their influence is minimal. The whole system is based on the rapport between the political journalist and this group of privileged readers. If we lose sight of this factor, we cannot understand the most characteristic aspect of our political journalism, perhaps of Italian politics in general: the feeling of talk within the family, with protagonists who have known each other since childhood, given to repartee, speaking a language full of allusions and, even when they dislike each other, wishing each other well. One speaks only for one's own pleasure, of course, as if a paying public did not exist.
>
> The relationship between the 1,500 readers and the political journalist is very close; each morning they have breakfast with him (if they read the paper with their caffelatte); they often invite him to dinner in person and make clear their admiration through colleagues or mutual friends. At Christmas, and also at Easter when it's particularly important, the political journalist receives from his admirers many cases of liquor. He's invited to all the parties. He's honored. If he asks something from public officials, he gets it more easily than the ordinary citizen. Incidentally, and a detail of some importance, in recent years, through private secretaries or a few joking words exchanged in the halls of Montecitorio [the Parliament building] the ministers and other gift-givers have been persuaded to switch from Italian liquor . . . to Scotch whiskey, cognac, French champagne, and even Russian and Polish vodka.[6]

This relationship may be exclusive, but its communication system is far from covert. Seven days a week, on the first or second page of most dailies, appears what is often called in the newsroom the *pastone romano*. *Pastone* is a mixture of edible refuse—hog feed. The pastone romano is not a forthright political essay; that role is usually given to the editorial. Instead it might be best described as a kind of ultimate extension of what American papers are now labeling *news analysis;* there is a skeleton of reportable fact, although it is often trivial, and a great deal of elaboration which can be read at almost as many levels as Symbolist poetry. This is the institutionalized channel of informal information, the arena for debate, or, more often, the reporting of debate, simultaneously part creator and part reflector of political stature and who is becoming what. Some French and English newspapers have played a similar role, although that tradition now seems attenuated; so have, on some occasions, the columns of such political journalists as Walter Lippmann in this country.[7]

There are Italians who deny much role in politics for the pastone. Luigi Barzini, Jr., an Italian journalist known widely in the United States, dismissed it as simply a collection of snippets taken from party handouts.

"Ministers and political leaders pay no attention to such stuff, and it's not a channel of communication; if they want to communicate, ministers talk to each other on the telephone."[8]

Whether he is more correct than Forcella is not as important as the undeniable fact that Italian newspaper front pages have for years been awash with political talk that almost seems designed to drive the unknowledgeable away. There have been some small signs of an attempt at reform since 1970. Several papers have reduced the pastone's length. After a radical overhauling of the front page, *Il Messaggero* discarded the pastone, for the most part, and substituted "Political News," made up of short notes about party affairs. It seems improbable that the reform will go very far, however; the spirit of the pastone romano runs throughout the Italian media, as we shall see, and all things considered, may even be on the rise.

For many decades Italian dailies have had another unique characteristic, the tradition of *la terza pagina* ("the third page"). It is a tradition that is changing and in decline, but Italian editors, journalists, and most intellectuals still take it seriously. The content of the third page might be described as stylish nonjournalism. When I first read Italian papers in the early 1950s, the standard forms were short, critical essays about the arts or the quality of life; interviews with eminent writers or artists; short fiction; bits of history and archaeology; pieces from foreign correspondents about matters cultural in their country of residence; and sometimes remarkable vignettes of the human condition very much in the style of what later came to be called New Journalism in the United States. Paying outlets for writers have always been scarce in Italy, and intellectuals such as college teachers fearfully underpaid; even the modest sums available through the third page regularly have attracted some of the best minds and talent in the country.

Such stuff was, however, even more elitist and of less interest to a middle-class reader than the political talk of pages one and two, and the gradual shift in content of the last few years represents, in most cases, the attempt to broaden appeal. Carlo Bo, an eminent contributor to the form, has referred, rather bitterly, to its "Americanization," and the word does suggest something of what has happened.[9] Toward the end of the 1970s there were more stories that an American editor would regard as conventional features, including travel pieces, and a substantial number of what the news business calls backgrounders, superficially analytical discussions of the context of ongoing major stories, such as the problems of the European Economic Community or the troubles in Ireland. The essential flavor clearly became less literary and intellectual and more journalistic.

After the third page the remainder of an Italian daily has usually looked a good deal like newspapers from countries elsewhere on the continent. The essential scheme of organization does not resemble American dailies so much as it resembles that of most U.S. newsmagazines. The news is arranged in compartments, each clearly labeled: local, foreign, business, entertainment, sports. Some Italian papers have women's sections, and most have a few comic strips, generally of U.S. origin and in translation. (*Peanuts* is called *Piccolo Mondo,* meaning Small World, and the ever-popular *Donald Duck* is *Paperino*.) The space allotments to each section are about the same from day to day, and so is the sequence in which they are arranged. There is a negligible amount of retail advertising, that is, display ads placed by local shops for specific items, which is not only the major share of U.S. newspaper income, but a major reason for reading the paper.

Newspaper reading is to a remarkable extent a matter of habit, and one gets accustomed to a particular arrangement and regards it as normal. Anyone who has moved from one city to another and has thus been forced to adjust to a different daily feels for a time a sense of frustration and annoyance. The Italian reader finds the structure of his paper normal, surely, but one can hardly help suspecting that the rigid pattern makes it too easy to discard whole areas of potential interest in advance and without a reasonable trial. Most human beings are mildly xenophobic, for example, and would seem less likely to read something formally labeled Foreign News than the American reader who finds stories from abroad mingled with local and national news and even tucked around Hollywood gossip columns.

Most newspapers in the United States are thoroughly structured, of course, but with the exception of sports and business sections this is hardly apparent to the nonprofessional reader. There have been no studies of exactly how the Italian reader uses his paper, but it seems reasonable that most have to make the decision to buy a copy on the basis of the attractiveness of only a part of its content.

There is one more factor that discourages wider readership of Italian newspapers. Most potential readers in that country find the prose of daily journalism difficult to read. To the foreigner who acquired his Italian through formal instruction that is a rather surprising idea. Italian is an easy language, especially for the English-speaking. Its orthography is thoroughly rational: a word is spelled precisely as it is pronounced, and pronounced precisely as spelled; with exceptions of *c, g, o,* and *e*—each with a single variant—a given letter is pronounced the same way wherever it appears. The alphabet is familiar, of course, and it is even shorter, since *j, k, w,* and *y* do not appear in pure Italian. There are innumerable cognates of other major languages because of some communal Latin heritage and the steady intake of foreign terms. There are some irregular verbs, but of the sort characteristic of all Western languages. Syntax and structure are close to English. An educated American can acquire sound working command of the language with relative ease.

The idea that most of the people on the streets of Rome or Milan would have difficulty reading a newspaper, therefore, seems preposterous. There are good reasons why it is not.

When an Italian acquaintance once complimented me on my Italian (Italians are invariably generous about outlanders' attempts), I commented that my knowledge of the language was functionally satisfactory, but that I was frustrated by my inability to understand much of the talk I heard on the streets or even on movie sound tracks (although I had no difficulty at all with broadcasts).

"That's easy to explain," he said. "You speak Italian. They don't."

He was being both flip and snobbish, but there was a reasonable point underneath. In any culture there are great differences between the language of ordinary people in ordinary situations and proper talk, and that is particularly true of urban patois; not only would an English-speaking foreigner be baffled by conversations overheard in Chicago, so might a native of Arizona. The distance seems greater in Italy, however, where there are varying infusions of dialect as well as an incredible nonverbal vocabulary of mobile hands, arms, eyebrows, lips, and untranscribable noises produced by vocal and respiratory apparatuses.

A historical inheritance is also involved. Italy's literacy rates have always been low by the standards of industrialized societies, because as late as the middle of the nineteenth century Italian was the common language only in Tuscany and Rome. Everyone else spoke some form of dialect or separate regional language. In most of these there was little written material, although modern scholarship has led to the publication of material in such tongues as Friuli and Romagnolo and Romano, the patois of the capital. But dialect cultures were essentially oral; the arts of reading and writing required knowledge of Italian, and learning that language simply was more trouble than it was worth for millions of citizens until well into this century. At the end of the Second World War a major effort was mounted against illiteracy. By 1951 the national figure was 14 percent; a decade later it was less than 8 percent, although illiteracy in most of the south was still around 13 percent; the national average was down to around 5 percent by 1971.

Clinical literacy, however, does not necessarily indicate the ability to read newspapers. One authority estimated in 1976 that one Italian citizen in three lacked that skill.[10] It was his further judgment that no one lacking secondary education could actually manage it easily, and almost 78 percent of the population at that time had only a certificate of elementary education. A survey of Milanese in 1976 asked, "Why do people read few newspapers in Italy?" The second largest bloc of replies, 27 percent, blamed "a language comprehensible only to a few people."[11] (The largest bloc, 46 percent, said "because there's television.") Other surveys, directed at nonreaders, have produced citing of such reasons as lack of time and dull content, which might be face-saving ways of saying the same thing.

Curiously, while most Italians may have problems with the Italian language, they have great respect for it, much more than the average English speaker for his. A modestly educated middle-class friend who was a salesman for a chocolate and spaghetti company once went to great pains to identify for me the precise location where, to his belief, the best Italian was spoken: just outside Sienna. (He felt there was a slight taint on that spoken in the city itself.)

The more sophisticated are equally conscious of the language. Both Ignazio Silone and, to a lesser extent, Alberto Moravia have been criticized in their native land on the grounds that they really do not write Italian very well. There has never been a significant movement in Italian literature involving experimentation with the language, with forms and structures; there have been no James Joyces or even William Faulkners. The cultural pressure is toward all the elegance one can manage, and the responsibility is entirely on one's own head. There are no copy editors on Italian newspapers. Every story, even those filed from abroad by correspondents, appears exactly as the journalist wrote it. (This affects the way the whole newsroom works, as we shall see later.)

The newspaper thus reads to the average Italian with even a secondary school education about the way *Rolling Stone,* compared to the *New York Daily News,* might read to most New Yorkers—manageable only with more effort than it is worth.

It is important to note that the comparison is with *Rolling Stone,* not the *Partisan Review.* Italian journalistic prose is not heavy going because it is overwhelmingly intellectual or reflective of dazzling vocabularies. It is, rather, stylized and in-group, sometimes to the point of being arcane. The language of journalism is like that in most cultures, but given the general low level of education, the gulf it creates between writer and reader in Italy is the greater.

There are some characteristics of general modern Italian that even those who are unschooled in linguistics can spot immediately as difficult for the plodding reader. One of these is the habit of turning nouns into adjectives, verbs, and adverbs.

Consider, for example, an article by an Italian scholar about Italian prose, which appeared in 1976. At one point he refers (and this is his own prose, not something cited as a bad example) to the *fascistizzazione* of the press in the 1920s.[12] It is an ugly word, upon both the page and the tongue, but at least its meaning is quickly clear. It is also fairly common usage. But consider the following, which is standard in the written language: the same writer is discussing an early historian and critic named Francesco De Sanctis. Seven lines later, and without further mention of the name, he refers to *lo stile desanctisiano* ("De Sanctis's style"). Additional difficulty grows out of the standard practice of reducing the capital letters of a proper name to lower case in such processing.

That device makes for harder reading, but at least it is possible to backtrack and find the name that was adapted into an adjective. When the writer assumes that the reader knows the meaning of the hybrid, but in fact the reader doesn't, the problem becomes more difficult. Italian political journalism is particularly bad in this respect. Since about 1960, for example, the phrase *corrente dorotea* has been commonly used in association with a group within the Christian Democratic (DC) party. It is almost never explained; by the 1970s it generally was used in reference to a faction of the conservative wing of the party. It has that curious label because of a famous meeting of DC leadership at a convent of Dorothean nuns in 1959. It would be a reasonable gamble that not one out of twenty of Italy's modest group of newspaper readers could explain it.

With the rise of terrorism in Italy in the late 1970s came a growing fear that the country might be coming apart, becoming a wasteland in which there was no real civil authority, and stylish political writers such as Alberto Ronchey described this with the word *sudamericanizzazione*

("South Americanization"). There really are no rules for the coinage of such nonce-words; a writer may string together almost any number of components, hang the proper suffix on them, and produce, presumably with a sense of consummated creativity, a new word all his own. My own favorite, cited later in these pages (it is too glorious to use only once) appeared in the Christian Democrats' paper *Il Popolo,* which, in a burst of fury over the weekly magazine *L'Espresso*'s attitude on a certain issue, described that publication, which had some indirect ties to the Agnellis who own most of FIAT, as *radicalautomobilisticodivorzista.*

Journalists, in particular, have also developed the habit of putting an Italianate cast on foreign words. Like all languages, Italian contains many foreign words integrated without change—*sport, weekend, cocktail, leader, killer,* and the like—but purists are more likely to be offended by the journalists' habit of devising naturalizations such as *absentismo, fanatismo,* and *nomadismo.*[13] The end product is the Italian equivalent of Franglais, and while it has not provoked the shouts of horror that that jargon has produced in France, the effect upon the average or potential reader may be off-putting. There also seems to be a developing trend to affected elegance in some cases; the phrase *pasticcio di mais* ("corn meal mush") has recently appeared, despite the fact that there is already a familiar and completely adequate Italian word, *polenta.*

It is difficult for Americans to sense a tight linkage between language and position in society; difficult to believe that a citizen could read a line or two of discourse and instantly decide it was for somebody else, not him. But it is true in continental Europe and in Great Britain. It is a particular problem for the political parties, led by intellectuals, which have attempted to organize the industrial proletariat. Palmiro Togliatti, the leader who built the powerful Italian Communist party after the Second World War, discussed it almost plaintively.

> To communicate with the workers. To "speak" with the workers. Among the best known of the leaders of our party who did not come out of the proletariat there are some who know how to speak to a crowd. But to converse with the workers, not as teachers or "leaders," but as comrades or, I should say, students . . . to collaborate with the workers in finding the path that is open to his class, to test the precision of direction and orientation—this few enough of us, this perhaps only Gramsci [Antonio Gramsci, first and dominant theoretician of the *Partito Comunista Italiano* (PCI)] knows how to do.[14]

The Italian press needs to learn how to speak not only with workers, but with an inattentive middle class. It seems possible that a perceptive entrepreneur could identify a level somewhere between the talk of the street and the sophistication of current journalistic prose and use it as a base for building genuinely popular papers.*

I asked one of the top editors of *Corriere della Sera* about this. He replied with a metaphor about clothes, touching the junction of his tie and shirt collar.

"Haven't you noticed how important all this is to the Italian male— the clean shirt, properly ironed, the right cravat?"

I had noticed; as a people Italians probably try harder to look well dressed than any other people on earth. There is no modish dishevelment.

"It's a matter of cutting a good figure. Personal style is everything. Well, it's the same with journalism. The reader would be insulted at the idea of the journalist trying to make it easy for him, and the journalist would lose his self-respect. Italians want their newspapers to cut a good figure, too."

The newspaper represents the chronic case of the pervasive elitism of Italian journalism. Newspapers are expensive. They are readily available only in wealthy urban areas. They are written in a language that is relatively difficult for the citizen with average education to read. Much of the most conspicuous content is in-group gossip, speculation, and dialectic for a very small group of readers. (If Forcella was right in his estimate of 1,500, the total might be 1,650 now.)

Furthermore, the newspaper audience at present is a nonexpanding elite. Italy is a poor country, but its economic development since the end of the Second World War has been remarkable. Italian politicians no longer speak proudly as they once did of the *miracolo economico,* but the fact remains that the gross national product tripled between 1955 and 1966, and per capita income, with inflation taken into account, almost doubled in the same period. Since 1970 the economy has been subjected to the vicissitudes of most Western nations, frequently writ large, but no one who has visited the country regularly over the past three decades needs statistics to convince him of the elevation of the level of consumerism. The 1950s was the era of the bicycle and the motor scooter; of the smell of wood smoke, even in the great cities, in late morning and the evening when meals were being prepared. At that time ice was rare, and mechanical refrigeration in family homes almost unknown, and housewives or their maids shopped for food every day, which was not as inconvenient as it seems because one-room shops and open markets were everywhere. More and more these days the urban Italian gets into an automobile, drives to something resembling an American supermarket,

---

*Such an attempt was, in fact, begun in late 1979.

does the shopping (maids are as scarce in Rome in the 1980s as they are in Washington), and comes home with armloads of packaged and processed food to stock the refrigerator.

What this has done to the quality of life is problematic, to say the least, but a great fulfillment of rising expectations is unmistakable. There has been a massive upward movement in Italy in the middle class. Italian newspapers have not been a part of this movement.

At an early point in all developed societies, newspapers were an elite medium (in England and the United States, for example, until about the middle of the nineteenth century). Then as education levels and affluence grew, newspaper circulation also grew. The industry's success has been based upon its penetration of the middle class, leading to the adoption of newspaper reading as one of the indispensables of the better life. In a few cases the newspaper industry has also been able to gain acceptance by a significant number of the poor and those of low status. The difference between the circulation figures of 314 readers per 1,000 of population in the United States and England's 437 per 1,000 seems to be explained in large part by wider acceptance of the newspaper by that bottom rung in the ladder of affluence.

But in Italy there are literally millions of people who own automobiles, live in comfortable houses, watch television, get a few day's skiing in the winter and a week or two at the seashore in the summer—and never bother with a newspaper. Newspapers are perceived as the properties of a very special and in some ways increasingly discredited group.

It has been suggested that circumstances growing out of the Second World War damaged newspaper readership as well.[15] The country's major papers were tainted first by association with the Mussolini regime and some were later forced to serve the purposes of a German army of occupation; when the war ended they, like the newspapers of much of the continent, changed their names to symbolize disinfection. *La Stampa* of Turin became *La Nuova Stampa,* for example, and *Il Resto del Carlino* became *Giornale dell'Emilia.* Since newspaper readers tend to be habit bound, some may have been lost through the change, although most of the original titles were later restored. Newsprint was also in short supply after the war, and the four- to eight-page papers of necessity eliminated features such as the "third page," which presumably were the chief attraction for some of the audience.

Both of these factors were short-range influences at most, however. A more persuasive explanation, at least at first glance, is that the rapid development of competition from two other media cut into newspaper audiences. First was the popular magazine, particularly the flashy weeklies which Italians call *rotocalchi* (plural of the word for "rotogravure"). The American visitor can only be astonished at the number of these. They feature flashy graphics, sensationalized politics, and much gossip, and Italians read them in enormous quantities. As a matter of fact, Italians consume magazines at the highest rate of any country in the world—325 copies per 1,000 of population, more than three times the rate of their newspaper consumption,[16] a proportion that continued to hold despite a slight decline in magazine circulation toward the end of the 1970s.

The extent to which the popularity of magazines cuts into newspaper readership is difficult to determine. Both magazine and newspaper readership are high in Denmark and Switzerland; Sweden has high newspaper readership and low magazine readership. Only Italy has high magazine readership and low newspaper readership. The variables in each situation obviously overpower any patent correlations.[17]

Certain factors do put magazines in a strong competitive position in Italy. Most are relatively cheap, compared to newspapers; in the spring of 1979, daily papers cost 300 lire, almost thirty cents, per copy. Well-made, glossy weeklies cost, at that time, 500 lire, or less than sixty cents. (In the United States, most dailies at the same time were fifteen cents, and *Time* and *Newsweek* were one dollar.) Magazines are more attractive, better displayed on newsstands, and in a few cases written in more understandable language.

Many people, including many journalists, would add television to the list of factors affecting newspaper readership. Survey research has indicated that in Italy, as in almost every other country, a majority of people say that their primary source of news is television, and that they trust it more than any other medium.

That does not mean, however, that great masses have stopped reading newspapers and turned to television and radio news. People do not drop a familiar medium upon adding a new one; when television was first introduced in the typical American community in the early 1950s, use of print media usually dipped briefly and then recovered, in some cases to above the original level. In Italy there has been almost no competition in content between newspapers and television; there had been little entertainment in Italian papers until the end of the 1970s and little local news on television. Italy's newspaper readers are a specialized group that quickly adopted television when it came along; it seems reasonable that most of the much broader television audience were *never* newspaper readers, rather than deserters.

Official television and radio in Italy are generated, produced, financed, and controlled by a government agency called *Radiotelevisione*

Italiana. It is invariably referred to as RAI, both in print and speech (where it is pronounced *rye*).

Broadcasting has always been under the control of the government in Italy, as in most European countries. Although RAI appears to be a freestanding state enterprise along the lines of the British Broadcasting Corporation (BBC), it technically is a private corporation with a contractual relationship with the government. There are few traces of direct interference with the corporation's affairs by its legal owners. The hand of party politics is visible, however, in almost everything RAI does. For years, including the early 1970s, the result was a rigorous censorship over all political journalism, which frequently reached the point of the ludicrous. There was, for example, a set procedure for reporting government crises. No politician's voice was ever heard, nor were his words quoted directly. Instead, party leaders appearing at the Quirinale (the presidential palace) for consultation with the president of the republic were each shown from the same camera angle and for the same amount of time; upon his exit, each was shown speaking at a microphone, but without sound; after a few minutes the next party leader was shown going through precisely the same routine. While this went on, a disembodied voice, which RAI calls a "speaker," read a carefully written and approved summary of what the man had to say. In every newscast, the last action of the *Telegiornale* news director before air time was consultation behind closed doors with a group of political censors over the finished script. Arrigo Levi, once a major RAI personality himself, described Italian politicians shown on television in those days as resembling fish in an aquarium. "Their mouths move, but no sound emerges."[18]

Since almost all civil unrest has political overtones, traditionally none was reported on the air. The Milanese who was delayed getting home at the end of the day by an uproar in the Piazza San Babila would never learn about it on that evening's news broadcast; the Roman who saw pitched battles with chains and monkey wrenches between radical students of the right and left could be certain that television would carry not a word of it.

RAI is a member of Eurovision (EVN), a network of European telecasting systems. As such, it is responsible for providing film of Italian news for other members, but for years no film of Italy's civil crises was ever available.

For more than a decade the major evening news broadcast typically began with the "fish in the aquarium," moved to a series of what television journalists call talking heads—RAI correspondents reporting from London, Paris, Bonn, sometimes Vienna or North Africa—and concluded with a feature or two about the monuments of the past and the beautiful countryside. Technically, Italian film and television crews have always been superb, but their reputation has been made by what they do when they are away from home. The coverage of papal trips all over the world, for example, has included technical showpieces such as the assembly from scratch of a satellite relay station in Uganda.

In May of 1975 a law providing for the "reform" of RAI was passed by Parliament. Its first provision was the establishment of a commission of fifteen members, politically balanced with representatives from the major parties, with wide powers to collect information and change both structure and executive personnel. Within a few weeks a new structure for broadcast news was in the planning stages. It established two news broadcasts, one controlled by the Christian Democrats, very much in the traditional style and identified as *Telegiornale 1* (TG1). The other broadcast, TG2, was basically reflective of the views of the parties of the left. (*Panorama* referred to the Socialist party as TG2's *"padre spirituale."*) TG2 also represented the Republicans and Liberals, both centrist but *"laico"* ("secular").

The development of a competitive spirit between the two gave powerful assistance to the breaking of old taboos. The staff of TG2 turned their attention to things Italians had never seen on television before. Its reporters covered national congresses of the major political parties, catching leaders for impromptu interviews and asking embarrassing questions. TG1 followed suit. Panel discussions on hot issues such as abortion were set up. Disorders in the streets began to receive coverage; so did domestic scandals.

To some extent RAI journalists were permitted to choose between the two services when the split came; the resulting TG2 staff, although considerably smaller, was considered by many to be the better, and out of some perception of that opinion has come considerable belligerence on both sides. The RAI establishment did not do everything possible to ease the path of the new division. TG2 began operations from an informal, if not awkwardly cluttered, studio because, its staff charged, RAI wouldn't provide anything better. TG2's work force was inadequate, not because few journalists and technical staff chose that direction, but because, they said, the RAI heirarchy managed the budget.

Major changes also came to radio. There are three radio networks under RAI's supervision; the prototype is the classic three services of the BBC. *Rete* (network) 1 and *rete* 2 carry a mixture of music, news, sports, and public affairs aimed at a general audience; *rete* 3 has always been modeled on the Third Programme. At the time of the TG1–TG2 split, the news operations of the two major radio networks were also divided between the two groups. There was little concern about the *terzo* ("third") program; as one magazine said, "It covers only about 15 percent of the country's territory, had a reputation for boring programs, and nobody wants it."[19]

Nevertheless, within a year the terzo began originating programs that would have been unimaginable earlier as RAI projects. Not only were they completely free of censorship, but they also involved the appearance of representatives of unconventional causes: militant feminists, organizers of inmate protests in Italy's appalling prisons and mental hospitals, homosexuals, and leaders of a movement to democratize the military.

These breaks with the past were not only a matter of the initiative of a few broadcasters. Media changes were only a part of a broad front of change that began moving through Italian culture toward the end of the 1960s. What happened might be summed up as a breakdown of conventions that governed some forms of societal behavior in Italy and some of the ways of thinking. Consider as one case the treatment of sexuality in the mass media. In 1960 there were no Italian publications resembling "girlie" magazines; there was no nudity in films, and too leisurely a look by the camera at the way Gina Lollobrigida filled a completely decorous blouse might get a film a government stricture against the admission of minors. There were no descriptions of sexual relations in popular literature, and even in the most serious work such things were handled with almost Victorian indirection; no scatological words were seen, or heard, in a public context. In every major Italian city, newsstands now display books and magazines (sometimes labeled "Swedish type" on the bands that seal them against browsers) that could be purchased in the United States only in porno shops.

In 1976 there appeared a new broadcast medium. It was called *radio libere,* literally "free radio," but "liberated radio" might be more accurate in spirit.

RAI's monopoly over broadcasting had been challenged several times in the courts over the years, but invariably was upheld, including a decision by the Constitutional Court as late as 1974. Then in January, 1976, RAI brought suit to shut down a station in Milan that had begun broadcasting on the unused portion of the FM band; the court of first jurisdiction denied the request, and the case moved to the Constitutional Court. On June 25, 1976, that body upheld the lower court, opening the way to private broadcasting in Italy for the first time. (Meanwhile literally hundreds of new stations had appeared.) The court held that RAI did hold a monopoly on *national* broadcasting, but only that, permitting the private use of both FM and television frequencies, which are short range. It also made clear that RAI's retention of any control had to be related to providing impartiality, comprehensiveness, and easy access, an echo of earlier decisions that had opened the way to the reform of RAI.

Thus in the spring of 1976 the FM band began to fill up with wildly undisciplined initiatives. There has not yet been an accurate census of the numbers involved, and estimates have varied greatly. By election time in June of that year RAI executives were estimating that there were 400 new radio stations, and in September the announcement of a new magazine called *Altrimedia,* devoted largely to instructions for starting up and operating a broadcasting station, referred to 800 stations.

Many of the new stations grew up around Milan and Rome. A correspondent for the *Washington Post* put them in three categories: political, commercial, and esoteric.[20] One of the most spectacular was in the last-named bracket. It was called *Radio L,* and among other programs it featured a late night recorded music show called *Vai a letto con me* ("Go to Bed with Me"). Some magazines, intrigued by this new kind of disc jockey, carried photographs of her: a young woman, blonde, wearing only a set of headphones and holding a microphone.

Such divertissements may have enlarged the horizons of the members of the RAI-conditioned broadcast audience, but their effect upon newspaper reading remains problematic. Even though "because there's television" was the most common answer to the question about low readership of newspapers in the Milan survey cited earlier, this does not indicate that one-time readers have relinquished the habit; as a matter of fact, newspaper circulation during the 1970–80 period remained relatively stable, and the rise of television simply provided a fresher reason for those who had never read.

The survey turned up some other rationalizations as well. In completing the sentence "I believe that journalists in Italy. . . ." 20 percent chose "exaggerate and distort the news, misleading public opinion." Another 23 percent were generous to the journalist but not at all to the institution, stating that Italian journalists "are serious and honest people, but are not free to write the truth." Twenty-one percent believed that journalists in Italy "are determined to direct political decisions through their work," which makes that group not altogether different from the 10 percent who believed them "a privileged and arrogant group which should be restructured." Only 15 percent felt that journalists' place in public esteem was "about right," and only 6 percent that they "do not have the importance they deserve."[21]

All this makes up a damning picture of public sentiment toward both the institutions and people of contemporary Italian journalism. Most serious journalists have been aware of that sentiment for a long time, and have been disturbed by it. Their concern was a primary force in the reform movement that peaked in the early 1970s, the rise and ebb of which make up a substantial part of this book.

Chapter 2

The Context of the Profession

This, as should already be apparent, is a personal piece of work. That circumstance may diminish its authority, but there seems to me no other way to do it honestly. Almost any analytical inquiry represents the analyst's judgments and perceptions, and the personal pronouns that appear here are to remind the reader of that limitation.

During the last decade or two there have been a good many books that attempt to describe national character. Englishmen have written books about the Americans; Americans have written books about the English and the French; an eminent Italian journalist has written a very popular book about the Italians.

Such books generally begin with a disclaimer which says, in effect, that of course there is no such thing as a national character, and that any attempt to generalize about a whole society is hopelessly oversimplified. I should like to associate myself with that kind of statement and proceed with my prejudices.

There are, it seems to me, certain major aspects of the profession of journalist in Itay that can be understood only in terms that have nothing directly to do with journalism.

For example, it is important to keep in mind that the news business is perhaps the most structured, the most demanding of unquestioning cooperation, of any intellectual craft in the world—and that Italians are individualistic and egocentric and structure-spurning to the extent that modern life permits it. That is a familiar stereotype, but living in Italy brings it back reinforced as with steel.

I remember a mob trying to get into a movie theater not long after my wife and I went to Rome in the fall of 1952; the crowd filled the street to the extent that traffic was blocked, and a pair of policemen decided to neaten the situation up a bit. They tried to form a queue.

"*Mussolini è morto!*" came a shout from the back.

The Duce has stayed dead, too, so far as that kind of discipline is concerned. Trying to get on a bus almost any time, or buying a little bread and salami in a popular *drogheria* around noon, or doing anything—absolutely anything—in a bank is an exercise in temper management for the non-Italian. I can remember when we foreigners, mumbling among ourselves, blamed the maids and cleaning women for this mind-bending rudeness. The maids are gone now, however, and *la signora* turns out to be far better at the game than the country girls ever were.

It is important to note that the technique is not personal. Nobody tramps on toes or snarls; nobody contends he was there first or, indeed, says a word. He or she is, instead, very much the individualist. The attitude is simply that all these other people obviously are concerned with some utterly different business than one's own; one goes to the window, or the counter, or the *cassa,* and gets it done.

Precisely the same attitude explains the spectacular awfulness of Italian driving. An Italian driver seldom deliberately cuts off another, or bluffs for the right-of-way. He is operating on a far higher principle; when he puts his hands on the wheel he is somehow seized of the knowledge that there are no other automobiles in the world but this one, and he is free to take it wherever he pleases, park it wherever he pleases, and drive it as fast as it will run under any circumstances. He is a human being gloriously alone.

When other machines turn up, he acts astonished and dismayed. At one time we lived at the north edge of Rome, across the Tiber, and I occasionally took a cab downtown. The route led through the Piazza del Popolo, a convergence point in those days for streets from five or six directions. All cab drivers went flat out on the relatively wide Lungotevere and slowed not at all as we headed into inner-city traffic; I soon learned to brace myself, because there would soon be a shriek of brakes, a fishtailing stop, and a driver looking over his shoulder, thunderstruck at the fact there were other cars in the busiest intersection in Rome.

La bella figura is so much a cliché in Italy that it commonly is used jokingly nowadays, but what it stands for is still central to Italian life.

At the humblest and most obvious level it is visible in the way Italians dress. Except for those whose work is extremely dirty, adult men traditionally wear neckties and jackets; they still tend toward white shirts. When it grows very warm, they will, under appropriate circumstances, open the collar and loosen the cravat ever so little; normally, however, the sidewalks in almost any Italian city are filled with manicured, buttoned-up, barbered males—and appropriately dressed women. Furthermore, they are carrying themselves with style, as if, though everybody else on the street may not at the moment be looking at them, it would only be natural if they did.

This extends even to the young who, like much of the young of the rest of the world, followed the example of the Americans in the early

1970s and went to blue jeans. In Italy, jeans and the accoutrements are often simply another—expensive—kind of fashion. The genuinely scruffy, fur-bearing, thong-footed guitar carrier in Italy almost invariably turns out to be some kind of Westerner other than Italian. The expression of *amour propre* through costume is so pervasive in crowds that it seems to have an inhibiting effect on the swarms of shabby young who wander throughout all the world's major cities in decent weather; they tend to avoid the center of Rome, for example, and concentrate primarily around the Piazza Navona. Romans have been idling in that elegant space for hundreds of years. Now it is generally filled by what the young call freaks. It is a scene from which most middle-class, middle-aged Americans would flee, but their Italian equivalents seem unoffended. On a hot afternoon Italians still sit on the benches and take the air amid, among other things, some of the grossest transvestites in the world. Piazza Navona has always been the world of the bourgeoisie, too, and that marvelous ability to concentrate on oneself provides much insulation.

La bella figura is much more than what one wears (or carries; construction workers and mechanics and street cleaners often carry their lunches in briefcases); it also extends to how one does one's job, whatever it is. The Italian waiter is a good example.

There is a trattoria in Piazza San Giovanni in Laterano in Rome which is one of the city's best, praised by Michelin and much favored by the neighborhood. It is invariably jammed at midday. One day I watched three American servicemen, identifiable, despite civilian clothes, by means of their haircuts, having a meal when the traffic was greatest. They were shown to a good table. One had only a Coca-Cola; the other two had plates of spaghetti with tomato sauce and a bottle of orange soda each. They were served not only with good manners, but with respect and style.

The respect is for himself and the perception others have of him; the ritual is for the better display of style.

The minor public official is an irritant even in the most civilized of societies, and so he is, frequently, in Italy, but for a reason different from the "I'll show this bum he can't rush me" attitude conveyed wordlessly by customs inspectors and railway officials and bus drivers in most of the world. In a movie of several years ago called *Avanti,* an American businessman whose father has been killed in an automobile accident in an Italian hill town comes to retrieve the body. Village officials accompany him to the crypt, and one sets up a folding desk, puts a stack of papers on it, and then unbuttons his jacket. In dozens of loops stitched to the lining are rubber stamps. He removes them one at a time and, with a solemn flourish, stamps the documents precisely so. Regardless of the comic license involved, the whole scene is wonderfully in the Italian spirit: the loving care of professional equipment, the precise execution of the physical requirements of the job, and, of course, the neatly tied cravat.

One can find evidence of the preoccupation with la bella figura throughout Italian life. The role of that feeling in shaping the kind of prose that Italian journalists write has been mentioned, along with what that kind of prose may have to do with low readership of newspapers. There is an effect beyond the comprehension of words on a page, however.

The creation of newspapers in most of the developed world includes as a critical part the functioning of what in the United States is called the copy desk. Here headlines are written, and, more important, the line-by-line, story-by-story editing goes on; the stuff produced by reporters is cut, sharpened, rewritten. It is through the copy desk that much of the style of newspapers with a lot of it, such as the *Wall Street Journal,* emerges. Copy editors not only make most news stories read better; the good ones are also walking libraries, spelling champions, and memory experts.

There are many reasons to believe that the quality of a newspaper is more dependent upon the copy desk than the brilliance of its reporters. In terms of the craft some of the greatest newspapers ever produced came out of England in the first few years after the end of the Second World War. Newsprint was scarce and rationed; such papers as the London *Times* and *Manchester Guardian* were reduced to ten or twelve pages. In large part through the efforts of the people on the copy desk—in the United Kingdom they are called subeditors—these papers produced thorough but remarkably condensed coverage of such matters as the Mau-Mau uprising in Kenya, the early flounderings of the United Nations, and the nationalization of much of British business and industry.

Italian newspaper journalism will never be saved by its copy editors, because it has none, except in a few special cases. The only function of the copy desk, in the familiar English-speaking sense of the term, is the writing of headlines and the selection of news stories. The writer is simply given a length and writes to it. No one else touches a word of his copy.

In the case of the major papers, the right of the Italian journalist to write what he pleases is undergirded by an in-house contract between the management and the staff. In the course of an interview directed at other ends I once heard the financial editor of one of the country's major dailies lamenting his problems with a correspondent he had sent to Venice for a piece surveying that city's economic recovery. When the piece came in, it was far too long for the space available, and in addition the section editor felt it was somewhat soft and overblown. Bound by the contract, he called his man in Venice and asked for permission to cut it. The reporter was reluctant, but finally consented with the condition that he select the parts to be cut. When his specifications came in, the financial editor disagreed almost in entirety. With the deadline approaching, the editor made his own cuts and sent the piece through. He was looking forward with some unhappiness, however, to the confrontation that was certain to develop when the reporter returned.

The lack of a copy desk function in Italian journalism costs a great deal. Foreign correspondents of the country's major dailies, with a few brilliant exceptions, file lengthy ruminative essays on the model of the nineteenth-century British papers' "diplomatic letters," which are carried, down to the comma, as originally dispatched. They are stylistically too difficult for the average reader and substantively too empty for the sophisticated one. The confluence of laws and contracts that prohibit the firing of a journalist and a prohibition against altering his copy in any way produces, in many cases, increasingly idiosyncratic performance. The sense of honoring individual uniqueness, laudable in many ways, takes its toll in Italian journalism.

Indro Montanelli, *Corriere della Sera*'s biggest name, left that paper to found a new one primarily for political reasons, as we shall see, but his conviction that style in Italian journalism was going to hell was part of it. Among the promises in the first issue of his new paper was "to create, or recreate, a certain journalistic tradition of seriousness and rigor."[1] This implied, of course, that the tradition had disappeared from the columns of *Corriere*. At another time, in a panel discussion on television, he complained that new entrants into the profession were clumsy workmen, especially left-leaners who had picked up some of the wooden rhetoric of Marxism.

Three years after Montanelli left, there was another clamorous exit from *Corriere della Sera,* and once again personal style was a contributing factor. Piero Ottone resigned as editor of the paper and was replaced by a man who had served for a long time as head of the reporting staff. The most important elements of that story were political, but an interesting sidelight was provided by the resignation from the staff of some of the paper's most eminent *collaboratori* for quite different reasons.

Collaboratori are regular, but part-time, contributors to Italian publications; for the most part, they write about books, plays, and music; or social criticism; or essays concerned with related matters cultural and intellectual. Within this group were several who feared that *Corriere*'s cultural pages were going to lose their high intellectual quality. One of them, Franco Fortini, set out his reasoning in a letter of resignation.

He had read and reread, he said, the first editorial of the new editor, and then decided to resign; he came to that step in part because, as another journalist summed it up:

The errors in syntax contained in that article were part, in his judgment, of a deliberate policy of reconciliation with the most backward element in the bourgeoisie, and were designed to annul the attempt at reaching intellectuals which thus far had survived in the pages of *Corriere*.[2]

There is another aspect of Italian *civiltà* with great effect on journalism. In the mid-1970s there began a series of revelations of corruption in many phases of Italian government and business, with the climax coming during the winter and spring of 1975-76 in the Lockheed bribery scandal. In the flurry of revelations a number of other U.S. corporations, including Exxon, Mobil, and Gulf, were identified, either through their own admissions to congressional committees or exposure in the Italian press, as heavy secret contributors to Italian political parties. Even though the exposures were almost certainly only a sliver of the reality, they were enough to indicate an extraordinarily pervasive practice.

The taking of bribes is not a habit unique to Italians, of course; highly placed Americans and Japanese and Frenchmen were being exposed during the same period. But it would not occur to most American businessmen, for example, that everyone with whom he dealt in a business relationship was on the take. The Italian businessman would assume it.

The taking of bribes, or the collection of graft, is only part of a broad pattern of corruption. Most of the sub-rosa activities in matters financial, whether in cheating on taxes or taking bribes or doing business through kickbacks, has an institutionalized quality. There are well-understood rules, the most fundamental of which is that the victims can afford it and deserve to be victimized (in many cases, of course, they insist upon it). As in other societies, the fact of widespread corruption says nothing whatever about what might be described as person-to-person morality. Italians are conspicuously honest in those relationships. Padded restaurant checks are rare, and so are cab drivers with a tendency to the long way 'round. I have had news vendors make a gift of a paper when they lacked change, and the tourist who mutely holds out a handful of money to a shopkeeper rarely gives up more than the stipulated price. In personal relationships, most Italians not only are fair but often generous.

Bribes and kickbacks and graft are something else, however. An eminent correspondent with whom I talked was unequivocal about the way it works in Italian journalism. "Every one of them is on the take. Every one." This from an American who has lived in Rome since the end of the Second World War, who identifies deeply and affectionately with the country, and who has been responsible for much distinguished correspondence in major U.S. newspapers and magazines—and who is a friend of most Italian journalists of consequence. "No exceptions?" "None."

In 1973 a young magistrate in Genoa began a series of investigations of corruption in politics and blundered into an Italian equivalent of the Nixon White House tapes—a safe containing complete records of illicit contributions by large industries to politicians and political parties. A list of journalists with sums attached was also found.

"When that one broke," said the American journalist, "I said to myself, 'Even they won't be able to bury this one.' Ha! Within two or three days the *bustarelle* were out and the whole investigation disappeared quietly from the papers."

Busta is the Italian word for envelope; from it comes the word for a bribe.*

Speaking to Italian journalists about bribes obviously is a delicate business, and although most of my interviews were leisurely and detailed, I did not often raise the subject. Sometimes comments were volunteered, or an anecdote, such as Barzini's, came up, and I did put the question directly to Arrigo Levi in 1977.

At that time Levi was the editor of *La Stampa,* a journalist widely known among Italians through his work on the national television network and his frequent byline in a wide variety of publications, including the country's best newspapers, several books, and magazines such as the international edition of *Newsweek,* for which he was a regular columnist. His many stretches of residence abroad, especially in the United Kingdom, have given him a cross-cultural breadth not common among Italian journalists, and go along with his personal openness and directness. He seemed an appropriate insider to ask about the assertion that everybody in the profession had some covert income.

He shook his head.

"I don't believe that," he said. "I would put my hand in the fire that no staff member of *La Stampa*—or *Corriere,* for that matter—takes bribes. Besides, Italian journalists make so much money they don't need to take bribes."

That dubious analysis was offered as a half-hearted joke, but it was clear in any case that he did not consider that kind of corruption a major

---

*Luigi Barzini sometimes quotes an illustrative remark of his own. In a conversation with another journalist, the name of a mutual professional acquaintance came up and, eventually, the absent colleague's education.

"*Che cosa ha studiato lui? Lettere?*"

[What did he study? Letters?]

"*No,*" said Barzini. "*Ha studiato le buste.*"

[He studied envelopes.]

factor in the country's journalism. He finally suggested, however, that perhaps there was some corruption among the *velinari*.

The name is from the word *velina*, light onionskin paper used for making carbon copies—what U.S. journalists sometimes call "flimsies." Velinari are independent operators who float around the press rooms of the Parliament and the executive branch selling inside information, tips, excerpts from unreleased documents, and similar material that the newsman may find useful. Levi said that *La Stampa* "doesn't use them much," and that he was trying to reduce it even further, but overall the velinari do a brisk business. In effect, the political reporter uses them the same way he uses press releases; the difference is that the source of press releases generally is known. The velinari, on the other hand, sometimes may be peddling something that is covertly paid for by somebody else.

When, a little later, the conversation turned to the qualities of young professionals coming into the field, Levi spoke of their passion for investigative reporting and exposé. (Woodward and Bernstein have had their effect on young European journalists.) He was asked if their zeal had been turned to the subject of corrupt journalists.

"No," he said after a moment. Apparently the idea had not occurred to him before.[3]

There have been at least a dozen books of criticism of the Italian press since 1967, most of them written by professional journalists. They have dealt in detail with the convolutions of ownership, the sins of politicians, and many other problems of the field. There is no mention in any of them of bribe taking. Italy has a half-dozen lively, frequently sensational weekly newsmagazines, most of which have regular departments covering the media. With a single exception, they have not mentioned journalists on the take.

The exception revealed more in what it did not do than in what it chose to do. The weekly *Tempo* for September 19, 1977, carried in large type on its cover the title "Report on the Journalist-Spies," with follow-up titillation in the subtitle: "Flimsies and Scandal: The Secret Service Infiltrates the Italian Press."[4] The article claimed that the Italian Secret Service, *Servizio Informazione Difesa* (SID), had in its files the dossiers of 149 journalists who had covertly accepted stipends from the agency during the previous decade. No names from the list were offered, however; instead, the bulk of the long article consisted of a "dictionary" of names that in one way or another were connected with SID scandals. Most of the episodes described were already part of the public record; most of the people listed were connected either with the Secret Service or the far-right *Movimento Sociale Italiano* (MSI) party. The name of Graham Martin, former American ambassador to Italy, appeared on the list, on the basis of the evidence developed by Congressman Otis Pike's subcommittee that Martin had channeled some $800,000 to Gen. Vito Miceli, then director of the Secret Service. Miceli used the money, said *Tempo,* to finance a journalist named Torchia in establishing a news service called *Oltremare* (Overseas). In turn, *Tempo* said, Oltremare transmitted false news. (It was true, however, that only far-right publications ever took Oltremare seriously, and they presumably knew exactly what they were doing.)

The story in *Tempo* proved nothing about the general level of morality among Italian journalists. The case that came closest to the mark was already well known; a star reporter on *Corriere della Sera* was on the Secret Service payroll, and his connections with them apparently helped him produce several important exclusives.

By and large, what the *Tempo* exposé established is not that journalists are corrupt, but that there are a lot of potential corrupters around.

In spite of what one is tempted to call a conspiracy of silence concerning bribes within the profession, there are some good reasons to suspect that some kind of venality is a good deal more common than the editor of *La Stampa* wanted to believe. The fact that it was a tradition at the beginnings of modern Italian journalism has been documented by an unimpeachable investigator, Giovanni Spadolini.

Spadolini probably had the highest prestige of any individual in the newspaper business in the late 1960s and early 1970s. He was the editor of *Corriere della Sera*. He also was a highly respected historian who began his career as an academic, then became editor of *Il Resto del Carlino* of Bologna before moving over to the leadership of the country's greatest daily.* Speaking at a professional meeting in 1967, he set out some details about press corruption in the Giolitti era.

Giovanni Giolitti was the leader of Italy for more than the first decade of the twentieth century, and they were, in many ways, good years. Industrial development bloomed, and with it a certain prosperity; a military adventure in Africa, very much the same kind of thing the English and French and Germans were up to, turned out successfully and made Giolitti a national idol; the delicate first steps of rapprochement

---

*Spadolini was abruptly fired as editor of *Corriere della Sera* by the Crespis in 1972, while that family still owned the paper, and circulation, income, and prestige were beginning to decline. He was elected to the Senate as a member of the Republican party, on the right wing of the center coalition, and became a prominent member of that relatively powerless body. He became a notable force in Italian journalism again in the winter of 1974–75 as chairman of a joint parliamentary coalition that held hearings and prepared legislation for subsidization of the press. In 1981 he became president of the Council of Ministers, the first prime minister since the end of the Second World War who was not a Christian Democrat.

with the Catholic church, and the church's entry into Italian politics, were taken. Giolitti also managed to blunt the thrust of socialism, rising forcefully throughout Europe. It was, in comparison to the struggle for unity that preceded it and the grotesqueries of government that were to bedevil Italy from 1915 onward, an almost serene and hopeful time.

In a speech to a conference on political journalism in 1967, Spadolini said that he felt obliged to publish in his new book

> accounts relative to the *bustarelle* from the Minister of the Interior to journalists. These included those most authoritative and above suspicion, such as the correspondents of *Stampa* or [*Corriere della*] *Sera* (parenthetically, the sums came to 100 to 200 lire a month in 1906, which is equivalent to around 300,000 to a half-million lire today [$450.00 to $800.00]). It must be realized that the list included all the political parties, including the Socialist and clerical opposition, with a revealing and remarkable price list by which not more than fifty lire a month was paid to Catholic journalists and not more than 100 to the Socialists and para-Socialists. I remember my uncertainties and many doubts before making public this sad and depressing list; but I overcame my reluctance, not only because of the obligation to the truth by which each of us is held, but also because it was well known by scholars of the subject that within two years all the documents from the Giolitti archives were to be published by Feltrinelli in three large volumes; one might as well have the courage to anticipate it rather than to thrust it brutally at the reader as the chief accusation hurled indiscriminately at everybody in a profession which did not merit such summary condemnation.[5]

The self-righteous outsider can amuse himself at length in the contemplation of what went through the heads of Spadolini's audience as he read those words—their eyes carefully fixed forward, faces carefully arranged to look serious.

Nevertheless such a picture probably is incorrect, flawed by a cultural difference not commonly perceived. A more accurate and understandable image might be that of, say, the earnest conservative parishioner who pushes for restrictive covenants to keep undesirables out of his neighborhood listening to a sermon about the concept that all men are one. If he thinks about this concept at all, he probably says to himself ". . . with the exception of this one little thing which doesn't really count."

I have in the process of these interviews come to know about fifty Italian journalists, perhaps a dozen of them fairly well, and three or four have become good friends. I seriously doubt that any of the latter two groups are corrupt or corruptible in the sense that their talents are for hire to the highest bidders or that an analysis of their work would indicate otherwise inexplicable changes in attitude. Further, I know a handful, particularly some connected with the rise of Journalists Committees, of whose devotion to the cause of elevating Italian journalism I am absolutely sure. It is most accurate, perhaps, to say that there is one subject upon which the typical Italian journalist cannot be trusted; it varies from journalist to journalist, of course, and the trick is to discover what that subject matter is and discount it.

The relationship between the briber and the bribe-taker is very commonly handled through a device that gives it a patina of legitimacy. In its story of "journalist-spies," *Tempo* referred to a list of seventy-five professionals listed by the Secret Service as "consultants." The system is said to be widespread throughout government agencies. A reporter assigned to cover a ministry may be asked to become a consultant to it. He (or possibly she, although there are almost no female reporters with such assignments in Italy) then prepares some kind of document and receives generous payment for it. In many cases, one hears, years go by without any reports at all, with the parties settling for an occasional lunch or a chat in the hall.

The more blunt, more old-fashioned approach, of course, is simply handing over money with no pretenses. The editor of an eminent daily somewhat reluctantly told this writer the story of a journalist on the staff of an unidentified paper who was transferred to Rome as bureau chief in late fall. In the middle of December he received a note from an unspecified cabinet minister which said, "Best wishes for the New Year." It was clipped to a check for a million lire, not a large sum (about $1,600 at that time), but enough to be a comfort in the winter months ahead. The new bureau chief returned it with an angry letter. The fact that the check was sent, however, seems to indicate that his predecessor had always behaved differently.

Most of the few references to bribery that came up in my conversations with professionals were indirect, but indicated that the speaker assumed that the custom was widespread. A leader of the Italian Press Officers Association, for example, used such a reference as an argument in favor of his specialty.

This is an association of professionals, almost all of them members of the Order of Journalists, who are spokesmen for Italian corporations, trade associations, and similar entities in search of a good press and more profit. In U.S. businesses such posts are usually in the public relations department, but the Italians dislike that phrase. The profession developed late in Italy, but is growing rapidly.

The head of the Milan chapter, Marco Betti, indicated that their most effective sales pitch went, in essence, like this: "You pay a journalist and he writes good things about you until he needs more money. You have no guarantee and no recourse. A company with a division which openly seeks good publicity will, in the long run, get more for its money."[6]

It is a persuasive notion, and perhaps has had something to do with the recent improvement in financial pages in major Italian dailies. Most press corruption is in connection with political matters, of course, but two other regular departments have traditionally been sinkholes. For many years financial "reporting" was notoriously venal, but a variety of factors associated with the reform movement that we shall be examining later have made the pages more interesting, at least, to the outsider, and it was a common observation among the professionals with whom I talked that the credibility of the information is also higher.

The other classically tainted department has been, not surprisingly, artistic criticism: the reviewing of plays, films, books, and art shows. During my first year in Italy I met an important critic who worked on a small but high-quality party paper. He regarded all his fellow critics as corrupt, and demonstrated by reeling off the prices per line for favorable reviews in various departments in a dozen different publications. The temptation to inquire about his own rates had to go unfulfilled.

Corruption of the press is simply a part of the endemic corruption in both the political and economic sectors in Italy. To the extent that journalists are believed to be corrupt, their credibility is damaged, and with it the status of the press in society. It unfortunately combines with the tendency toward the politicization of practically everything to make a raging cynicism about all establishments another characteristic of modern Italian life.

The Latin passion for politics is one of those eternal reservoirs of popular humor (perhaps the only one unrelated to sex): get three Spaniards together and you get four political parties. The reason there are so many revolutions in South America is that so many people still haven't been president. The Italian voter casts a blank ballot because there are only thirty-four parties listed and none really represents his thinking.

Stereotype or no, most Italians do take delight in politics. Political discussion is a basic outdoor sport. Sometimes it becomes almost institutionalized, as in the vast cathedral square in Milan. This is a favorite site, of course, for scheduled political rallies, but there is also a long tradition of alfresco argument; on a pleasant Sunday afternoon there is likely to be a group of fifty or so men standing in a loose circle with two shouting principals in the center, the kind of thing that in the United States automatically suggests a fight. But this is argument, not physical violence, and although there is shouting, tempers are not really high. Spectators stand silently, listening with an air of judicious gravity. Something like it goes on regularly in the central piazza of every city in Italy.

People with that kind of interest will be good voters, obviously, and Italians are. In recent national elections more than 90 percent of the eligible have cast ballots, in spite of the fact that voting is not a simple action. In the national election of 1976, for example, Romans also voted for local and regional administrative officials, and thus had to deal with four different paper ballots, one of which required writing in a series of names in order of preference. The voters seem inexhaustible, despite the fact that elections are more frequent in Italy than in any other country.[7]

It is frequently said that such figures are not very significant because voting is compulsory in Italy. This is not true; there are no penalties under the law for not voting. The fact is recorded on the nonvoter's identity card for five years, however, which provides a certain amount of psychological persuasion.

Even in nonelection years, party politics is always before the eye and ear in Italy. Although there are recent predictions that the number of outdoor meetings will decline as party leadership turns to radio and television, throughout the 1970s the *comizio* ("mass meeting") continued to be a common spectacle, the bunting-draped platform set up in the piazza, the preliminary parade through the streets with huge banners, the amplified music, and the rhetoric flooding tinnily from bullhorns. Party headquarters, down to the neighborhood level, are usually identified with a conspicuous and permanent sign; a working-class neighborhood is certain to have a highly visible Communist Party headquarters. The national offices of the Christian Democrats occupy a palazzo that dominates the Piazza del Gesù on one of Rome's busiest streets, and the view from one of the most tourist-frequented spots in the world, the arches of the Galleria Colonna in the heart of Rome, is dominated by an ancient triumphal column and a huge sign on the top floor of the building across the square identifying the headquarters of the Social Democrats. Italy is a country of superb walls, sweeping surfaces that order and define the landscape; the walls are covered with posters, and most of them are political.

Further, the social institution that many would feel has been the most dominant of all over Italian history, the Roman Catholic church, is a powerful political entity; it plays partisan politics openly and is perceived as much as a political as a spiritual institution by most of its friends as well as its enemies.

This is not to say that most of the Italian population is deeply interested in politics. Politics in any society seems to be a passion of a part of the people—not necessarily an elite, as conventionally defined, it should be noted; many of high socioeconomic status in any society are hostile to any political system. But the group committed to politics as the primary thing that matters is made up of those who persevere in the endless detail that eventually produces governance, of one sort or another. That part of the Italian population goes about it with more passion than the equivalent part of most societies.

Several reasons for this suggest themselves. They are a people hooked on words, immersed in both a verbal and oral tradition, possessed of a lyrical and elegant language, the exercise of which they love; politics is a language game.

Like most parliamentary democracies, Italy's is based upon proportional representation, a system that makes it perfectly reasonable to organize a party in hopes of winning two or three seats. European politics since the First World War has seen a gradual shrinkage of that tendency; Britain has had three parties, and only two major ones, for decades; Germany has had no more than four since the end of Hitler. There were signs in the Italian election of 1976 of the same trend, but still nine parties contested that election, and all but one of them won a place in Parliament.

The passion for politics has helped give the country a dramatic history. Italy as a modern nation is about a hundred years old, and has always been among the less powerful European nations, but through it have swept all the shattering thrusts of political change—successful early colonialism, anarchism and the Socialist scission, near defeat in the First World War, fascism, catastrophic defeat in the Second World War, the abandonment of the monarchy, the rise during the Stalinist era of the largest Communist political organization outside the Soviet Union. Almost every modern political idea of significance has had a run in Italy.

The superficial signs of the political way of life are easy to see in Italy. Of more consequence but less immediately visible is the politicization of the institutional structure of the society.

Party politics and the process of governance, for example, are fused together in ways not common elsewhere. In the first place, political parties—which, as someone is always pointing out, are not even mentioned in the U.S. Constitution—are creatures of government as well as its creators.

In the 1976 national election campaign the two biggest Italian political parties spent *twenty* times as much money as the two major British parties in their 1974 election. A substantial amount of this came directly from the government, under legislation passed in 1974. Specifically, the Christian Democrats had a total income of about $29 million.

Of that, the government contribution was about $18 million. The *Partito Comunista Italiano* (PCI) had a total income for the campaign of about $31.4 million, of which the government contributed about $12.5 million.* Each party, incidentally, overspent its budget and ended with a deficit for the campaign.[8]

That financial relationship simply puts in concrete terms the articulation between parties and public institutions. Enterprises that are, of necessity, in the public sector in any society, but that are generally relatively sanitized of direct partisan infection, are highly political in Italy. The Biennale of Venice, for example, is an international festival of the arts, particularly well known for its film showings and display of painting and the plastic arts. It is of worldwide importance, and a source not only of considerable tourist revenue, but of national pride to Italy.

Most of the Biennale's financing comes from the government. Out of that inevitably grows the fact that its eighteen-member governing board has been carefully chosen along political lines, representing the country's political parties, the municipal administration of Venice, and the trade unions. Even honored guests are picked with political considerations in mind. This means that political sensitivities are carefully observed—and can be expertly manipulated. Something of the sort happened in 1977, when the director of the festival, a Socialist, announced that the theme of that summer's exhibition would be cultural dissent in Europe.

This was admittedly a timely and significant theme, but it also seems artful politics. The Socialists during the electoral campaign of 1976 attempted to establish their independence from their former coalition partners, the Christian Democrats, by attacking them energetically, refusing in advance to be part of any DC-led government regardless of the election results, and insisting that any proper government would have to include the Communists. This gave a superficial impression, at least, that the Socialists were allies of the PCI, something that may have contributed to the disastrous Socialist losses in the voting.

The problem then became that of establishing independence from the Communists, and at least one American reporter, Sari Gilbert of the *Washington Post,* saw the choice of the dissent theme for the Biennale as a means to that end.[9] The Italian Communists were embarrassed; although busily demonstrating their own independence from Soviet communism, they also have always gone to great lengths to avoid giving gratuitous offense. Their embarrassment was not eased when the Soviet ambassador to Italy complained and announced that his government would not participate in any future Biennale if the theme was carried out. The wran-

---

*Conversion to dollars is made on the basis of 850 lire equals 1 dollar.

gling went on for months, and finally ended with a much more modest Biennale than usual, still vaguely on the theme of cultural dissent but much diluted, and gloomy prophecies that the whole institution was doomed.

Most aspects of Italian culture have political color, including even the funerals of national cultural heroes. I have an Italian friend who had high-level connections with the Italian movie industry for years. He also is politically conservative. When he was asked if he was going to Roberto Rossellini's funeral in 1977, he looked surprised and said, "Good lord, no. It'll be a Communist show." He was absolutely correct; the city of Rome, with a Communist administration, took over the staging of the affair and only PCI members spoke. Although the director's death was big news in all the Italian media, *L'Unità,* the PCI's daily, gave it by far the largest play, filling pages with photographs and laudatory rhetoric, all set out in subtly proprietary tones that would have given the unknowing a clear impression that Rossellini was wholeheartedly one of theirs. In fact, he was only an occasional, vague sympathizer.

But then the movie business in Italy has always had a strong political framework. Most of the movies of the first postwar decade, the golden era of Italian filmmaking, were subsidized by the government. The hopeful producer made a proposal to the department of subsidization in the Ministry of Tourism and *lo Spettacolo* (a generic term that covers all phases of theatrical entertainment, including music), generally including a script, a tentative cast and crew, and his own professional record; the ministry would then decide how much assistance they would provide toward the cost of production. The system had its virtues; superb short films accompanied feature showings in Italian movie houses long after they had disappeared from the United States, and they were financed almost entirely through government grants. It was also, however, a system that encouraged political caution. Once the film was finished, the government provided more help through subsidization of the price of movie tickets that kept them cheap.

Much the same system was applied to all the other *spettacoli:* opera companies, theater repertory companies, symphony orchestras. Thus there was a great burgeoning not only of productions but also of audiences; in the early 1950s it was possible to get an excellent seat at a first-class play for a third of the Broadway equivalent. Some kind of state subsidization of public arts is found in most European countries, of course, but there generally is some kind of organizational buffer between the politicians and the players. In Italy, however, the successful recipient of subsidies has had to be a person of great political sensitivity.

The government-controlled broadcasting system is the ultimate example of politicized bureaucracy in almost any country. The structure and history of RAI is set out elsewhere in this book. On paper the organization appears very close to the common pattern that was modeled in great part on the British Broadcasting Corporation (BBC); a pattern so common, in fact, that the United States system is the only major exception. The broadcasting systems of other nations not only are under government control to some extent, but are also dependent on their governments for much of their financial support.

The distance that the broadcasting entity keeps from the intricacies of party politics is one of the chief indicators of differences among broadcasting systems of different countries. The BBC apparently is the most removed, although there is a steady thread of political activity throughout its history. The French system has been considerably more politicized than the BBC, and *L'Office Radiodiffusion-Télévisione Française* (ORTF) was particularly so during the regime of Charles de Gaulle.

But Radiotelevisione Italiana is a political institution down to the selection of the unseen toilers who read voice-overs for news film. Every position of consequence is filled by a person whose political identity is clear, and the mix of identities is critical. The result is a system haunted by a typical Italian irony. In almost everyone's opinion, RAI has always attracted the brightest talents in Italian communication; and in almost everyone's opinion, RAI is muscle-bound, inefficient, and generally incompetent. When one asks a knowing Italian a question about RAI, the answer comes not in words, but a gesture.

Two other points about politicking in the public institutions of Italian society should be mentioned. First, the public official usually maintains his ties with his party and thinks of himself as that party's representative as long as he is in the job. Although it is far from being the rule, Americans are accustomed to seeing people in important appointive posts change as they grow into the job. There have been dozens of people among Supreme Court justices, Federal Communications Commission (FCC) members, comptrollers of the currency, cabinet members, and even district attorneys who have changed political color on the job to the extent of actively opposing the men and the party who appointed them. Congress usually contains members who have switched parties. That very rarely happens in Italy. The function remains political, and the functionary a politician.

Secondly, it should be apparent that the prevalence of this system in Italy has not meant that the Christian Democrats have been able to impose thought control and guarantee their own eternal dominance. There are many Italians who might insist that the DC tried and, in ways not seen and to extents not easily measured, succeeded. But the steady burgeoning of the Communist party and the number of votes it attracts indicates something less than successful suppression. The range and vigor of the arts has demonstrated that talent cannot be ultimately corrupted through government subsidy; it is a safe generalization that most of Italy's eminent artists of whatever medium have been anti-DC, and some of them savage critics of the regime.

Until the beginnings of its reform in the mid-1970s, the major institution that most clearly demonstrated the effect of party politics was RAI. Even there the most visible effect was a disinfected torpor; the politicians in command operated, consciously or not, on the principle that the way to prevent the opposition from saying hurtful things was to let no one say anything at all.

The point to emphasizing the pervasiveness of politics as a force in the society is not primarily that of short-term effects. It is, rather, the significance of a process: the fact of politicization, almost regardless of particular dogma, does condition the ways Italian society is unlike other Western societies, and it has profound effects, of course, upon the Italian journalist.

The phenomenon is not all on the surface. Deep within the economic structure is a relationship among business, the state, and political parties of which many Italians are not aware. A substantial part of industry is now controlled by holding companies that are a mixture of government and private investment.

These holding companies are the biggest of a total of almost two hundred companies with government involvement; altogether, by 1980, these enterprises had debts of more than $20 billion. They had an aggregate deficit of $1.5 billion in 1976. Since most of the debts are owed to Italian banks, the collapse of these firms would be catastrophic. At the same time, the government is a heavy investor in those same banks; the system is Byzantine, with failing government-financed companies forced to borrow money at what were then high interest rates (12 to 15 percent was common by the end of the decade) from government-financed banks. In 1976 Parliament made provision for an additional $7 billion subsidy to help sustain the system for the remainder of the decade.

"The crisis is a crisis of responsibility," Guido Carli, once head of the Bank of Italy, pointed out to a reporter. "The heads of public corporations are evaluated not on the basis of their efficiency but on their party loyalties."[10]

All this means that the Italian businessman, even though his own firm is entirely in the private sector, also has to be a knowledgeable politician and a committed one to an extent far beyond the vague conservatism of most businessmen in the United States.

If the owners and publishers of the major Italian dailies are political men, their employees are even more so. Ties with politics—intellectual, emotional, and institutional—sharply distinguish the Italian journalist from the average professional in Britain or the United States. French journalists also tend to find joy in politics, of course, as do those from Latin America, but a case can be made for the Italians as the ultimate example within the profession in the West (and in Eastern Europe, for that matter; the successful Soviet-bloc journalist has enormous political sensitivity, but it is for consensus politics; he essentially is a vessel for received truths). The process by which the Italian journalist comes into the profession is in the broad sense political, and both the trade union and the national professional society to which he belongs and by which he is licensed are deeply involved in direct political activity. In no other major country are the connections so pervasive.

There are still American journalists who refuse to vote, although not as many as fifty years ago; there are many more, resident in states in which it is necessary to declare party affiliation in the primary election, who abjure that part of the electoral process and vote only in general elections. Politicians and their activities are constantly discussed in American newsrooms, of course; political parties a good deal less; and partisan evangelism is seldom heard at all. The managing editor of most major American dailies would be hard put to identify with certainty the party commitments of more than half his staff.

This does not mean that the American journalist has no interest in the processes through which his government works or the influence of those processes on his society. Research has repeatedly shown that most journalists in this country are attracted to the profession in part because they are somewhat reform-minded; they see it as a way to help better the world. But most American journalists do not see party politics as an effective method for bringing about that kind of change; their sense of social responsibility is more closely linked to their profession.

This can be reduced to the assertion that professionalism, however loosely and erratically it may be defined, simply means more to the American journalist than to the Italian. This does not imply that the American journalist thus acquires superior virtue. He is, in a sense, the poorer; he has weaker commitments, less certainty, and is probably much more likely to be bored by what he does. But if he is forced to make a deliberate choice, he generally will put professional considerations above acting on personal political beliefs.

Not so the Italian journalist, if one judges by a traditional provision of the national agreement that establishes wages, hours, and conditions of work for all professionals in the country. Article 32 of the national journalists' contract for 1977–78 reads:

> In the case of substantial change in the political direction of the paper, or in the case of assignment of the journalist to other publications owned by the same company but with substantially different characteristics, an assignment which impairs the professional dignity of the journalist, the journalist may ask for dissolution of his contract and receive severance pay equivalent to being fired.[11]

The last clause means, under Italian contracts, a cost so great to the employer that few will undertake it: a month's pay for each year of service to the company, plus a special indemnity ranging from an additional thirteen months' pay for top editors down to seven months' for ordinary reporters. It thus would cost a major daily around $27,000 to disaffect a reporter who had been with the paper for ten years and just short of $100,000 to fire a managing editor with twenty years' service.

It should be pointed out that this notion did not originate in Italy, but in France in 1935. A special section of the journalists' *code du travail* provides a formula for compensation for the offended journalist when there occurs

> a notable change in the character or orientation of a newspaper or periodical, if the change creates, for the person employed, a situation which impairs his honor, his reputation, or, in a general way, his moral interests.[12]

Perhaps significantly, the word *political* appears in the Italian version, but not in the French. It has been used primarily in regard to political shifts, however, and under its provisions a highly paid French editor sued for damages totaling about half a million dollars in 1979.

The provision regarding a change in political direction puts a powerful tool in the hands of the journalist; if he is bored or unhappy on his job and wants out, he can add a handsome bonus to his severance pay if he can convince a magistrate that his political morality has been offended. For this reason management tends to handle expensive help with great care, usually through the device of continuing salary while refusing to carry work which is at variance with the publication's policies.

Indro Montanelli was not so easily placated. Montanelli has been for almost fifty years one of the best-known Italian journalists. He was for many years a distinguished foreign correspondent for *Corriere della Sera;* he has written many books, generally political comment, and coauthored a series of histories of Italy. Always a conservative, he rebelled when *Corriere* began to swing sharply to the left after the firing of Giovanni Spadolini, and retaliated by founding a new newspaper in the summer of 1974, taking with him twenty-five veteran staff members. The entire group later filed an action against *Corriere* under the provisions of the contract. The courts eventually threw out the case; if it had been upheld, it might very possibly have bankrupted the paper.

Judging by the rhetoric in the Montanelli case, the suit for damages had more than a little lust for revenge in it, although the money alone made it worth undertaking. But some genuine political sensitivity of a sort quite unknown to American journalism frequently is also involved in leaving a job. When Italo Pietra left *Il Giorno* of Milan, for example, he knew he had to go, but he was not openly angry and lawsuits apparently never crossed his mind.

Il Giorno, the major competitor of *Corriere della Sera,* was the property of *L'Ente Nazionale Idrocarburi* (ENI), a conglomerate with holdings in many fields, including petroleum and industrial chemistry, which had been established by a brilliant maverick industrialist named Enrico Mattei. Pietra was its responsabile, and his deepest commitments were to two ideas that seemed contradictory. He was a hero of the Resistance, a serious Socialist, and at the same time devoted to the memory of Mattei, a Christian Democrat who had been an empire builder in the style of the robber barons of the nineteenth century in America. In the process of rising to the top he fought against the classic big names of Italian industry. Pietra went through the list during an interview with me, making contemptuous references to other industrialists who owned newspapers: the Agnellis, Montis, and Perrones. That sounded like the good Socialist, but the awed respect for Mattei did not. The contradiction was compounded by Pietra's carry-over of loyalty to Eugenio Cefis, Mattei's protegé and heir. Cefis was at that point becoming, in the eyes of most people in Italian journalism, a hot-eyed monopolist threatening the whole structure of the press. Nevertheless Pietra never wavered in his devotion to him and, in time, simply cut off conversations that became critical of Cefis.[13]

Even more surprising than the enthusiasm for both Mattei and socialism, however, was my realization that Pietra knew very little about the detailed, day-to-day news operations of the paper. The point of the provision in Italian press law for a responsabile is just what the word implies, the designation of someone who assumes final responsibility for violations of the law and serves as a formal target in civil suits. The law specifies nothing, however, about what else he does, and the national journalists' contract specifies only certain restraints upon whatever authority he might choose to exercise. The responsabile who is interested only in one aspect has been common on papers published by political parties, but uncommon on major dailies. At the time Pietra and I talked, for example, Spadolini was responsabile of *Corriere,* Ronchey of *La Stampa,* and Alessandro Perrone of *Il Messaggero;* all were deeply involved in supervision of the generation of the daily paper. Pietra was not; he simply left all that to a pair of highly capable managing editors, while maintaining close control of the paper's political tone and content.

There were two reasons for Pietra's leaving his job in June, 1972. One was corporate infighting; his friend and protector Eugenio Cefis, under fire from several sides in the conglomerate, lost control of the paper to an in-house competitor who, in effect, fired Pietra, although permitting time for the formal process of resignation. It was unnecessary to push, however; Pietra felt it was time to go—not for business reasons, but because Italian politics, his only real interest, had shifted. The center-left government that *Il Giorno* had generally backed and that, although not precisely his own, he lived with comfortably, had moved to the right.

In the summer of 1960, in an atmosphere of tension following the failure of two rightist-leaning governments, the Christian Democrats tilted the other way and put together a government supported by the Liberals, the Republicans, and the Social Democrats; equally important, the Socialists agreed to abstain. This "opening to the left" stance endured, with various changes, until the early 1970s; for a variety of reasons beyond the scope of this book, it is now remembered with regret and even bitterness by almost everybody, including those most deeply committed to it.

By the summer of 1972, the center-left was gone, more by erosion than by overthrow; an unremarkable longtime Christian Democrat functionary named Giovanni Leone was the president of Italy (with the assistance of the votes of the far-right *Movimento Sociale Italiano* [MSI]); Giulio Andreotti was prime minister and head of a "centralist" government.

"It was," in the words of one of the historians of the Italian press, "a whole new contest which, in Pietra's judgment, made his presence in the direction of the paper no longer supportable."[14]

Although the circumstances of his leaving were different in some respects, Giovanni Spadolini saw his dismissal from the post of editor of *Corriere della Sera* as similarly tied to the fortunes of the center-left government: ". . . because I precisely represented the center-left line at *Corriere,* the crisis of that group . . . was, for my leadership, most serious."

Many observers thought that the owners, the Crespi family, were more interested in money than in politics, and that Spadolini was fired largely because of the skidding fortunes of the paper. Spadolini's explanation did not rule that out as an element, but he still felt it was largely a political matter, pointing out that to old conservative readers, his line was dangerously leftist, while it continued to appear conservative to the burgeoning forces on the left. "Look," he told an interviewer, "during that period I was under seige on two fronts."[15]

Within the context of American journalism, such linkage between politics and presumably independent newspapers appears strange indeed; it would have been unbelievable, for example, that the editor of the *New York Times* might consider, as a matter of conscience, stepping down when the Rockefeller wing of the Republican party lost out in the 1964 convention. But that kind of Italian political sensitivity is only one tie. The choosing of a replacement for Pietra at *Il Giorno* provides an example of another kind.

The new publisher of the paper, Raffaele Girotti, solicited a wide range of opinions about his presumptive nominee, according to his own account: from other journalists, including the redoubtable Montanelli; from leaders within the business community; from President Giovanni Leone; Giulio Andreotti, then head of the government; Arnoldo Forlani, secretary of the Christian Democrat party; Flaminio Piccoli, director of press subsidization and other government participation in media economics; Amintore Fanfani, an eminent party leader; Francesco De Martino, leader of the Socialist party; and its secretary, Giacomo Mancini.

The process was informal, obviously, and no one had an absolute right of veto, or at least the only dissenter to the appointment of Gaetano Afeltra did not. Francesco De Martino, who was a friend of Pietra's, disapproved. That opinion was counterweighted, however, by the support for the appointment from the party's secretary, Mancini.

Politics seems to have been an even more forceful presence in the replacement of Piero Ottone by Franco Di Bella as editor of *Corriere della Sera* several years later, in the autumn of 1977. Precisely what went on never became entirely clear. In September, Ottone resigned as editor and accepted a high-level corporate position with Mondadori, a publishing firm with interests in books, magazines, daily papers, and broadcasting; its properties included the highly successful weekly newsmagazine, *Panorama,* and a fine new daily called *La Repubblica.* Some serious and highly reputable Italian journalists have insisted that there was no more than meets the eye in that action; that the new job offered not only high pay, but wider and more imaginative possibilities than the continued nursing of a *Corriere* that was still a long way from financially well.

The sizable segment of the press bent toward the left, including Mondadori's own *Panorama,* had a different story. According to *Panorama,* Ottone was a victim of developing closeness between the Rizzoli family, which had acquired *Corriere* from the Crespis, and the Christian Democrat party. As the Rizzoli empire rapidly expanded, it ran up monumental losses; the need to find salvation fit nicely, according to *Panorama,* with a growing conviction on the part of Fanfani, in particular, that the party needed better representation in the press.

Fifteen years earlier that idea would have been preposterous, but by 1973-74 three of the country's four top general dailies were anti-DC and the fourth was hardly supportive. The fact that the party's leadership felt that much had to be done was clear. Flaminio Piccoli, the party's press specialist, laid it out at the Christian Democrats' national congress in March, 1977. It is an illustration of the extent to which not only political commitment, but action, may be expected of the Italian journalist by politicians.

> It is clear that all Christian Democrats who work in the field of journalism should associate themselves with the party, giving their work the stamp of the values that the DC represents. To make this happen it is important that, while still protecting individuality, we not lose our way by taking many roads, in personalized initiatives; that we instead redirect everything toward unity, making our role in the mass media increasingly competent and functional.[16]

Even more important than encouraging more political action among working journalists, it might be assumed, was major influence at the top levels of ownership. That fitted neatly, according to most left-oriented publications, with the Rizzoli organization's desperate need for cash. Through their connections in European financial circles they raised billions of lire; the amounts and sources involved varied from one account to another.

The politicians who made it possible, the story goes, began to apply pressure to remove top-level journalists whose attitudes they disliked; getting their own man in *Corriere,* the largest and generally assumed most influential paper in the country, was high priority. Whether or not that was true, some of the Christian Democrats made no attempt to hide their feelings about Ottone.

Regardless of what Ottone actually felt, or the relationship that he had with Rizzoli, there is no question that the atmosphere within the organization was increasingly tense. Nor was there any question of the openly political character of the hiring of his successor.

In searching for a replacement, the owners were seen in the chambers of the powers of the Christian Democrat party—the presidential palace, the Senate, the party headquarters. The approval of Fanfani, Andreotti (then premier), Piccoli, and Bettino Craxi, new secretary of the Socialist party, apparently was solicited before Franco Di Bella was named to the post. Di Bella was an old hand at *Corriere,* and a safe one.*

When it comes to criticizing "public authority," he told the staff of *Corriere* at his meeting with them as nominee for editor, the criticism should be "as usual, documented, never generalized"; there should be "a sharp, constructive turn" in reporting, "eliminating any suspicion of a prearranged program of systematic discrediting of institutions."[17]

All this does not mean, of course, that the Christian Democrats in 1977 installed a party hack as the editor of the country's biggest newspaper. In the first place, even the dullest politicians who survive very long are smarter than that. More importantly, the person who runs the news operation for a major daily has to be of a high order of competence. The owners of any publication, however profoundly politicized they might be, are also concerned with solvency. The trick is to find an administrator of great professional competence who is also a passionate believer in what his bosses believe to be the best politics. If he is not to be found, it is both easier and safer to ease off on the political requirement.

The name most talked about as successor when Ottone's intention of resigning became known was that of Alberto Ronchey. He had glorious credentials: former editor of *La Stampa,* distinguished correspondent, author of some thoughtful books. An associate of Fanfani quickly made it clear that Ronchey would not be considered for the job.

"Ronchey is a preacher," he said. "Good editors are from among the parishioners."[18]

Interestingly enough, Piero Ottone had also been seen primarily as a proven editorial administrator when he was hired after the displacement of Giovanni Spadolini. He was never much of a political man, and *Corriere*'s turn toward the political left was largely an effort to build a new audience and make the paper more responsive to what he saw as the spirit of the times. The owners of the paper and their political partners found that uncomfortable, in time, but they felt, it seems, that they could find a replacement with the same credentials who might be safer politically.

There is another tie between journalism and politics in Italy represented by the character of the journalist-politician, a type more visible in that country than this one. Only 3 percent of the members of the U.S. Congress in 1974, for example, were journalists—16 of a total of 535. Over 6 percent of the Italian Parliament that same year were members of the profession—60 of a total of 945.

More striking than the differences in numbers is the number of party

---

*He was, however, forced out of *Corriere* in June, 1981, by the revelation that he was a member of a secret Masonic lodge called P2.

leaders in Italy who are professional journalists. Among the sixty in that Parliament were Giulio Andreotti, several times premier; Pietro Ingrao of the Communists, who was to become president of the Chamber of Deputies in 1976; Ugo La Malfa, longtime leader of the Republicans and one of the most respected figures in the country's politics; Giovanni Spadolini, exeditor of *Corriere della Sera*, who played a leading role in the Senate from the day of his arrival; Giorgio Almirante, leader of the far-right *Movimento Sociale Italiano;* Arnoldo Forlani, secretary of the Christian Democrat party; and Luigi Longo, a leader of the Communists since the end of the Second World War. The president of the republic from 1964 to 1971, Giuseppe Saragat, was also on the list.

All these were *professionisti* in the national Order of Journalists. Among the members of the *pubblicisti* branch (free-lance writers) of the Order of Journalists was Enrico Berlinguer of the PCI, and Saragat's successor as president, Giovanni Leone.*

Most of these did not come into the profession through the regular process. At the end of the Second World War a group of about a hundred political figures who could be expected to take leadership roles in the rebuilding of Italian politics were given what amounted to honorary status as professional journalists; the action was a quick certification of their lack of any Fascist taint and provided them a respected and visible place in the system. The only journalism most have ever practiced has been in the party cause. Several have been editors of party papers, although they cannot, under Italian law, stay in that post after election to Parliament (because members of Parliament have immunity, and editors have responsibilities under the law that require that they be prosecutable).

In any case it would be misleading to give the impression that all Italian journalists are ideologues or precinct captains. To the contrary, when it comes to specific issues and particular politicians, most Italian journalists, very much like those of any other country, are skeptical and carefully detached; the leftist orientation of most newsmen in that country grows primarily out of deep, often very bitter, cynicism about the Christian Democrats; they are equally cynical about the Communists, and end up being Socialists, which has the additional attraction of being the party of many intellectuals.

The big difference between the Italian journalist and his equivalent in most other societies rests in his seeing almost everything outside his

---

*The word *pubblicista* is commonly misunderstood by English speakers; even one of the standard Italian-English dictionaries translates it as "publicist." It has nothing to do either with publicity or *pubblicità,* the Italian word for advertising. It simply means a freelance writer, and is almost identical to the German *publizist.*

intimate personal relationships through a political lens. The American journalist normally would not see the quality of education, or law enforcement, or the state of the water supply primarily as partisan political concerns. The Italian journalist sees them, and a hundred other elements of the social dynamic, as politics and the terrain of politicians. Furthermore, things he has not thought about before, but with which he must begin to be concerned, he will analyze first as political phenomena. The question of prohibiting the eating of shellfish from the bay of Naples because of contamination a few years ago was treated as a political issue; so were the provisions of the reform bill for higher education passed in 1973. And so, of course, in part because of the activism of the Catholic church, were both divorce and abortion.

The key word is *politicize*. Like most *-ize* adaptations of nouns, it is a graceless word, offensive to the ear. But the point is the *process* of transforming all manner of things into essentially political phenomena. This process is frequently seen as deplorable in the United States; there have been recurrent cries of "Let's keep politics out of this!" since the country's beginnings. That objection has been used in reference to issues ranging from foreign policy to low cost housing. American journalists would probably be better practitioners if they more frequently examined the possible political dimensions of the stories they cover, but Italian journalists' insistence on the political lens sometimes produces journalism with profoundly disfunctional effects, eroding the credibility not only of Italian political institutions, but of Italian journalism as well.

This chapter has dealt with some of the social and cultural contexts of the practice of the journalist's profession. These factors will be frequently reflected as the analysis proceeds. Their influence on shaping the way the journalist develops, however, is obviously secondary to constraints and rewards of the elaborate system through which one enters the field. Now we need to look at that system in detail.

Chapter 3

Becoming a Professional

When an Italian citizen decides on a career in journalism, he or she takes the first step into a bureaucratic system that has origins more than a hundred years old. It is a system that asks the surrender of a certain amount of control of personal initiatives and preferences; in the past, in the Mussolini era, admission was used as an enforcer of Fascist orthodoxy. In recent years the nascent journalist has no longer been open to direct political pressure, and the rewards and protection to be gained from membership seem to outweigh whatever loss is involved, but there is still a single path to professionalism, and, at the final stage, a single definition of professional competence.

There are no formal education requirements. The candidate must be at least eighteen years old at the time he presents himself for the first examination. The whole process of candidacy and examination demonstrates clearly how the neophyte's perceptions and commitments are shaped from that first moment of tentative self-selection.

It is important to note first that the stipulations that follow are matters of law. Statutes passed by the Parliament established the Order of Journalists and defined most of the essential characteristics of the profession. The regulations include detailed guidelines for a preliminary examination, the *Esame di cultura generale*. The device was established originally for the benefit of older journalists who had only a grammar school education; it is seldom used any more, however, since it is waived for holders of secondary school diplomas.

In theory, the process of beginning an apprenticeship consists of simply applying to the newspaper at which one wishes to work and making a good impression. In practice, the successful applicants are usually accompanied by a discreet letter or telephone call from somebody who knows somebody. When I asked one of the editors of a major daily how he chooses an apprentice he replied, "Well, I look for a good background in economics and political science. Then there's a whole list of questions of my own I like to ask, but I generally don't get to ask them, because the boss calls, and he's heard from a cabinet minister, or it develops that this young man is a cousin of one of the owners, or. . . ."

He shrugged amiably. Good job openings are, and always have been, rare in Italy, and there always have been more hopefuls for journalism than posts for them. Under such circumstances, a system of accommodation to friendship, family ties, politics, and business connections is inevitable. The young journalist generally is not only well educated, but well connected.

Once accepted, he begins work. The minimum salary that he can be paid is stipulated, as are minimums for all grades and categories of journalists, in the national contract negotiated between the National Federation of the Italian Press (FNSI) and the publishers' organization, the Federation of Italian Newspaper Publishers (FIEG). Under the 1977–78 contract, the monthly minimum for an apprentice after three months' service was about $242. Almost every journalist of whatever category is paid above the minimums set out in the contract, however; the apprentices on *Il Giorno* in Milan, for example, by the mid-1970s were making slightly less than $600.

Even so, the apprentice is cheap help, and the law and the contract go to great lengths to make certain that management does not take advantage of that fact. Several conditions, such as the amount of time he can be used as a correspondent in another city, are specified, and in any case he can remain an apprentice for a maximum of three years; he has to take the examination for professional fitness at the end of eighteen months; if he fails, he may try eighteen months later. Failing that, he must leave the profession.

The nature of his activities within the news organization, beyond the specifications of the rules, will vary somewhat from job to job. In the things that really matter, however, the experience of newsroom apprentices is remarkably the same, not only in Italy, but in every other country as well. There seems to be universal agreement that apprenticeship is one of the best, if not the best, way to train a journalist. Even in the United States, the country by all odds most infested with journalism schools, there are many editors who prefer to hire those basically ignorant of the mechanics of the business and train them on the job.

Training journalists on the job consists of throwing them into it, beginning with simple things that require a minimum of specialized skills—writing routine obituaries, for example. From that point on, the beginning journalist is expected to "pick it up" as he goes along. He not only receives no instruction in any formal sense, he generally receives little generalized advice. The introduction of a young man from City College of New York named A. M. Rosenthal into the apparatus of the *New York Times* was described by Gay Talese in this way.

... he was startled by the soft voice of a stranger behind him, a lean and homely-looking man wearing glasses, asking, "What's your name?"

"Abe Rosenthal."

"What do you do?" the man asked pleasantly.

"I'm the City College correspondent."

"Do you need paper to type on?"

"Yes."

"Do you know where we keep the paper around here?"

"No."

"It's over there in that box," the man said, and then he proceeded to walk down the aisle, to grab a batch of paper, and to place it on Rosenthal's desk.

"Do you know how to slug a story?"

"No," Rosenthal said.

The man showed Rosenthal where his name should go, at the upper left-hand corner, with a single word to describe the subject of the story.

"Do you know what you do after you finish your story?"

"No," Rosenthal said.

"You give it to that copyboy standing over there."

Rosenthal nodded.

"By the way," the man said, "my name is Mike Berger."

"Thank you, Mr. Berger."[1]

That is a very characteristic kind of on-the-job training. A newsroom is an extraordinarily busy place. There is no time for teaching why or considering alternatives, at least for those who are in a position to do it best. Trial and error is the vehicle, and sharp observation the critical tool; the best pupil is one who does not repeat an error committed out of ignorance.

There is, therefore, very little conscious learning; there is rather a growing sense of the complex structure and dynamics of the job situation, of being able to predict what those with whom you work will do next, and in turn conducting yourself so they can carry out their jobs, confident that you, too, are predictable. Rather than a sense of learning, there is a growing sense of mastery of subtle skills, which somehow are all the more satisfying because they are never really defined.

Sometimes this is called learning through indirect cues. It runs throughout newsroom operations and is not restricted to ignorant beginners. I have been studying for the past several years the persons who work on foreign desks in the major dailies in Sweden, Yugoslavia, and Italy. It is these people's jobs to decide what foreign news goes into the paper and what is discarded. (There is always far more available than space allows.) With rare exceptions, only experienced staff members get such an assignment. I always ask if they, at the time they moved onto the foreign desk, received any instruction—any formal discussion, even ten minutes with their superior, on what guidelines they should use in the selection of news. Invariably—and the word is used literally—the answer has been no.

"Then how did you learn to make judgments about news from abroad?"

"Well . . . you just learn. You know."

"Not exactly."

Puzzled silence, generally touched with condescension for an unworldly professor who would ask a question the answer to which is so obvious.

"Well . . . you just pick it up. There are other experienced men on the desk, and you watch them, and then pretty soon you know."

In terms of the efficient operation of the system, this obviously is a good way to teach and learn, even though few alumni go as far as A. M. Rosenthal, who became editor of the *New York Times*. Some psychologists have stressed for years the effectiveness of "involved" learning, in which the situation is "real time" and "hands-on," and there are few situations more involved than, for example, trying to write a news story against a deadline in a specific number of words when you do not know how to count them.

It is efficiency gained at some sacrifice of intelligence and judgment, however; it substitutes mind reading and horseback empiricism for understanding. The neophyte does not think of challenging the news judgments of his betters because he is too busy trying to figure out what they are and to develop a built-in set of his own that will work the same way. Learning on the job reinforces—indeed, requires—the acceptance of all the practices and attitudes of the newsroom as it operates at a given moment. It makes change difficult, and reduces foresight and challenge. The beginning Italian newsman who has to show considerable congruence even to get a chance at the profession is inevitably shaped for the mold much more finely through the apprentice experience. After eighteen months, the apprentice takes the *prova di idoneità professionale* ("test of professional skill").

The National Council of the Order of Journalists administers the test, which generally is given twice a year, in April and October. The examining commission consists of two judges of the Court of Appeals of Rome and five professionals, each of whom has been a member of the order for at least ten years. Five alternate professionals are also named, and the full list is published in the Official Gazette (the Italian equivalent of the *Federal Register*).

The written examination must be taken first, and admission to the oral component depends upon passing it. The examining commission sets out at least six *argomenti* ("topics"), or areas of the contemporary scene within which the writing is to take place. The commission supplies the essential information. The candidate must then, as the regulations put it, write a summary story or simulated spot news story. It is specified that these fall within the general categories of domestic politics, foreign affairs, economics, *cronaca* (roughly speaking, "local news"), or sports. The candidate may write in the particular journalistic form used in his job—candidates from broadcast news prepare the script for a broadcast, for example.

The law specifies elaborate bureaucratic ceremonials to prevent cheating and guarantee fairness in grading. The topics and materials to be used are agreed upon by the commission just before the session begins. The paper upon which the candidates write is furnished by the commission, an inheritance from the traditional Italian devotion to stamped official paper for any document of importance. Two members of the examining commission are in the room at all times, and when the exercise is finished, a system of numbered double envelopes and wax seals provides anonymity during the evaluation process. That process takes place immediately, and the commission gives a yes or no judgment as soon as it has finished reading what the candidate has produced.

The test is not easy. These were some of the topics specified for the written exercise in the spring proceedings in 1975.

> Domestic politics:
> A new fact of Italian political life is the proposal by the PLI [Partito Liberale Italiano] for the formation of an anticlerical bloc among Social Democrats, Republicans, and Liberals.
> What are the positions of the three parties toward the proposal and the foreseeable repercussions of the bloc, if it is formed, on the political life of the country?
> Foreign policy:
> The Suez canal will be reopened soon. Your newspaper has directed you to leave for Egypt for a series of articles on the affair. Today, before leaving, you are to write an article which sets out the economic and political repercussions of the reopening of the waterway for the countries on the shores of the Mediterranean, and particularly for Italy.

Economy:

The council of agricultural ministers of the European Economic Community will meet in the next few days to put an end—at least it is hoped—to the notorious "wine war" begun by French winegrowers, who, among other things, have called for a total halt in imports, in clear violation of the Treaty of Rome.

Since the French government cannot completely satisfy their demands, the growers have erected barricades and obstacles to keep wine-carrying ships from docking.

The candidate will summarize the various aspects of the situation, indicate the reasons that have led to the "wine war," and the precautions taken by the Italian government.

"Hard" news is the area in which most Italian journalists spend considerable time during the apprenticeship period and the early years of professional status. Some reporters spend their career there, of course, but essentially it is a station on the way up, closely comparable to what is sometimes referred to in U.S. metropolitan journalism as "cityside."

Cronaca nera is a loosely defined subcategory involving sensational stories, scandals, and disasters, for the most part. ("The priests," said an acquaintance who had been on the committee of judges several times, "always choose to write cronaca nera.")

The test in the spring of 1975 provided a couple of topics for those who chose that category. One was a complicated hypothetical situation in which a series of thefts from the National Agricultural Bank seemed to be tied to some officers of the bank, and the candidates were asked to address themselves to the formulation of logical analyses of what happened and why people in such jobs might turn down the primrose path. The second choice in the category was succinct and classic. Fire in a hotel: 14 dead and 37 hurt; scenes of panic during a terrible night.

Other categories that the candidate may choose are more specialized: fashion, the current scene, labor, politics, and sports.

The candidate who passes the written test is then eligible for the oral test which usually takes place the next day. The law sets out very specifically the material to be covered during this test (which, incidentally, is public). The candidate must demonstrate his or her knowledge of—

1. the elements of the history of journalism;
2. the elements of sociology and of the psychology of public opinion;
3. techniques and practices of journalism;
4. judicial standards relating to journalism; the elements of civil rights; the legal regulation of the profession of journalism, including

contractual matters; provisions of both administrative and criminal law relating to the media; laws relating to literary rights;
5. professional ethics.

In addition, the candidate also has the opportunity during the oral test to demonstrate some particular competence that he has acquired during his apprenticeship. He notifies the commission three days before the session that he wants to discuss some aspect of the current scene; the law suggests it may be "in the sector of domestic politics, foreign affairs, economics, customs and culture, art, theater and motion pictures, sports, fashion, or in any other specific field of which he might have acquired knowledge during his apprenticeship."[2]

The commission hears all the candidates, then immediately gives a decision on each. The quality of the written test is taken into account in this final judgment.

European students have developed specific techniques for taking oral examinations. The candidate prepares a series of little speeches, in effect, topical blocks carefully organized for style and clarity, complete with an occasional arcane reference to demonstrate erudition, and a witticism or two. The trick in preparation, of course, is to anticipate the questions; after that, the chief skill is adapting the rote material to a question to which it is almost, but not quite, relevant. European academic humor is full of stories about the extremity of some efforts, but when the student is good at this, it is obviously a satisfying game.

Almost all candidates for membership in the Order of Journalists in 1975 were university products, and thus were prepared in the traditional sense; an examiner's question about professional ethics, or press law, or the other specified area, was the same as pressing a button. The machine produced a smooth torrent of words and not very original ideas.

There is a quality of show business about the whole thing, of course. Although I was, so far as I could tell, the only "public" present, there were a good many people around. The number of examiners in this case was eleven—the five alternate professional examiners sat in, along with the five regular examiners and the presiding judge. About twenty or thirty other candidates, most of those scheduled for that day's examining, also sat in, listening intently and sometimes taking notes. It was distinctly a time to cut a good figure, and most candidates made the most of it.

For that matter, so did the examiners, who frequently made rather pat speeches of their own incidental, or antecedent, to asking a question. The choice of the members of the commission is in the hands of the administration of the Order of Journalists, and it is a delicate matter. The group must be balanced in terms of political orientation, types of media, and geography. No professional may serve as a member for two years in a row, although a good many have appeared several times over a period of years. That, too, may be a matter of politics, although not in the most invidious sense. There is a plethora of good professionals who are Socialists, or something like it, and many Christian Democrats; there is an adequate supply of Communists from which to choose. There are, however, few distinguished professionals on the political far right in Italian journalism. Although nobody ever said as much, I gathered this might be part of the explanation of the repeated appointment of Vanni Angeli, a bright and provocative man who called himself a Monarchist and was for several years managing editor of *Il Tempo*.

A total of 206 eligible apprentices applied for the test in 1975, and 203 actually took it. Only 25 of these were women. The largest single group was from Milan, not surprising in view of that area's dominant role in Italian journalism; there were 62 Milanese, 56 Romans, 20 from Bologna, 14 from Turin, and 13 Neapolitans. The remainder were from eight other regions.

A total of 145 were from daily papers; 36 from magazines; 17 from radio and television; and 8 from news agencies. I saw no more than 30 or 40 of them, but almost all of these were young, under thirty, I should judge, although I saw one male who was clearly middle-aged.

I suppose it should also be added that I found the twenty or so whose examinations I heard a rather disappointing lot. They seemed to me impressive in the nuts and bolts departments for which they had prepared in advance, but anything that moved afield was likely to show, it seemed to me, that they were not very well educated. That is a curious thing to say about Italian journalists, and may be simply a fluke due to the small group I observed. Some of the commission members seemed to have the same feeling, however, and their questioning became sharper as the day went on.

A basic problem seemed, at least on that occasion, to be a surprising ignorance of recent and contemporary Italian affairs. The candidates tended to speak in slogans or the kind of encapsulation characteristic of the more plodding Marxists. One particularly glib young man, in discussing the Fascist era, was speaking in code, for all practical purposes, and an aging professional member of the commission took after him to see how much he knew in concrete terms about that period. The questioner was in no sense pro-Fascist, but he obviously felt it would be a good thing if the candidate knew something hard-edged; eventually his questions began to deal in detail with constraints on the press under Mussolini. By that time the glibness was gone, the young man was sweating, and the examiner finally dropped the line of questioning. That kind of thing happened several times; even an outsider got the impression that this particular group of young people knew little about the country in which they grew up, and that seems strange in Italy.

Overall, however, the group was not subpar (and, I repeat, I heard less than 10 percent of them). Of the 203 who undertook the examinations, 11 failed the written test and were not admitted to the oral; another 16 did not pass the oral. The overall failure rate thus was 13.3 percent. That is lower than the 17 percent average rate in the years 1965–75, and a touch lower than the median 15.2 percent. There seems to be no discernible pattern in the number of failures, although it is possible to speculate around the edges. Failure rates were extremely low for the first two years of the present system (1.6 percent for 1965; 4 percent for 1966) and that might be accounted for by the fact that people who had been, in fact, working professionals for some time were getting themselves qualified under the new legislation; one might explain the sudden leap to 22.8 percent the third year by guessing that the fact of almost everybody's passing led to a flood of unprepared people who assumed passage was automatic. But how does one explain a failure rate of 33.6 percent in the fall of 1972 and a rate of 9.7 percent in the spring of 1973? Or something close to a doubling of the rate between the fall of 1974 (7.2 percent) and the spring of 1975 (13.3 percent)? The most obvious explanation might begin with the fact that this is a tightly controlled trade union, and that new members are admitted to the club essentially on the basis of the leadership's perception of available jobs. There are no data, to my knowledge, to permit serious investigation of that premise.[3]

Given the cheery corruptibility of so many Italian institutions, it is almost reflexive to wonder if some fixing goes on during the tests. There seems to be none. I asked directly about it in a good many interviews, and always drew surprised denial, even from the rare few who are opposed to the Order in principle. The administrative officers of the Order work hard at the business of being Caesar's wife, in regard to both financial considerations and political pressure. Their control is tight, its limits clearly defined, and they operate efficiently.

Protests against the process are rare. Marco Sassano, a member of the staff of *Avanti!*, the Socialist daily, failed the examination for the second time in May, 1972. *Avanti!* ran an editorial attacking the decision as "an act of political reprisal for the democratic, anti-Fascist, and libertarian attitudes influenced by Sassano through the newspaper and his journalism."[4]

The affair received broad play in the Order's official magazine, *Rassegna*, which reprinted the *Avanti!* editorial and carried a letter from

Enzo Forcella, a major figure in the reform movement about which we shall hear a good deal later, supporting Sassano; Forcella did not support the charges of political reprisal, but simply attacked that particular commission of examiners as union hacks.

That concession made to both sides of the issue, the administration of the Order made clear their own outrage at such a charge. (The article in *Rassegna* was entitled "Slander by *Avanti!*") The commission was called into session again, Sassano's materials examined once more, and he again failed. The members further charged *Avanti!* with "violation of the elementary rules of professional conduct,"[5] and officially suggested to the regional association of the Order of Journalists, with which all disciplinary action must begin, that they might want to take disciplinary action. Since any such proceedings are not made public, it is uncertain if the association did so, but by 1976 Marco Sassano was not a member of the Order nor a member of the staff of *Avanti!*

It hardly seems necessary to belabor the point that this elaborate system tends to fix not only day-to-day newsroom practices but basic attitudes and commitments in a rigid pattern of "this is the way it has always been, this is the way it is today." It is an extraordinarily effective way of forcing the newsman into elimination of personal alternatives, of developing a standardized self-perception. With the loftiest of ends in mind and while emphasizing possession of skills and intellectual qualities that all would agree are most important for journalists anywhere, the selection and certification process tends mightily to produce not only well-educated and well-connected elitists, but men who think alike about the role of a major social institution that is desperately in need of change.

That pressure toward conformity is reinforced by the Italian journalist's automatic membership, upon certification, in the national Order of Journalists.

The laws of the Republic of Italy officially establish twelve professions: lawyers, engineers, architects, chemists, doctors of agricultural science, actuaries, surgeons, veterinarians, pharmacists, *dottori commercialisti* (holders of degrees in business and economics), and journalists. The orders of lawyers, surgeons, and pharmacists go back to the early part of the century; most of the remainder were established during the Fascist era. The Order of Journalists is the youngest; it was established in a law officially promulgated on January 3, 1963.

The fact that an institution is defined and established by law obviously is an enormous protection for the people in it. The protection begins with the availability of a job. Under Italian law it is illegal to publish a newspaper or magazine or run a broadcast news operation, except under special and limited circumstances, which has anybody other than members or apprentices of the Order on the payroll. It is also a legal offense to practice journalism (or any of the other codified professions) without being a member. Both a fine and a jail sentence can be imposed for violation of either requirement, and it happens occasionally. In mid-January of 1970, for example, early in the collection of material for this enterprise, a writer was fined 150,000 lire (then equivalent to about $240) for the "abusive exercise of the profession of journalist." He had written some articles for a sports daily without being a member of the Order; his defense was that they were only publicity, not journalism, but the court disagreed.

Part-timers are barred from membership in the roll of *professionisti* in the Order; that group is limited to full-time paid employees. (There is a separate listing for free-lance contributors, *pubblicisti*, but it clearly represents second-class status.) The law also establishes the validity of a national professional contract that specifies minimum salaries and the hours and conditions of work throughout the country. Violation of the contract's provisions thus becomes an actual violation of the law.

The Order of Journalists is the youngest of the twelve orders in part because the struggle to get it established took twenty years. A self-selected cadre of anti-Fascist journalists, including historian Luigi Salvatorelli, met literally within hours after the fall of the Mussolini government in 1943 to start work on the rebuilding of the profession. That initiative was obliterated when the Germans occupied Italy, but the drive started again as soon as the war in Europe ended.

The beginnings of the formal canons of professionalization of journalism in Italy go back much further than the postwar years, however. The official history of the Order of Journalists[6] reflects a great sensitivity to the common charge that the present systemization is essentially Fascist, and points out that as early as 1877 there was an organization called *Associazione della stampa periodica italiana,* and that it set up categories of practitioners: *effettivi,* the full-time professionals; *pubblicisti,* established free lances; and *frequentatori,* "personalities of the worlds of politics and culture." In 1901 came the first initiative for "judicial recognition" of the profession; a bill to that effect was introduced in Parliament by Luigi Luzzatti, later a prime minister of Italy. Seven years later legislation accomplishing that purpose was passed. Its focus was much more specific and functional than the establishment of an abstract principle. It provided for reduced railroad fares for members of the press, and thus began a custom that still continues. Those who show the *tessera* ("identity card") of the Order of Journalists still receive large discounts on railway and airline fares and travel free on the *autostrade,* the country's superhighway system.

Much more important than that unsurprising reflection of the classic Latin culture of insiders, however, was the mechanism that made it possible for the journalist to use it. To get those cheap railway fares he had to be registered in *l'albo,* literally, "the album," or the registry of those officially identified as journalists. The registry of journalists was the essential device for the control of the profession during fascism, and it was the direct predecessor of the Order.

The basic Fascist decree governing the press was issued in 1928. It provided for an organization based upon inscription in an official registry; inscription was denied, of course, to those less than ardent in their enthusiasm for the regime. Jews eventually were also banned. The issue facing the reformers of the profession when Italy became free in 1944 was the retention of the concept of the registered professional. The matter was easily decided. Although the decree of 1928 was officially overturned toward the end of 1944, there was general agreement to retain the registry and certain other aspects of the old law relating to unionization and fringe benefits. In October of that year the newly reconstituted *Federazione Nazionale della Stampa Italiana* proposed to the "Italian and allied authorities" the establishment of a *Commissione Unica,* which would maintain and protect the registry until affairs could be put sufficiently in order to make some major decisions. This involved, in effect, the retention of the principles codified specifically under the Fascist decree, the most important of which was restriction of the practice of the profession to those inscribed in the registry. As the Order's history put it: The FNSI had three possible paths: to abolish, purely and simply, the professional Order; to develop *di nuovo* a decree or a series of emergency decrees to regulate the profession; or to accept the legislation of 1928 with some indispensable corrections.[7]

The Commissione Unica, which was to supervise the institutional development of the profession for the next two decades, was appointed by the minister of justice in consultation with the FNSI and the undersecretary of state for the press and information. The latter post in the new government did not long endure. The FNSI protested violently against its creation from the beginning; the title was abolished within a few months and the functions assumed by the undersecretary of state to the president of the council of ministers. In practice, the supervisory commission was made up, throughout its history, of professional journalists. A substantial number of those over the years were also members of Parliament.

It was clearly understood by everybody involved that the commission's essential duties were custodial, until something better could be worked out, and at its inception no one anticipated its long life. The general assumption was that the first postwar convention of the National Federation of the Italian Press, the journalists' trade union, would settle everything but the details.

That meeting was held in Palermo in 1946, and its most important business was the discussion of the implications of licensing journalists. The outcome was never much in doubt, but the leader of the opposition to retention of the registry or establishment of an Order set the issue out in terms that forced the profession to face what they were voting for. His name was Vittorio Gorresio.

Gorresio had been a reporter on *Messaggero* when the Mussolini government fell, and was a prime mover in the reestablishment of the national trade union of journalists. The most important years of his career were spent on *La Stampa*. That newspaper is the least politicized of the country's major dailies, and considering the fact that he has been, among other things, an eminent political reporter, Gorresio is in that tradition. His salary has been paid, in effect, by Giovanni Agnelli, who through his control of FIAT has been for decades the dominant figure in the Italian equivalent of the National Association of Manufacturers, but Gorresio has repeatedly attacked the conservative wing of the Christian Democrats. His writing and thinking have been clear, functional, and unpretentious. It is almost impossible to find anybody in Italian journalism who speaks ill of him.

Some of that professional respect goes back to the Palermo meeting of 1946. Gorresio spoke in favor of a cause that was not only lost, but overwhelmed. He also spoke, however, to both the conscience and the intelligence of his colleagues. A decade later those who were pressing most strenuously for the establishment of the Order were still, obliquely, answering him.

He had only one argument. It was a simple one. There is no way, he said, to reconcile freedom of the press with government certification of reporters. That system, he said, was Fascist, regardless of the gloss put upon it, and more political than professional. A closed profession simply suppresses free thinkers and innovators, and journalism needs both.

To journalists in several countries that appears not as an argument but a patent truth. But Italian governments, along with most others on the continent, traditionally have had a qualified view of what constitutes free expression. During the same year as the Palermo meeting of the journalists, the Constitutional Assembly was drafting the first constitution of the new republic. It was proclaimed in its final form January 1, 1948. Article 21 begins in a way that would warm the heart of the most passionate civil libertarian.

> All are entitled freely to express their thoughts by word of mouth, in writing, and by all other means of communication.
> The press may not be subjected to any authority or censorship. . . .

But goes on:

> Distraint [sequestration of publications] is allowed only by order of the judicial authorities, for which reasons must be given, in the case of offenses definitely laid down by the press law, or in the case of violation of the provisions which the said law prescribes for identifying responsible parties.
> In such cases, under conditions of absolute urgency and when the immediate intervention of the judicial authorities is not possible, distraint may be applied to the periodical press by officers of the judicial police, who shall communicate the matter to the judicial authorities within 24 hours. If the said judicial authorities do not ratify the measure within the next 24 hours, the distraint is withdrawn and is null and void. . . .
> Printed publications, performances and all other manifestations contrary to morality are forbidden.[8]

There was an attempt within the constitutional convention to throw out some of these provisions; the authorization for police sequestration in "urgent" cases provoked particularly heated discussion. The protesters were overwhelmed by a coalition made up, interestingly, of the Christian Democrats and the Communists.[9]

Gorresio, speaking in Palermo on behalf of what amounted to a minority report drafted by an absent colleague, Armando Zanetti, in opposition to both a registry and an Order, also was overwhelmed. Almost the entire leadership of the profession represented at Palermo rose to speak in favor of a controlled and sanctioned profession. Some of the talk dealt with the problems of installing a new form of organization; it would be easier to "modify institutional norms," some said, through a controlled group of journalists working toward the same objective. This reasoning was too blatantly political and manipulative, apparently, for most of the assembly; most other arguments were much more functional. They were summed up in the final resolution passed, almost unanimously, by the Palermo meeting. It began:

> The national Congress of the press, meeting at Palermo, has examined the problem of the juridical regulation of the journalistic profession, and it believes that the defense of the liberty of the press and the independence of the profession are not in conflict with the existence of a legally recognized Professional Order of Journalists since in a democratic country such an Order cannot be regulated except by its own actions in open meetings of journalists and the executive actions of elected bodies recognized by law.[10]

Behind this were largely economic concerns. An Order would provide a way of keeping too many newcomers from drifting into the field. Tightly organized, it automatically had some bargaining power which its leaders knew it would need. One of them, Enrico Mattei, made a final summary speech at Palermo that laid out grimly the argument that counted most with the majority of delegates.

> It would be much nobler if we could take our inspiration from other democratic countries, such as England and the United States where professional orders, national labor contracts, and apprentices do not exist, and where journalism is a kind of grand arena open to the four winds; where one arrives and departs with unlimited ease, where it is not obligatory to have identity cards, job turnover is steady, and the best elements, the most energetic, the most intelligent, the most dynamic, overcome and displace without pity the less aggressive in the competition, assuring journalism access to new energy and fresh ideas in a continual renewal. . . .
>
> Comparisons with other countries are always useful, as long as one does not forget the irrepressible diversity of psychology and of the economic and social ambience that contrasts one people with another. . . .
>
> In America, in England, with much higher average income, it is easier for a man who has some intellectual capacity to find a job and a salary. In Italy an individual who may have spent his youthful years in journalism, pouring out the best of his energies and of his intelligence will find difficulty in maturity in finding work anywhere and will be a misfit for all his life. . . .
>
> Let us not delude ourselves: the idea of unlimited freedom for journalistic activity is an advantage for only one group, the publishers; the little and medium-sized publishers, above all, have already demonstrated in this respect a truly worrisome lack of scruples.[11]

The Palermo meeting was not devoted entirely to the issue of establishing an Order; several other resolutions were passed, including one that provides a striking insight into the qualified nature of freedom of the press in Italian eyes. It reminded the assembly, in the process of working out new press laws, to develop some that would protect children

> . . . from the pernicious influence of many publications which, under the pretext of diverting their audiences with stories of crime and loose morality, contribute powerfully, through their cupidity and single-minded commercialism, to influence the young not toward a healthy belief in order and courage, but to yield to the worst instincts of violence and the undisciplined society.[12]

There was also a certain amount of talk about the establishment of a national school of journalism. This was not a new idea to Italian journalism; four journalism schools had been established by the Fascist regime, at the universities of Perugia, Rome, and Trieste, and at the Catholic university of Milan. These had disappeared, but they also seem to have been discredited much earlier simply as educational institutions. The conferees at Palermo saw a single national school, presumably supervised by their national organization, as a means of instilling high standards of both craft and ethics. It might also provide in particular cases a bypass of the apprentice system, the legality of which was under question. There was general enthusiasm for the idea and a commitment to get started. From time to time during the decades since there have been announcements from officers of the Order that the establishment of such a school is imminent, but the first steps have never been taken.

Resolutions dealing with news agencies and the potential of broadcasting were passed, along with those stipulating in some detail certain desirable organizational characteristics of the presumptive Order of Journalists. The final statements of the meeting have justifiable overtones of triumph; the journalists of Italy had proved that they could meet together and act through democratic methods in genuine unity, of which professionalism was the cement and to which politics and geography were incidental.

Now began the long process of getting legislation establishing the Order through Parliament. During the next twenty years the protection of the registry, of the exclusivity of the profession, remained in the hands of the Commissione Unica (its members changed occasionally, but always included journalists who were also deputies or senators) and, for lack of any other guide, on the principles set out in the legislation of 1928.

The business apparently took so long because of a combination of complicated matters that needed resolution and what seems to have been a widespread resistance to the idea outside of journalism. The structure of the new organization had to be worked out in detail. Its relations with the already powerful printers' unions went through several modifications; in the beginning it was assumed that the two groups would be somehow linked. It did not work out that way; today they are quite separate. Although journalists and printers sometimes work together on both political and labor-management issues, they also sometimes are at odds. A system of adequate medical insurance and pensions had to be worked out, involving the establishment of an *Istituto Nazionale di Previdenza dei Giornalisti Italiani "Giovanni Amendola";* this body includes representatives of the Order, the Italian publishers' association, and the government.

If the complexity of such arrangements was not enough to establish a slow pace (the first complete draft of the proposed law did not appear until 1956), certainly the general climate of hostility against the legislation would have been. From the beginning it had the embarrassing handicap of opposition from the most eminent Italian of the time, Luigi Einaudi, first president of the republic. Einaudi was not a journalist and hence was not involved in discussions within the profession, but he took a public position very much like that of Gorresio, rather impatiently dismissing the possibility of reconciling freedom of the press with government accreditation.

Einaudi did not seriously lead an organized opposition, however, nor did anyone else. Most of the arguments were highly specific, even technical, but not all. A number of members of the national assembly, for example, were disturbed by the assumption that professionalism in journalism was completely analogous to professionalism in medicine or engineering. All other professions, it was pointed out, had a specific body of knowledge. Once a candidate demonstrated that he had mastered a sufficient share of it, he was automatically admitted; the measures were objective, and anybody who wanted to try was free to do so. The consent of those already in the field was not necessary. In journalism, however, the aspirant had to find someone who would hire him—a completely subjective judgment by one person—before he could even begin to prepare. Furthermore, as the law was drafted, his employer had to certify his abilities before he could be admitted to his examination of professional competence. The body of knowledge involved in journalism was modest, in comparison with learned professions, and even judgments about craft skills varied widely.

There were also serious arguments exploring potential conflicts between the proposals and the country's new constitution. Most of these dealt with one facet or another of article 21, which guarantees to every person the right to express freely his own thoughts, but others referred to article 4, dealing with the right to work; article 18, concerning the right of free association; and article 41, which establishes the right to start a business. After the eventual passage of the act, many of these constitutional arguments were to be carried to the Constitutional Court, which found the Order substantially constitutional.

Perhaps the major overall reason for the slow movement over the years remained the fact that, as one of the leaders, Leonardo Azzarita, put it in 1955, "The registry of journalists does not have many friends." By the last days of 1962, however, it had acquired enough friends. The Chamber of Deputies passed the legislation establishing the Order on December 12 of that year; on January 24, 1963, the Senate approved; and on February 3, 1963, it was promulgated by the president of the republic, Antonio Segni. The process had taken almost seventeen years.

Law number 69, of February 3, 1963, is about six thousand words long. It is divided into four sections (the Italian heading is *titolo*), six chapters (in Italian, *capo*), and seventy-five articles. Accompanying it is a set of bylaws ("Rules for the Execution of Law no. 69"), which have been added to and changed from time to time; these bylaws provide definitions and spell out the details of implementation.

Article 1 sets up the Order and describes its members: *professionisti* are those who practice journalism "exclusively and continously"; *pubblicisti* are those involved in frequent, paid journalistic activity, even though they carry out another profession or responsibility.* For the sake of repetition to avoid confusion, the reader is reminded that the word *pubblicista* has nothing to do with publicity or advertising.

Article 2, headed "rights and duties," probably was more exhaustively explored and frequently redrafted than any other. The final version is brief and more pragmatic than high-minded.

> Journalists have the irrevocable right of freedom of information and of criticism, limited only by observance of laws protecting other people. It is their obligation to respect the substance of the facts, always observing the responsibility imposed by loyalty and by good faith.
>
> News that is inaccurate must be set right and errors corrected.
>
> Journalists and publishers are required to respect news sources as a professional secret when circumstances require it, and to promote the spirit of collaboration among colleagues, cooperation among journalists and publishers, and trust between the press and its readers.

---

*In recent years there has been added a special additional list (*elenco speciale*) made up of working journalists of foreign nationality and nonjournalists who are permitted to serve as responsabile of "technical, professional, or scientific" publications.

It is interesting to observe that, under the law, information about news sources has been privileged in Italy, while the news business in the United States has labored for decades to establish the idea with little success. Many American journalists have gone to jail on contempt citations since the early 1970s because they refused to talk to prosecutors or grand juries, and the issue is, in this country, the most sensitive and difficult among the relationships between authority and the press.

Nor has the issue been as simple in Italy as reading article 2 would indicate. The problem is a conflict of laws; a part of the criminal code specifies that those refusing to answer a judge's questions about sources of information are subject to arrest and imprisonment of up to three years. Prosecutions under the criminal statute have been very rare, but a 1980 case drew particular notice because it involved the Red Brigades' assassination of a police officer and the possible participation of the son of a Christian Democrat leader. In contesting the indictment, the journalist's attorney called for the matter of conflicting statutes to go to the Constitutional Court, the country's highest, for resolution. Meanwhile some members of the profession fear a growing vulnerability.[13]

The remainder of the first section of the law deals with the mechanics of the organization. Like many associations of licensed professionals, the Order of Journalists puts much authority in the hands of local units; most decisions eventually made at the top begin with action either in a *sezione*, the smallest subdivision, usually made up of journalists from a single city, or with a regional council. Any disciplinary action must begin in the regional council.

In 1979 there were fourteen regional councils: Piedmont-Valle d'Aosta; Lombardy; Veneto; Trentino-Alto Adige; Liguria; Tuscany; Friuli-Venezia Giulia; Emilia-Romagna; Lazio-Umbria-Abruzzi-Molise; Campania; Calabria; Puglia-Basilicata; Sicily; and Sardinia. The original law set up twelve, but Calabria was later split off from Campania and Trentino-Alto Adige from Veneto.

The cumbersome Lazio-Umbria-Abruzzi-Molise arrangement would seem, at first glance, almost ridiculously big, since Rome is in Lazio. Actually it reflects accurately the curious geography of newspapers in Italy; there is not a single daily newspaper in Umbria, Abruzzi, or Molise, despite the presence of major cities such as Perugia and Pescara.

The work of the Order in each of these fourteen regions is under the direction of a regional council, made up of six professionisti and three pubblicisti; the council chooses officers from among its members. The council's basic responsibility is the maintenance of the lists, which gives it control over additions, suspensions, and transfers. (Journalists are registered in the region in which they work; if they move permanently to another region, their registration is transferred.) The law of 1963 goes into great detail about the regional council's conduct of affairs; article 13, for example, simply sets the date for the treasurer's report and approval of the next year's budget. There is also a national council, which serves as an appeals court.

More importantly, the national council serves as liaison between the Order and the Italian government. The presence of the Ministry of Justice is constant in the affairs of the Order, although actual interventions have been rare. The price paid by professional journalism for special status and protection under the law is the concession of the right of oversight of the profession to the national law enforcement agency.

The relationship goes back to the immediate postwar years. The Commissione Unica, established to protect the registry along the general lines of the law of 1928 while a new arrangement was being worked out, was officially appointed by the ministry.

And the national council of the Order is, in a particularly Italian kind of way, something of a creature of the ministry. Article 16, which begins the second chapter of the law of 1963, says, "The National Council of the Order of Journalists is hereby instituted, and is legally represented within the Ministry of Justice."

Article 21 of the Order spells out the relationship.

> The minister of justice exercises surveillance over the National Council of the Order.
>
> He can, by decree, and upon the advice of the council, dissolve a regional or inter-regional council that may not be able to function regularly; when the date of the election of a new council established by the law has not been observed; or when the council, after being requested to observe the obligations imposed on it, persists in violating them.
>
> In the same decree the minister will nominate an extraordinary commission, chosen from among professional journalists, who will function until a new council can be elected, which must take place within ninety days after the decree of dissolution.

Article 44 provides that each regional council deposit a copy of its registry each January with the authorities—the court of appeals for the region and the Ministry of Justice in Rome—as well as with the National Council of the Order. The names of new members must be submitted within two months of admittance to the Order to the procurator, the minister, and the court of appeals of the region.

The courts may also be involved in various disciplinary actions, depending upon the circumstances. They are totally responsible for the enforcement of article 45.

> No one may assume the title, or practice the profession, of journalist if he is not inscribed in the registry of Professionals. Violation of this provision will be punished as specified by articles 348 and 498 of the penal code. . . .

The disciplining of members normally rests with the regional council of the Order. One entire section of the law, a total of 21 articles, is devoted to disciplinary matters. As set out in article 48, those who are guilty of "not conforming to decorum and professional dignity, or acts which compromise his own reputation or the dignity of the Order, are subject to disciplinary procedures." The regional council originates the action.

Four levels of disciplinary action are available to the regional council. The most innocuous is the official warning to a journalist, administered for minor lapses "in the observance of his obligations." Censure may be imposed for more serious lapses. Suspension from the profession "may be imposed in cases in which the member has by his conduct compromised professional dignity." The supreme penalty is expulsion, in cases where the member by his conduct "has gravely compromised professional dignity with the result that his continuance in the Order is incompatible with that same dignity." A member who has been expelled can apply for readmission after five years. There is an appeals procedure for these sanctions as well; the appeal must begin in the council of first jurisdiction. If the appeal is lost there, it may then go to the national council.

Not only the guilty party may appeal, however. At both levels the appropriate public official may also make an appeal, presumably, in most cases, because the accused was found innocent. Regardless of the appellant, however, the national council must take into account the formal written conclusion of, in effect, the representative of the Ministry of Justice before the deliberation of the case begins. The judgment is made by a special panel of professionals. After it is delivered, any of the interested parties—the defendant, the council, or the civil authorities—can request a new appeal in the regular courts, and once on that track the case can move up through the system to the highest appeals court in the country.

From the moment he steps into the examining room for the final leg of the test for professional competence and faces a committee that is headed, not by a journalist, but a magistrate—from that point forward, the journalist is part of a profession that is tied to civil authority at almost every turn. Government defines the profession; government gives its corporate decisions the force of law; government protects the people in it from outside competition, and permits them to protect themselves against the possibility of too many qualified competitors.

To the American journalist that cozy togetherness can only seem frightfully dangerous. From the government, a journalist in the United States receives nothing but the protection of that ingeniously drafted negative sanction that begins the First Amendment to the Constitution: "Congress shall make no law. . . ." He carries no required documents. He cannot be punished for transgressions special to the way he makes a living; he can be found libelous, or slanderous, or criminally obscene, but only under statutes that apply to the whole population. He can run away from his alimony payments, change the name he uses in bylines, and peacefully go to work in Roanoke or Seattle or El Paso without in any way jeopardizing his right to be the best possible journalist he knows how to be. And he may come to work some morning to find alongside his desk a youth with a pocket full of writing instruments who says, "I'm the new guy the city editor told you about; I graduated in English from Bard College, and he says I should go along with you to learn all about covering city hall, because he said something about having other plans for you."

Whether or not he thinks about it often, the American journalist is a remarkably free man, and the system within which he works produces a press that also is, by the standards of any other country, remarkably free. It is an inviting jump to the notion that the Italian journalist, working under restraint imposed by press laws and with the government close at hand in most professional decisions, would feel much less free, and that his work would show it.

To judge by the content of newspapers and magazines, the Italian press is reasonably free, particularly in regard to what would seem the area of greatest vulnerability. The government has been criticized constantly, vigorously, and frequently viciously; so has the Vatican. Chapter 8 discusses the media during the electoral campaign of 1976, when the magazines went to particular extremes in labeling the Christian Democrats as corrupt and fascistic. Among the national dailies, *Il Messaggero* of Rome has been particularly strident. (Its front-page editorial on election day in 1976 was headed "We Must Save the Country!")

For a period in the mid-1970s *Corriere della Sera* had, for the most part, a highly critical tone. There have been repeated examples of behind-the-scenes pressure by the government upon various newspaper owners to alter the news or to get somebody fired. Almost every journalist interviewed in the course of this study had a stock of such stories.

Government officials and political leaders in the United States also bring pressure on newspaper owners and editors, particularly those who are their friends or are like-minded. The custom probably reached its peak during the Nixon administration, which was frequently on the edge of paranoia about media hostility. The pressure ranged from attempting to get Dan Rather of the Columbia Broadcasting System (CBS) fired (as John Kennedy had once tried to get David Halberstam fired) to trying to persuade businessmen to advertise in the *Washington Star* rather than the *Washington Post*. Connections between powerful businessmen and powerful politicians are much closer in Italy than in this country because of the government's deep involvement in corporate affairs, as well as an increasing amount of government subsidization of the press.

The question is not so much whether government, any government, will apply pressure, but the kind of results it gets. Results depend upon the tools it has available for the job and the ability of journalists and management to resist or to take evasive action.

There is a certain amount of protection in the bureaucratic nature of the news-handling system, of course. In any news enterprise of reasonable size there is a set of interlocking command posts in effect, in which it is easy for instructions to somehow disappear. Heavy-handed publishers such as Colonel Robert McCormick and William Randolph Hearst were repeatedly infuriated at the way stories they wanted printed were not, or ones they tried to kill were printed.

Changes within Italian newspapers during the 1970s also made resistance easier. The conduit for the publisher is, because of the structure of the editorial staff, the direttore responsabile. He, like the American editor, speaks for the owner. With the development of Journalists Committees and unquestioned trade union power—Italian journalists can, and do, shut down their papers on a moment's notice—the responsabile and the staff often had something close to an adversary relationship, particularly on some major papers. Indirect pressure, gentle hints, and suggestions, therefore, frequently have gone unheard; direct orders risked bringing on a confrontation.

Hence, criticisms of parties, politicians, and the ruling government have continued. Amintore Fanfani, as the best-known figure in the Christian Democrats, has received the worst press of any politician in any Western country with the possible exception of Richard Nixon. In the late 1970s several publications tried strenuously to identify Giovanni Leone, president of the republic, as a Lockheed graft recipient and finally drove him from office. Aldo Moro, once president of the council of ministers, and Giulio Andreotti, premier of the "government by abstention" that took over after the elections of 1976, were often reported skeptically and occasionally accused of fraud. The most visible elements of the police and the high command of the army have also been handled in critical terms much more often than with even faint praise.

Italian politicians, like politicians everywhere in the West, are generally too cautious to fight back directly, although Fanfani occasionally has done so. Any overt act of suppression would cause an uproar. Therefore another means has been found: the utilization, sometimes on very thin pretexts, of the country's press laws.

In 1975, for example, a reporter named Fabio Isman of *Il Messaggero* and Italo Pietra, responsabile of that paper, were arrested and charged with instigating for abortion and therefore contributing to delinquency. The charge was based upon the fact that Isman had reported from a press conference a statement by a leader of the Radical party strongly advocating abortion. There was no question of the accuracy of the report. Isman said, in astonishment, "I'm being taken to court for reporting direct quotes, without a line of comment, from the statement of the secretary of a political party. It's absurd."[14]

A former judge interviewed by *Panorama* found it absurd, too. Furthermore, the authorities waited for two and a half months after the story appeared to act. Clearly the charges were designed as punishment for *Il Messaggero* and the two journalists, and as a broad hint about future conduct.

Perhaps the most arrested Italian of recent years has been a journalist named Marcello Baraghini. Unlike Isman, he was a deliberate opponent of the system that controls the press, and hence presumably was always aware of what he was getting into, but his case demonstrates in a different dimension the extent to which the laws can be used. Any periodical in Italy must have a responsabile, the symbolic figure who can be punished, and under the provisions of the law setting up the Order of Journalists the responsabile must be a member of the Order. Baraghini made a career—at least, a short one—of signing on as responsabile of publications that could not find another professional who would do so. Some pornographic magazines were included, because he was against the obscenity statute. The magazine that caused him a jail sentence in the spring of 1976, however, was something called *Against the Family,* which advised children about self-defense against abusive parents. It was the 145th complaint against him; Baraghini had already been through four trials, had been found guilty twice, but had escaped jail. Signing for *Against the Family,* although he had no part in its production, got him a sentence of a year and a half in jail.

In 1972 the co-responsabile of *L'Ora* of Palermo, Etrio Fidora, was sentenced to a year in prison for defamation by means of the press. He also lost the right to practice the profession for a year, a penalty authorized in the penal codes held over from fascism. Both the Order of Journalists and the National Federation of the Press protested the latter element of the sentence furiously, on the grounds that professional discipline was their prerogative.

Harrassment of journalists and publications has sharply increased in recent years, and much of it seems to be carried out with a touch of the vindictive. Italian legislation dealing with the press ranges widely, beginning with the prohibition in article 21 of the constitution against publishing material "contrary to good moral practices." Repeated attacks upon the constitutionality of these laws has brought some small erosion in favor of freedom. Nevertheless, such regulations as article 656 of the penal code, which prohibits the "publication or diffusion of false, exaggerated, or tendentious news" that might serve "to disturb public order," continue in force. A sizable share of the material in almost any issue of any newspaper might be found, at least in the minds of some judges, in violation of such broad and subjective standards. The Constitutional Court upheld its legitimacy in 1972.

Such are the weapons that the government has at its disposal to intimidate Italian journalists. It is probably for this reason that the authorities have seldom used the oversight granted them in the law that established the Order in 1963 to try to control the profession.

Professional discipline has instead, for the most part, been left to the profession. The extent of such activity is hard to determine. The legal consultant for the Order has described internal disciplinary procedures as happening "often enough." A more specific figure is said to be impossible for two reasons. In the first place, such actions are not made public except in very special cases. Secondly, in practice all such actions are carried out through the appropriate regional council and whatever accounts exist are buried in regional archives. It seems surprising that the central office of the Order has no information about such matters, but apparently it does not.

This means that specifics would require a lot of travel and a lot of digging into the Italian bureaucracy. At one point I wrote to an Italian friend, a member of the Order, and asked him to make inquiries. After some exploration, he reported back, "It might be easier for you to get the information, because as a foreigner you would not be suspected of ulterior motives."

The obfuscation, in my judgment, does not mean that there is any scandal in the facts; it is not meant to conceal either the lack of disciplinary action or the overuse of it. It is simply in the tradition of the Italian way of doing things, and "often enough" is probably a fair answer.

Only one case in the years covered by this study has received any attention in the media. It involved the relationship between a journalist named Giorgio Zicari and the Italian Secret Service, known as SID. Zicari was the star local news reporter of *Corriere della Sera,* and had a series of remarkable scoops from that murky area where politics and crime overlap, beginning with a series of exclusive articles about the investigation of the Piazza Fontana bombings of December 12, 1969. He followed with other articles over the next few years, concluding with a set of coups from the investigation of the Fumagalli plot, a plan for a series of assassinations and sabotage by a secret Fascist group. By this time Zicari's journalistic competitors were beginning to suspect something, and since the SID was the basic investigating agency, a connection with them seemed likely. The uproar, including repeated questions in the Chamber of Deputies, became considerable in late summer of 1974, and Zicari finally admitted that he had performed one chore for the agency, at their request, without any compensation, and with the knowledge of his superior, Franco Di Bella.

He had interviewed Fumagalli while wired with a concealed tape recorder and a microphone in his trousers and then turned the tape over to the SID. He had done it gladly, he said, because he was convinced it was necessary to help save the nation. The management of *Corriere della Sera* fired him the day after his admission and called for the regional council of the Order to investigate with an eye to discipline. At the conclusion of the proceedings he was suspended from the profession for two months.

There were no allegations, apparently, of Zicari's performing other chores for the Secret Service, nor did any details of anything they might have been doing for him over the years become public. Most of the discussion seems to have centered on Zicari's contention that Franco Di Bella, then *Corriere's capocronista* (a post akin to, although not identical to, that of city editor), not only knew of Zicari's relationship with the SID, but encouraged it. Di Bella denied it. The whole controversy popped onto the front pages again three years later when Di Bella became editor of *Corriere.*

Even if it does occasionally punish its members, the Order for the most part, and from its beginnings, has functioned chiefly as a protector of the profession from both management and public authorities. The law of 1963 provided that the procurator of a region could initiate disciplinary action by the Order—that is, within the court system—as well as the regional council. In 1970 the procurator of Rome tried to make use of that provision. He began prosecution under the criminal statutes of a journalist for "defamation by means of the press"; he simultaneously requested that the regional council take disciplinary action. The council refused to do so, citing the principle that those charged with crimes are innocent until proved guilty, as well as article 21 of the Italian Constitution, which provides freedom for the individual to express his own thoughts. The Order then proceeded to press for, and win, an amendment to the original legislation that removed the right of the procurator to initiate such actions.

The Order also lodged the strongest possible protests in the cases cited above—the codirector of *L'Ora* who was suspended from the profession through the provisions of the penal code; Isman and Pietra, charged with incitement to delinquency; and Baraghini, the True Believer in freedom of expression who was willing to put his head on the block to help secure it. This last case is perhaps the most striking illustration of the organization's tendency to automatically fight for its own. Baraghini has never been any kind of insider in the relatively small world of Italian journalism. The journalistic establishment, however, was unequivocal in its reaction to his sentencing.

"For thirty years we have been waiting for the abrogation of Fascist regulations," said Alessandro Curzi of the executive committee of the National Federation of the Italian Press. "The case of Baraghini, the first journalist to stand on the threshold of prison, has finally triggered the problem, and we will do what's necessary; if by June [1976] the Parliament has not eliminated the regulations concerning crimes of opinion, we will push for a popular referendum to abrogate them to be held in 1977."[15]

Baraghini did not go to jail, as it turned out, and there was no referendum, but the point was unmistakable. If there is a presumption in law that the accused is innocent until proven guilty, it is lightly held compared to the familiar trade union presumption that a brother accused by outsiders is almost certainly in the right.

Americans in particular are inclined, in analytically evaluating rules, laws, and regulations, to push their possible application to the most extreme test. What is the maximum abuse, we tend to ask ourselves, that can be inflicted upon me or the body politic by a really ingenious abuser? What is the far limit of authorization provided to a government more ill-intentioned than this one? We seem to have a tendency to try to define those outer limits when making rules or laws, rather than to assume that the normal course of events will follow predictable lines and that laws simply provide standby authority for use in cases of extreme emergency. Other democratic societies, open and free, find the latter idea easy to live with. The British, for example, have been able for years to live with the Official Secrets Act, which, on paper, has an astonishing potential as a tool for authoritarianism. Almost all continental countries have a legal provision very much like the Italian law cited above which permits action against news that may disturb public order; the idea goes back to the middle of the eighteenth century. On the rare occasions when a publication is sequestered or an editor arrested, there is not only protest, but indignation, almost a reaction of "Well, sure, it's a law, but everybody understands you're not supposed to use it."

It is in this spirit that Italian journalists, most of them highly suspicious of government, live with equanimity in a situation that gives government the necessary apparatus for control. Some show a remarkable confidence, if not naiveté, about their ability to fend off the bad things about government involvement while getting a larger share of good things. Employees of *Agenzia Nazionale Stampa Associata* (L'ANSA), the national news agency, struck in 1975. Along with speeches about freedom and professional integrity, they demanded that the government increase its already considerable subsidization to the point where the service would be free to any paper requesting it.

Which is, it seems, a variant on an old saw; there are some journalists who believe that it is possible to have your freedom, and sell it, too.

Chapter 4

The Profession and the Union

The Order of Journalists could not exist without its parallel organization, the National Federation of the Italian Press. Structurally they are much alike; both are built on regional organizations that have a good deal of authority; each has a national council, although the federation has a more elaborate administrative apparatus. The new professional, upon certification of his competence, usually becomes a member of both. Membership in the federation, the trade union, is voluntary, but at the end of the decade 92 percent of the profession belonged.

The chief difference between the two organizations is in function. The Order is a creature of the law, described in detail in the country's statutes. It is primarily concerned with the process through which a candidate becomes a professional journalist and the adjudication of cases arising from violation of the law. The federation is an energetic, and of late aggressive, trade union, bargaining about hours and wages and conditions of work. Its only connection with the country's legal system rests in the fact that the national journalists' labor contract is recognized as binding by law, and the federation represents the journalists in negotiations with the publishers' association, the Italian Newspaper Publishers Federation.

Historically, the federation is long antecedent to the establishment of the Order. It evolved in 1908 from an organization that was founded in 1877, and the Order was the result of the federation's work. The federation has been so good at negotiating that it has drowned, in tides of lire, any real opposition to the present structure of the profession.

The offices of Federazione Nazionale della Stampa Italiana (generally written as FNSI; in conversation, one sometimes hears *Federstampa*) look as if they might go back to the beginnings of the organization. Corso Vittorio Emmanuele II is, by Roman standards, a very long street; it rises in the Piazza Venezia and runs westward to the Tiber, where it ends in an ornate bridge that is a primary conduit to Vatican City. It is a street jammed with traffic, dirty, and largely without buildings worth any particular notice, a commercial neighborhood in gentle erosion. Number

329 is only a few hundred meters from the river. It is a squarish, dust-colored nineteenth-century office building.

The aging open-shaft elevator hauls one to the second floor and the offices of FNSI. The place is cold, almost without decoration, reminiscent of a railroad station. The outer furniture seems chosen at random; most of it is black and heavy. Inside, in offices and conference rooms, there is more of the same. It seems, in short, the classic nest for an unimportant and obsolete bureaucracy.

In fact, it is the center of the forceful direction of the best paid and most exclusive trade union in Italy, one which has, in less than thirty years, brought the salaries of the professionals that it represents from the threadbare level of most European journalists' compensation to very near the top of the world scale. Far from being threatened or sniped at by government, it has been steadily reinforced by it.

There are some significant differences between FNSI and professional groups or trade unions in the United States. The leadership of such groups in this country is generally bureaucratic; eminent practitioners are seldom deeply involved in professional politics. The point is irrelevant, of course, so far as most trade unions are concerned, but the tradition carries over into the most high-status professional groups. Seldom has the president of the American Medical Association been a distinguished medical man, or the president of the American Bar Association a genuinely eminent jurist. American journalists' organizations have followed the same pattern. The American Newspaper Guild, which is closer to a parallel of FNSI than any other U.S. group, has had among its activists only one major national figure, Heywood Broun. Even eminent academic organizations seem to chose career organization men as leaders as often as they choose luminaries in the field.

In contrast, almost all the journalists mentioned frequently in this book have been active in FNSI's affairs, even though they may have held no formal title as officers. Gorresio, as we have seen, was one of a small group that started putting the profession together again as soon as Mussolini fell; he was a dominant figure in national meetings throughout the early years of the organization and led the losing fight against the establishment of the Order. Luigi Barzini, Jr., was president of the Roman regional association throughout the 1970s. Indro Montanelli, until leaving *Corriere*, spent much of his time on assignment outside the country, but has both spoken and written forcefully about the problems of Italian journalism and FNSI affairs. Mario Missiroli, longtime editor of *Corriere della Sera*, was president of the federation until his retirement in 1968. Paolo Murialdi became president in 1974. He was a well-established newspaperman, having been managing editor of *Il Giorno* for seventeen years, but his national reputation has rested on his work as a historian and analyst of the Italian newspaper press. He is cited repeatedly in these pages.

With his assumption of the presidency, Murialdi left full-time editorial work (a special provision of the law of 1963 permits members who have public or trade union leadership roles to continue as *professionisti*; others who are out of the profession for more than two years are dropped); the presidency is an active and involved job.

The Italian love for dialectic and politicking explains some of the tendency of the eminent to take on major roles within the union. It produces at the biennial national meetings of the group an examination of the issues and problems of journalism that professional meetings in the United States do not normally produce. Taken as a whole, the talk at FNSI meetings is high-level indeed.

But the National Federation of the Italian Press does not get its strength from good talk or even reformist zeal. The strength comes from a lengthy document, revised and reissued about every two years, which is entitled *Contratto nazionale di lavoro giornalistico* (literally, the National Contract of Journalistic Labor). It covers, in detail, the implementation of every journalistic vocation in the country; salaries, hours, vacations, pensions, health care, working conditions. It is remarkably generous to the journalist.

The signatories are the president of the Italian Newspaper Publishers Federation and the president of FNSI. Generally negotiations continue over a period of several weeks or even months. Most year-to-year changes have sweetened the figures for the journalists, meaning higher salaries and overtime provisions and reduced working hours.

In the years between 1970 and 1976, in the contracts negotiated during the first years of an aggressive new union leadership, two new elements were incorporated. The employees of all periodicals are now covered in almost precisely the same terms as newspaper journalists, in whose almost exclusive interest the contract was originally drawn. Secondly, the new role of the Journalists Committee is reflected in almost every article. No significant management options have been taken away, but a requirement for consultation is now attached to most important management decisions. That requirement, in turn, makes easier the process of organizing for protest, and in the case of a few major publications some significant powers have been taken from the editor through supplemental in-house contracts; we shall have a longer look at that phenomenon later.

A good sense of the contract can be obtained through a summary look at its provisions; a few passages appear in full, however, because of their uncommon character.

After preliminary definitions and terms of application, the contract begins with stipulations concerning the powers of the editor. The name of any person nominated for the post of editor must be transmitted to the Journalists Committee before notification is given to any third party, and at least forty-eight hours before he or she assumes the new post. The powers of the editor are specified as those set out in his contract with the publisher, as long as no provisions of the journalists' contract are violated, of course, but the details of the editor-publisher agreement must be made clear to the Journalists Committee; in fact, it must be the new editor's first official act.

The primary purpose of this provision is the clarification of the "political-editorial program" of the publication or broadcast operation. It has been pointed out that for many years Italian journalists have had a contractual right to collect very heavy severance pay if they resign as a matter of conscience in case of a change in political line. Obviously a formal statement makes it easier for the dissenting journalist to argue his case.

This provision means more than that, however. It has reflected the concerns of the reformist wing of the profession about Italian politics in general and the reformists' attempt to do something about these concerns through the newspaper. For this reason, in two of the country's larger papers, the agreement drawn up in the mid-1970s was not between the publisher and editor at all, but between those two and the Journalists Committee. The supplemental in-house agreements for both *Il Messaggero* and *Corriere della Sera* reflected far more the leftist passion of the committees than the centrism of the editor or deep conservatism of the owners.

The national contract gives the editor the power to hire new employees and, so long as it is for "technical-professional" reasons, to fire employees. He also, with some qualifications, is given the right to direct the interpretation of the agreed-upon political line and to supervise the mechanics of assignment and getting out the paper.

FNSI has been working for years at reducing working hours, with much talk about the *settimana corta* ("short week"). The 1969–70 contract specified a thirty-six-hour week for journalists in all the major cities, with a thirty-nine-hour week in the provinces; the 1977 contract wiped out the distinction, and the entire profession moved to the thirty-six-hour short (no more than five days) week. Most of the rest of Italy still works on a six-day week, including the public schools. The 1970 contract specified that the journalist could not be required to work more than eleven hours at a stretch; the 1977 agreement specified ten (art. 7).

The first reaction of an American reporter to that kind of work week would be astonishment. The second would be a question: how do they get the paper out? Even if the papers are considerably overstaffed, how is it possible?

Before answering the question, let us look, in the name of coherence, at another part of the contract that raises the issue even more forcefully. Article 19 deals with holidays and other days off. Nothing in journalism anywhere so well demonstrates what a really effective trade union can do. In 1976 the text of article 19 read this way.

> Considered as holidays are:
>
> *a*) Sundays
>
> *b*) the four national holidays (April 25 [National Liberation Day], May 1 [May Day, added in the 1967 contract], June 2 [Anniversary of the Republic], and November 4 [victory anniversary for the First World War])
>
> *c*) and the following other holidays: January 1; January 6, Epiphany; March 19, St. Joseph's Day; Easter Monday; Corpus Domini; June 29, St. Peter's and St. Paul's Day; August 15, Assumption Day; November 1, All Saints' Day; December 8, Immaculate Conception Day; December 25 and 26; and the name day of the patron saint of the city in which the journalist is located.[1]

All of these were at that time traditional Italian holidays, marked in most cases by the closing of public institutions such as government offices and schools. In March, 1977, the Italian Parliament struck several from the list; the four national holidays were reduced to two, April 25 and May 1, and the religious holidays to eight. There was no way for the next journalists' contract to restore them, of course, but it did provide for compensation for those days at the familiar bonus holiday rates.

The remainder of article 19 lays out in detail the complex formula for the calculations: the basic scale for holiday pay is one day's pay plus 80 percent.

It is of interest to pursue the question of "Who's keeping the store?" from one additional direction, that dealt with by article 23. In the 1977–78 contract, that article guarantees to all members of the Order the following paid vacation time:

- twenty-six *working* [italics added] days for those who had been in the company up to five years;

- thirty working days for those who had been with the company between five and fifteen years [in the 1969 contract the figures for eligibility were, respectively, eight and twenty years];
- thirty-five working days for those who have been with the company more than fifteen years [the 1969 figure was twenty years].[2]

In addition, any established holiday that falls within the vacation period does not count as a vacation day. The fact that the provision is for working days pushes the elapsed time even further along. For someone with fifteen years service in 1978, for example, a vacation that began on June 1 lasted through July 12, including an extra day for St. Peter's and St. Paul's Day (June 29), calculated on a basis of twenty-six working days per month, the figure that is used throughout the contract.

Since the contract requires that vacations be taken between the first of May and the first of November, some very shorthanded summer months would seem inevitable.

This is not the case to any significant degree, of course. The answer lies in requiring service and paying overtime; the prodigious number of days off granted the working journalist is not time out at all, but, in most cases, a mechanism for paying him or her more.

In addition to the elaborate formulas set out in article 19, other provisions that helped raise the total are:

1. higher pay for night work (defined as that which ends after 11 P.M. or begins before 6 A.M.). Most of the country's major dailies are morning papers, which means that a sizable number of their staff members qualify for the premium;

2. the *indennità redazionale,* which translates as "bonus" and amounts to an extra month's pay, granted on June 30 of each year, to which is added another month's pay, identified simply as a sum due the journalist for no specific reason;

3. the "thirteenth month," paid in December and amounting to a contractual Christmas bonus; it came to something more than a month's pay. The thirteenth month device is a matter of law, and applies to all hiring arrangements in Italy.

All this adds up, it will be noted, to fifteen months of pay a year for every journalist. And there is more:

4. an automatic salary increase for every two years of seniority; the contract specifies at least 6 percent of the minimum scale for the position, plus an *indennità di contingenza,* which does not refer to actual contingencies, but to a vague idea approximating a bonus for

good behavior, and which is calculated by another formula (for 1977, the figure ranged between $38.50 and $44 minimum per month);

5. and finally, Italian journalists, along with most trade union members, are on the *scala mobile,* an escalator provision based upon the cost of living, the addition of which in no way affects the application of any provisions of the contract.

Even a quick look at all these provisions for extra pay reveals not only why Italian journalists are experts with a pocket calculator, but how actual compensation can routinely reach the level of 150 percent of the stated salary. Precise figures on who makes how much are almost impossible to come by. Minimums are established by the national journalists contracts. They seem modest, but it must be remembered that they are minimums.

The following figures are for the 1977–78 contract, and represent the basic monthly minimum for each category, converted to dollars on the basis of 850 lire to 1 dollar.

Apprentice after first year	$250.00
Staff with less than eighteen months experience	344.00
Staff with less than ten years	430.00
Staff with more than ten years	435.00
Department head or bureau chief	490.00
Managing editor	534.00

The contract does not cover editors or associate editors, whose higher pay scales are a matter of negotiation, but it does provide for the minimum increase that must be added to their salaries when a new contract goes into effect; the stipulation is pro forma and the sum small, in any case.

The most significant thing about these contractual minimums, however, is that they mean nothing; no professional of which this writer knows has ever received as little as his category's minimum, except during a brief period when two papers were run as cooperatives. Apprentices are sometimes held to the minimum, but general practice pays them more. FNSI and the Order both keep close watch on the number and longevity of apprentices, a process designed as much to prevent the employer from using cheap help as the new journalist from being exploited.

The larger question remains: how much money do Italian journalists make? It has been asked by a variety of people. One of the most curious was Giuseppe Caroli, a Christian Democrat member of the Chamber of Deputies, who headed a special committee charged with looking into salary levels in many fields, including journalism. He paid special attention to *Il Messaggero*. One of the newspaper's managing editors saw the investigation as hostile and punitive, asserting in a conversation with me that the deputy had been outraged by the paper's swing to the left. What Caroli saw apparently startled him. He made it clear that the figures were very high. My informant at *Il Messaggero* cheerily admitted that at least his was, and said that if they would give him the chance he would be happy to demonstrate that he deserved it. He mentioned no figures, however, and efforts to dig out specifics from the Caroli investigation ran head-on into the statement that no information at all had been released by the committee. (This was in the early summer of 1977.) Indeed, some political journalists to whom I talked expressed doubt that anything would ever be released.

One story had it that the committee had made inquiries about the total compensation—not just salary, but perquisites, allowances, and speaking and writing fees—of U.S. congressmen for purposes of comparison with Italian legislators. A few weeks after the information was forwarded from Washington, the rumor had it, the committee announced that the information would not be used, after all, to protect the privacy of the Americans. Some journalists said that the real explanation was somewhat more crass; the Italian figures for legislators were embarrassingly higher. The concern about privacy, however, is believable; Italians have a profound sense of privacy about money, particularly their own.

Nevertheless, some did volunteer their salaries during my first interviews in 1970; a few other figures came from journalists talking about each other, or could be deduced. One salary at that time seemed to be known to everybody in the business; on several occasions when I brought up the subject of compensation the first remark was "Do you know that Giovanni Spadolini has a salary of three million lire a month?" That, in the predevaluation lire of the time, amounted to about $58,000 a year.* Salaries clearly have risen since the beginning of the decade, however, and Piero Ottone, Spadolini's replacement as editor of *Corriere della Sera*, undoubtedly did a good deal better than that.

Most of the people about whom I got specific information in 1970— I have not pursued the question in recent times, since considerable sensitivity seems to have grown along with the salaries—were in the range of $1,300 to $2,000 a month. These were people near the top of the profession, however; a political writer on a national daily, one of the managing editors of *Corriere della Sera*, the director of a specialized news agency, and the like. The most modest salary volunteered was that of a young man

---

*L620 = $1.00.

who had been with an American wire service for five years; he made, at that time, $500 a month, not very much above the minimum. Surprisingly, he felt it fair, and was happy with it. A good pattern of raises was ahead of him, and he knew he would do better.

The general satisfaction with salaries and fringes is a striking aspect of the profession in Italy. In literally hundreds of conversations over almost a decade I heard complaints about every conceivable aspect of the journalist's life except pay; it is literally impossible to remember a single one, or find it mentioned in my notes. On the other hand there were dozens of volunteered comments that went something like "All things considered, we make as much as American reporters, maybe even more." A survey of professional journalists in Milan in late 1976, discussed in detail in chapter 9, revealed substantially the same kind of satisfaction.

That is a bit difficult to understand in the light of the figures listed above, although the claim of being the second-best-paid journalists in the world may indeed be correct. Worldwide, journalists' pay is appallingly low, including countries with a tradition of a strong and high quality press, such as the United Kingdom and Japan, and Italians rank so well in part because so many others do so badly. And if they are in second place, they are still considerably behind their U.S. equivalents, at least in official compensation.

There were several dozen U.S. newspaper editors who in 1970 received more than Spadolini's $58,000, and heaven knows how many television anchormen. The managing editors of most dailies were making more than $25,000, the figure for one at *Corriere della Sera* (and *Corriere* always has been regarded as the best-paying paper in Italy). The $18,000 salary of the political writer on *Il Messaggero* was close to that of one at the *Baltimore Sun* or the *Detroit Free Press* at that point, but still behind.

Whatever their incomes, most Italian journalists with whom I have had contact live well. When I set up interviews, several suggested that we talk in their homes. Such invitations are not common; traditionally, middle-class European families live in modest housing, to free as much money as possible for the more visible life of the promenade, restaurants, and, increasingly, something other than the cheapest automobiles.

Comfortable circumstances for the Italian journalist in some cases represent another benefit of the national journalists' contract. My first trip to Turin, in 1970, took an unexpected course but, so far as I was concerned, a fortuitous one. *La Stampa*'s editor at that time was Alberto Ronchey. I looked forward to meeting him, but the paper was struck by its printers before my arrival. There was a ceremonial meeting with Ronchey in the hall in between his shuttle trips among the rooms that held various negotiating teams; then he turned me over to a young man he introduced as a member of the staff. His name was Paolo Garimberti. After a tour of the place (*La Stampa* was the first Italian paper to adopt U.S. newspaper architecture, with a huge open newsroom rather than the traditional maze of small offices), Garimberti said that he and his wife were commissioned to take me to dinner, and suggested that we go to his apartment for a drink. That is an uncommon invitation to a stranger in Italy; one goes to a bar for a drink. Garimberti had been in the United States only briefly, but it apparently was long enough to learn the conventional American amenities. He was from Genoa, and had begun his career on *Corriere Mercantile,* a small shipping paper there.

His wife was beautiful and the apartment elegant, including a handsome lobby with a fountain in it. I was much impressed by everything, including both Garimbertis. He became *La Stampa*'s correspondent in Moscow and was, by the late 1970s, one of its biggest names. When I returned to Rome I described the experience, including the apartment, to a journalist friend.

"Sure," he said. "He used his severance pay from Genoa to swing the deal for the apartment."

The reference was to article 27 of the contract, which deals with severance pay in case of resignation or firing. When a journalist resigns, in most cases, to accept another and better paying position, he is entitled to a month's pay for each year, or fraction of a year, that he has worked for the company. If he has worked fifteen years or more (the figure in earlier contracts was twenty) he receives in addition a fixed indemnity ranging from seven to thirteen months' pay, depending upon his position. When a long-term Italian employee of an American news service, United Press International, resigned to take the directorship of another news service, UPI wrote him a check for the equivalent of about $25,000. There is no limit to the number of times a journalist can do this during his career, and on some occasions resignees actually have been rehired by the same employer and have started the cycle all over again. The contract carefully specifies, however, that in such cases only the seniority acquired since the beginning of the new employment counts in calculating severance pay the next time he quits.

The costs to a publication or RAI of firing an employee are much higher than in the case of an amicable dissolution of the relationship. In practice, genuine firings of the by-god-we've-had-enough-of-you-clean-out-your-desk variety are by this time almost unknown in Italy because of legislation passed in 1971. This specifies, in broad terms, that no one can be fired from any job without "just cause." Although the legislation does not mention journalists, it has been generally assumed that it applies. Allan Jacks, who worked for the Associated Press in Rome for more than twenty years, pointed out in a conversation in 1975 that no employer in journalism had yet found a cause "just" enough to fire anybody.

Journalists were substantially safe from being fired before that particular legislation was ever passed, however, because of the cost of letting someone go. The national contract continued to carry the same provisions, in part, perhaps, because of the desire for backup in case the 1971 law does not hold up. The 1977–78 contract provided for a special indemnity, in addition to the severance pay described earlier, as follows:

> To those holding the post of editor or associate editor, the equivalent of thirteen months' salary.
>
> To a managing editor, special Rome correspondent, or chief of the Rome bureau, ten months' salary.
>
> To section or division editors, such as a city editor, sports editor, or foreign editor, eight months' pay.
>
> To any other professional, seven months' pay.

Under these circumstances it is cheaper simply to work around a discontented or inefficient staff member, particularly if he is highly paid; an example was cited in the opening section of this book.

The indemnity for being fired runs throughout the contract as a convenient yardstick for extra compensation under a variety of circumstances. Any journalist who has reached the age of sixty with at least three years of service to his employer may resign and, in addition to the month's pay for every year compensation, collect the indemnity for being fired. In case a publication is discontinued, each staff member receives the same indemnity; the same is true in those cases where a journalist's job is moved to another town and he does not care to follow it. The journalist who resigns because of pregnancy also receives these benefits, and in one of the more curious provisions of the contract, the staff member who marries, in addition to getting a paid twenty-day vacation for a honeymoon, also has the privilege of quitting the job and receiving the extra indemnity along with seniority pay.

There will be occasion to refer to other provisions of the contract, related to power instead of money, elsewhere in these pages. Financial provisions for sickness, death, and pensions have been generous by European standards. In case of injury or illness, for example, the journalist's job must be held for him for one year. If he has between five and ten years of seniority, he receives full pay for the first five months of that period and half pay for the next five; the figures scale down to three months of each for those with less than five years of service. In the 1976 contract permanent disability, in addition to the sick leave provisions cited above, called for a payment of approximately $41,000. Death benefits, in addition to a final salary settlement equivalent to being fired, totaled about $35,000. At that point such insurance cost the journalist about $2.35 per month. His employer made an equal contribution; a substantial government subsidization provided the remainder. Retirement pay ranges from about $2,000 to more than $18,000 per year, depending upon variables such as salary and length of service.[3]

Before concluding the discussion about money, a reminder of some other considerations that enhance the Italian journalist's economic condition should be mentioned. One of these is represented by that exquisite phrase, *in omaggio,* which means literally "as a compliment," but which signifies in the marketplace as getting something for nothing; another is the more commercial *sconto,* which means "discount." Journalists in Italy get some things in omaggio as a legal recognition. An earlier note pointed out that the first step toward recognition of journalism as a special profession was the turn of the century law that granted practitioners much reduced railroad fares. They still get them, and reduced air fares as well. They are excused from tolls on the autostrade, which is not so trivial as it might seem; the tolls are high.

And, although somewhat in decline, there is still the widespread habit of giving journalists discounts on most of the things they buy. One shows the professional identification card, and some kind of discount frequently is forthcoming. One does not, however, haggle, despite the folklore held dear by some tourists that the only reasonable conduct in Italy is the same as in a bazaar in Marrakesh. Better yet, one deals with the same people over and over, which makes it easy to dispense with any ceremony at all. The journalist who eats at a particular restaurant regularly simply pays a smaller check, in many cases, than someone at the next table with the same meal. And a new vacuum cleaner or a set of automobile tires or a new typewriter will be available at a handsome reduction.

For an indeterminate number of journalists, there is another source of influence, the quiet income from those who want to assure themselves of appropriate treatment in the press. On that point there seems to be nothing to add to the discussion in an earlier chapter.

Even this summary of the works of the Order of Journalists and the National Federation of the Italian Press makes it clear that there are few job holders in any society as well off as the Italian journalist. In the United States probably only senior-grade civil servants and tenured professors in rich universities possess such a combination of complete job security and good salaries. There are thousands of people in American life, and in American journalism, who make far more money than the top Italians, but there has never been any tradition of security. The television anchorperson in Pittsburgh or San Francisco may indeed make two hundred thousand dollars a year, but if the ratings of the newscast slip from first to third and stay there he is likely to find that he is making nothing at all. Such well-paying enterprises as Time, Inc. at its peak always retained the weapon of instant dismissal; there were people who commanded intellectual empires at *Life* one day and found their traps piled in the hall the next, waiting for the movers. A reporter covering the State Department for the *Baltimore Sun* may be extravagantly praised one week and fired the next. There has always been a catch-as-catch-can, dicey atmosphere throughout the history of the mass media in America, and it is tempting, at least, to think that some of their accomplishments may be related to that.

One of the questions that continuously has interested me in my investigations of the Italian journalist is that of his feelings about that golden groove. Ever since Gorresio fought the battle of 1946, there have been those who have been doubtful of the social usefulness of the fat and happy journalist. The perquisites and protection and the self-satisfaction that accompanies them have been attacked from time to time, sometimes eloquently. This, for example, from an unsigned article in *Il Mondo* in 1960:

> It is not only a question of people that the condition of journalism is sad; we have the impression that the conception of it is all wrong. If one wishes to think about remedies, it seems strange and deplorable that the professional organizations assist in silence the destruction of the profession which now is underway. The good salary, the pension, the thirteenth month, the paid holidays, the special indemnities are very important, beyond doubt; but professional dignity, independent thinking, and high quality journalism must have more than a secondary part. Why does the Federation of the Press never get involved in these essential problems? And why, for their part, do journalists not understand that the heart of these problems, regardless of their political tendencies, is not the defense or condemnation of a political sector or of a proprietor, but the defense of their rights, of their profession, of their excellence as journalists rather than as spokesmen? Certainly the problem is immense and at the right time will have to be confronted at its source.[4]

Ten years later that kind of talk still turned up in my interviews occasionally. The most impressive individual to speak against the concept of the Order was Paolo Murialdi, then president of FNSI, in a private interview in October, 1979. He seemed to regard the problem more as one of logic, however, than as a matter of urgent need for change. Beyond that, I found only one or two working journalists who were willing to criticize either the concept of the Order or the functioning of the national contract, and none who was willing to make any connection between these things and the professional problems about which he might feel deeply. When asked directly about their feelings about the Order and the possibility of conflict with genuine freedom of the press, for example, most shrugged it off politely: "Well, you know. . . ."

The most outspoken critics of the system were those on the edges of the profession, administrators or managers, or those no longer active in a newsroom. In a 1975 interview, for example, Marco Betti, president of the Press Officers Association of Lombardy, spoke to me openly and vigorously against the Order, primarily because he feels the profession "should be open to anybody good enough to get in." He pointed to the low number of apprentices and the long process of breaking in, which means all the originality and initiative is squeezed out of them.

One of the 1970 interviews was with a journalist who was head of a specialized financial news service. Although Italian, and a member of the professionista branch of the Order, he was openly contemptuous of Italian journalists as a group, and particularly critical of the national contract. "What can you do with a man who is required to work only six hours a day?"

Most management people among my respondents echoed some variation on that idea. The editor of a couple of specialized magazines who had spent twenty years on *Corriere della Sera* and its satellite magazines was against both the Order and the contract, saying that journalism had become simply another job because it was controlled by a bureaucracy interested only in money.

But interestingly enough, Vittorio Gorresio, who led the opposition to the retention of the registry of professionals in 1946, in our conversations more than twenty years later, spoke favorably of both the Order and the contract. So, over the years, have the rest of the working reporters.

Thus, when serious talk about reform began in the late 1960s, none of it was aimed at changing any important characteristics of professionalism, as Italian statutes define it, or the process of professionalization, as both the law and the trade union contracts specify it. Certainly there has been no discussion, at least on the part of people who have some capacity to do something about it, of increasing the amount of competition within the profession or of cutting loose from any of the anchors that make it so secure. I have never agreed with a former newsman who assured me that Italian journalists as a whole were lazy, self-centered, elitist, and pompous. He thought they became that way because of the Order and FNSI and the benefits corollary to them. I would not agree with that; but those among the profession in Italy of whom that description is accurate can be certain, because of the system, that they can continue to be so without fear of either penalty or rebuke.

The satisfied elitist, however, was not the important figure in Italian journalism in the 1970s. A reform movement that more or less began with the decade was to make a significant difference in both the profession and the industry, and its rise and decline illustrated the essential character of the system. Because reform ultimately was tied to changes in ownership and economic control of Italian mass communications, it is necessary at this point to consider those elements by way of preface.

Chapter 5

Newspaper Owners, Politicians, and Purity

It is not difficult to begin a description of Italian media ownership, but it is almost impossible to determine where to end it. A comprehensive account of the games of proprietorship during the 1970s would fill more than one volume the size of this one. Exposure to only a modest amount of detail can prove addictive to the investigator. One gets hooked on the question of who was behind whom when he acquired what, or feinted acquisition while his real objective was something altogether different, or what political debts had to do with it, and so on endlessly.

For years I felt that, considering the fact that I was in the country only a few weeks a year, I was staying reasonably well informed, until a story surfaced in 1977 that the Swiss branch of the house of Rothschild had bought 49 percent of a major Italian publishing company. I mentioned it with some surprise to an Italian friend. He smiled wisely.

"Rothschild," he said, "always has had 49 percent of that company. From the beginning." As, his tone implied, we insiders always have known.

So much for feeling well informed. One never really gets unhooked (was it true that the money used by the Libyan dictator Muammar al-Qaddafi to buy a sizable percentage of FIAT was passed on to Angelo Rizzoli to set up the private television company Telemalta?), but my concern in this project is with journalists, not owners. And the most important questions have little to do with financial detail, but with the Italian journalists' perception of owners as a class; with the journalists' beliefs about what the owners were up to in all the buying and selling; and about what politics, eternally and inevitably, had to do with all this.

We can begin with a summary generalization: the newspaper industry in Italy in modern times has never been profitable.

That makes it difficult to explain the fierce efforts in recent years to buy up major papers, the first by Eugenio Cefis and the second, which overlapped it in time, by Angelo Rizzoli. We must begin with a description of an institution that had to die before the corporate infighting of the 1970s could take place.

There is an Italian phrase *editori puri* ("pure publishers"). The word *editore* does not refers to the editor of a publication, but his boss, the person or the institution that owns it.

Editore puro is the standard phrase in the field for owner-publishers whose primary interest is in journalism. It is generally regarded as enlightened ownership, and to describe a media baron with the term is regarded as a compliment. That is not a uniform judgment; one of my journalist friends who sees the chief function of the press as political sardonically defines a "pure" publisher as one who will do anything for money. The most common attitude, however, is that the owner with a single-minded devotion to the news business is likely to produce a more serious and responsible product than one to whom his journalistic property is a small tail on a large corporate dog.

Until 1960 the ownership of almost all American media was in the hands of owner-publishers, even the networks; the great names that come first to mind are Hearst, Pulitzer, McCormick, Ochs-Sulzberger, Luce, Wallace, Knight, and the first broadcasting giants, Paley and Sarnoff. (For decades the only newspaper owner not preoccupied with the news business was the Anaconda Copper company, which held newspapers in Montana.) That kind of ownership was one of the great strengths in U.S. journalism, and has always been much admired by the Europeans, who almost from the beginning have had to live with the product of intellectually absentee owners.

The pattern of ownership in Italy of major papers has always involved wealthy outsiders. In 1882, for example, a sizable packet of stock of the new Milan paper called *Corriere della Sera* passed into the hands of an industrialist named Benigno Crespi. In 1920 the FIAT company (meaning the Agnellis) acquired a third of the stock of *La Stampa*. One-half of the stock of *Il Messaggero* was acquired in 1915 by the Perrone brothers, manufacturers of armaments and other steel products.*

All three of these papers functioned, at least for a time, under the direction of *puri* who controlled the major interest in each paper. Then in 1925 both *Corriere* and *La Stampa* were briefly suspended by the Fascist government, which ordered the sale of the remainder of the stock to the industrialist who, in each case, already owned a portion; to the Crespi family, in the case of *Corriere,* and in the case of *La Stampa* to a reluctant

---

*The other member of the four national independents, *Il Giorno,* was established much later, in 1956, and was from the beginning a corporate child.

Giovanni Agnelli, who made it clear, but to no avail, that he did not want to own any more of it.[1] The same action was taken against other local and regional papers that the regime did not like, *Il Mattino* of Naples, *Il Gazzettino* of Venice, and *Gazzetta del Popolo* of Turin. The Perrones acquired the rest of *Il Messaggero* without government pressure; the paper never had any difficulty with the Fascist regime.

There was a brief flurry of talk at the end of the Second World War about throwing out all collaborators with the Fascists, publishers and journalists alike, but unlike France and Germany, where ownerships were radically altered and sizable numbers of journalists punished, a bit of symbolic behavior served in Italy. Some titles were changed for a few years, then restored. No newspaper owner who wanted to retain his publication lost it, nor was any journalist penalized; within a year after the defeat of the Germans, things were pretty much back to the old ways.[2]

Thus the Crespi family still owned *Corriere,* the Agnellis *La Stampa,* and the Perrones *Il Messaggero* when the reform movement in the profession began to gain thrust in early 1970. None were actually editori puri. Yet two of these owners functioned in a way to which even the most suspicious journalist would find it difficult to take exception, following what might be considered the second-best line for ownership. If the entrepreneur of the media is not to be primarily interested in what his communications enterprises do, he should hire good people and let them alone. This, essentially, is what happened with both *Corriere della Sera* and *La Stampa*.

The Crespis made no attempt to take over the actual control of *Corriere della Sera* when Mussolini encouraged them into acquiring total ownership. The first great editor of *Corriere* was Luigi Albertini, the part owner whom the Fascists forced to step down. (He retreated into seclusion and spent the rest of his life writing what is still regarded as a masterpiece, a history of the coming of the First World War.) He was succeeded by a variety of short-term editors who were used up in accommodating a variety of authoritarianisms, first Italian fascism, then German nazism, then the armies of occupation and good-hearted but ignorant committees growing out of the resistance movement. Then, in 1952, Mario Missiroli took over and reestablished the grand style. Missiroli was a major figure in Italian life, and for years the dominant figure in Italian journalism. His actual successor was Alfio Russo, competent but not awe inspiring; his spiritual successor—his dauphin, as the common Italian expression had it—was Giovanni Spadolini. All of these men were, of course, hired and paid well by the Crespis; none apparently had to suffer instruction about how to be the editor of what was said to be the greatest paper in the country. The Crespis were rich from the textile business and benevolent overlords of what they saw as their Milan; it was enough that *Corriere* brought credit to the city and to Italy.

In the early 1970s *Corriere* began to lose money, although it had traditionally been one of the rare profitable papers in Italy. Some members of the family grew restive. In 1973, ownership was divided among the four heirs of three original Crespi brothers. Within a few months three indicated their desire to get rid of the paper, and at that point an editore pura emerged. She was Giulia Maria Crespi Mozzoni. By this time Spadolini had been fired and replaced by Piero Ottone, a sound professional who had proved his competence on *Il Secolo XIX* in Genoa. Giulia Maria wished to exercise her option and buy out her relatives, but needed help to acquire two-thirds of the stock. She brought in as equal partners Gianni Agnelli of FIAT and Angelo Moratti, head of a company active in petroleum, cement, and other fields. She made it clear, however, that the newcomers would have no connection of any sort with the paper, and that their support was to be regarded more as a public service than as an acquisition. Giulia Maria Crespi was in charge, as "president of the board of directors with particular responsibility for editorials," that is, the paper's stand on political issues.[3] Her tenure was brief, during which the most spectacular event was the resignation (or firing) of Indro Montanelli. In July of 1974 the paper was abruptly sold and became part of the Rizzoli empire, at which we shall take a longer look later.

Since Mussolini forced its sale, *La Stampa* has had to do without an editore puro, but it has made do very well with Agnellis. Both Giovanni Agnelli and his nephew, also named Giovanni but usually called Gianni, have been content to hire fine editors and give them free rein. Editors such as Alberto Ronchey and Arrigo Levi have responded by producing a paper that many have considered the best in the country.

The Agnellis are one of the most visible families in Italy. Gianni, the eldest, was president of the Italian equivalent of the National Association of Manufacturers and may be Italy's last old-fashioned tycoon. He had planned to run for the Senate in the election of 1976, but stepped aside when his younger brother Umberto announced his intention of running at the same time. (Umberto was elected.) The Agnelli sister, Susanna, is one of the best-known women in Italy, an independent feminist and a veteran in politics.

Nevertheless there is no attempt to influence anything in *La Stampa*. Arrigo Levi was both specific and forceful about that while he was still editor. (He resigned in 1978.)

"I see Agnelli for lunch about once a month, although it's been six weeks now, in fact," Levi told me in 1977. "We don't travel in the same circles, and I don't feel I know him well." After a moment he added, with a slight shake of the head, "It's very strange. I don't think there's been a newspaper in history owned by someone who paid so little attention to it."[4]

The cynical explanation that comes immediately to mind, of course, and which would be, in the case of many editors, correct, is that Levi was so docile and so predictable that the owner had nothing to worry about. But Levi, far from being docile, sometimes was a prickly man, and that extended to sharp criticism of his boss.

In December, 1976, for example, FIAT announced it was selling about 13 percent of its stock in a private transaction to Muammar al-Qaddafi, the dictator of Libya. Speculation arose immediately that Levi would have to go; he is a Jew, a 1948 volunteer in the Israeli army, and he had provoked Qaddafi's anger by publishing a piece ridiculing him two years before. On that occasion Qaddafi had tried to get him fired; when that did not happen, the dictator unsuccessfully attempted to organize an Arab League boycott of FIAT. But with his stock acquisition, he had seats on the fifteen-member board of directors of the company and much more clout.

Levi did not help matters by publishing an editorial attacking the deal, saying that it grew out of Italy's economic weakness, and making clear that it in no way changed either *La Stampa*'s perception of what Libya represented or the independence of its own editorial line in the future. Levi's observance of the old custom of Italian papers that calls for editorials written by the responsabile to be unsigned, representing the voice of the paper rather than someone's personal opinion, reinforced this stand.

For the only time during his editorship, according to Levi, he consulted Agnelli in advance. He called him on the telephone, read him the editorial, and announced that it was running in the next issue.

"He said, 'Well, that's going to make it harder. I hope it doesn't interfere with the deal,'" Levi reported. "That was all."

Levi was not particularly suprised at that attitude. Several decades before, the Franco government of Spain had been unsuccessful in their attempts to receive friendlier news stories in *La Stampa*. In 1970 FIAT had an enormous contract for building an entire automobile manufacturing complex in the Soviet Union. The Soviet Union did not like *La Stampa*'s Moscow correspondent at the time and brought pressure to have him removed, as a matter of courtesy to a client with delicate feelings; the Soviet ambassador was even said to be involved. *La Stampa,* then directed by Alberto Ronchey, instead left the correspondent there until the Soviets found an excuse to expel him; upon his return to Italy he wrote a series of articles saying things about the USSR he could not say in Moscow, and *La Stampa* gave them heavy play.

Similarly, in 1971 Gianni Agnelli refused to interfere with the operation of *La Stampa* in the face of furious demands by a political leader who might be assumed to be his natural ally. In early January, Vittorio Gorresio began a long series of investigative reports on Italian politics, in preface to the national elections of 1972. Eventually there were about seventy articles. In midsummer he struck a nerve with a profile of Amintore Fanfani, longtime leader of the conservative wing of the Christian Democrats, then president of the Senate, and one of the most powerful politicians in the country. Soon after it appeared, Fanfani called Agnelli—not the editor, Ronchey, it should be noted, but Agnelli himself—and demanded to see him.

Gorresio was in the Senate building when Agnelli appeared for the interview, and listened to the uproar that filtered through the closed office door. When Agnelli finally reappeared, he said mildly to Gorresio, "Fanfani is very displeased." That was all he had to say, and Gorresio never heard again from him about the matter. Several years later an interviewer, Giampaolo Pansa, asked Agnelli about the confrontation. He replied:

> I met Fanfani at the Senate. He began arguing immediately, condemning the lack of responsibility of certain papers. He said that the moment was critical, that it was time that politicians and industrialists remember the responsibilities they have in common. Then he added that one cannot risk compromising personal positions for the entertainment of some "irresponsibles." I never saw Fanfani so irritated; even his voice changed. I continue to be fascinated by the ability that political men have, in common with others, to raise a calculated row.[5]

The significance of the episode was summed up by Indro Montanelli when the Gorresio series appeared as a book. Montanelli at that time was still a member of the staff of *Corriere della Sera*, and he pointed out in a commentary that Fanfani had asked the proprietor of *La Stampa* for the head of an impertinent reporter because of two articles published the previous July.

> For those who have doubts about the independence of the great national newspapers, let us remember that this proprietor, regardless of the close relationship which he, as president of FIAT, must maintain with the political powers, turned the request over to the editor Ronchey, who replied that the firing of Gorresio would mean firing him as well. And it stopped there; with Ronchey and Gorresio still in their jobs, and Fanfani fuming in impotent rage.[6]

More surprising than anything Agnelli has done—or refused to do—is something he once said about owning newspapers.

> Personally, I would prefer that industrialists did not own newspapers, with the exception of *24 Ore* [a financial paper]. Can you imagine what might happen if the *New York Times* was the property of General Motors?[7]

Gianni Agnelli may not be an *editore puro*, but if the journalist must work for an owner whose heart and soul is not in the newspaper that employs him, the Agnellis have been models of the next best way to have it.

The dominant newspaper of a great city is a part of the city's character. Those who think they know New York but seldom read the *New York Times* delude themselves, and few among the legions of detractors of the *Chicago Tribune* would contend that the image of the city is the same without it. *Il Messaggero* reached its one hundreth birthday in 1978, and during most of that century it has been *il giornale del capitolo*. It has not, in recent years, been a great newspaper; there are countless Romans who would agree with the response of a friend of mine to a mention of the paper.

"It has no character," he said. "When fascism was in power, it was Fascist. When the Nazis arrived, it became Nazi. After the war it was piously Christian Democrat. And now that it is stylish to be radical, it's radical."

Still, and for better or worse, it is the paper that is most identified with Rome. Certainly there were many who, during the 1970s, regarded *Il Tempo* as better, and many who would have said the same thing of *Paese Sera*. But in mid-decade *Il Messaggero*'s circulation was bigger than any other, 315,000 against 260,000 for *Il Tempo* and 200,000 for *Paese Sera*.[8] There was a good deal of experimentation with the paper, both in content and format, during the 1970s; some of its many critics would find "experimentation" much too pretentious and something like "fooled around with" much more accurate.

The paper began as a simple local news sheet and had a variety of owners over its first several decades; it was converted into a *giornale d'informazione* by new owners in 1911. They were bankers and industrialists. Four years later they, in turn, sold it to two brothers, Mario and Pio Perrone. They also were primarily industrialists, but with an interest in newspapers; they had inherited *Il Secolo XIX* of Genoa from their father in 1908. Both papers remained Perrone property until 1973, and *Il Secolo XIX* still is.

Among *Il Messagero*'s post–Second World War editors was the highly capable Mario Missiroli, who spent six years there before moving on to the editorship of *Corriere della Sera*. He was succeeded by a family member, Alessandro Perrone, who increasingly immersed himself in the paper for almost twenty-two years. When I met him in 1970 he was *direttore responsabile* and a member of the board of directors of the company that owned both papers, along with his two sisters, his cousin Ferdinando Perrone, and Ferdinando's two sisters. Ferdinando was chairman of the board. Lest that seem too much detail about the Perrones, it should be pointed out that the alignment of the board was to be a critical factor in events that brought not just reform, but revolution, to *Il Messaggero*.

In 1970 it was in many ways an old-fashioned newspaper. In appearance, it closely resembled, say, the *New York Journal-American* of the 1930s without the huge black banner lines. The editors had a particular fondness for splashy pen and ink drawings on the front page that "reconstructed" a crime, picturing the most violent moment of the action, and on the inside jump page a map and heavy black arrows, dotted lines, and crumpled figures. They managed to find such a story on most days, although it might mean settling for a fatal traffic accident. This artwork so dominated the front page that everything else was hung around it, and the man responsible for front-page makeup was a high-status specialist at the head of a staff of five.

In 1972–73 Perrone set out to change the paper. He began by striking out in the attempt to attract more circulation. Encouraged by some influential members of the paper's staff, he began moving the paper to the left. *Il Messaggero* began making approving noises about divorce and even abortion. Front page editorials began reflecting hostility toward the Christian Democrats.

The business relationship between Perrone and his two sisters, operating as a bloc, and his cousin Ferdinando and Ferdinando's two sisters was always bumpy; they had been in court in some kind of contention no less than thirty-nine times since 1950.[9] Disagreement reached its apogee in June of 1973, when the Ferdinando bloc abruptly sold their shares of the company to Edilio Rusconi, owner of a highly successful string of magazines, mostly directed to women. Along with informing Alessandro of the sale, Ferdinando, as chairman of the board of directors, also informed him that he was fired.

That was easier to announce than to carry out. The stock was divided equally between the two families; Alessandro Perrone controlled as much as his cousin, and he simply refused to accept the dismissal. He instead met with both the newspaper staff and the printers, seeking support. Rusconi meanwhile named one of the senior wise men of Italian journalism, Luigi Barzini, Jr., as editor. When Barzini arrived to take over his office he found the premises barricaded with most of the staff inside, dug in and fortified with seige supplies of cigarettes, whisky, coffee, and even some food. Barzini, a man with considerable concern about personal dignity, withdrew from the whole business and returned to his handsome villa on the outskirts of Rome.

Inside the barricade, the journalists and printers had not only promised their support to Perrone, but were also working in his behalf. The way they went at it sets out again the remarkable implicit alliance between politics and the press in Italy; they called upon prominent members of Parliament, asking for government action to keep Rusconi from gaining control of the paper. The conversations were informal, and the full list of persons solicited is not available, so far as I know; typical, however, was a long session with Ugo La Malfa, the most eminent of the Republicans, urging his support on the grounds of the Republican party's classic anticlericalism and belief in free inquiry.

The ad hoc committee also went to court seeking to have the firing of Perrone ruled invalid, both on the grounds that he was a member of the Order of Journalists and therefore covered by the national contract as well as invoking the recently passed legislation requiring "just cause" for dismissal.

Perrone's own activities were most striking of all. They were summed up this way by Ferruccio Borio.

> *Il Messaggero* continued publication under its old director, Alessandro Perrone, who did not lose the opportunity to respond openly to the ideological demands of his staff. The political line of the paper moved from the center-left to strongly radical positions. This was less due to Sandro Perrone's convictions than to the wishes of the most activist group in the newsroom. Sandro Perrone's own ideas rest on a moderate anticlericalism with "some moments of libertarian disrespect when the situation demands it." But his deeper aspiration, that of remaining in his post as editor, whoever might be the publisher, led him to broad concession in the search for backing. . . . At that point Perrone also turned to the Socialist party [*Partito Socialista Italiano* (PSI)] secretary, Francesco De Martino, who, through his close collaborator, Aldo Ajello, assured him of the unconditional backing of the Socialists; naturally, on the condition that a certain political line be followed.[10]

Perrone was soon to lose the battle, and *Il Messaggero* as well. He retreated as far as Genoa, where he had acquired complete control of the other family newspaper, *Il Secolo XIX,* and resumed the role of editor and, indeed, editore puro.

With his departure from the capital, the major papers, with the exception of *La Stampa,* were left in the hands of new owners of which neither precise identity nor intentions were known. They shared another characteristic: all were running up enormous deficits.

The common talk of the news business for years in Italy identified only three dailies as money-makers: *Corriere della Sera, La Stampa,* and *Il Messaggero.* By 1972 all were losing money and *Corriere* and *Il Messaggero* had new owners. Outside of a few small town papers with marginal profits, Italian newspapering had become a business of losers and has remained so.

It has stayed alive through a variety of strategies. For many years the sale of newsprint has been under control of the government, and a special tax is levied upon all other buyers of paper to provide a hefty discount for newspapers. Most transactions within the business, from building new plants to the sale of copies on the street, receive extraordinary exemptions from taxes. Newsprint, in addition to its artificially low price, also travels at reduced rates by rail; there are special rates for telephone, telegraph, and teleprinter service.

Government is also limitlessly involved in the media in more complex ways, as it is in all Italian business. Essentially, and despite the reiteration of official noises about independence and enterprise, the Italian economy has moved a long way from both, to a mixture that a noneconomist might call state capitalism. Central entities in this process are huge conglomerates, umbrella organizations covering industries and businesses that have no functional relationships. This has been the trend throughout the industrialized world, of course, including the United States (where it is quickly destroying the remains of American editori puri), and there are some linkages to government in most cases, if nothing more than that of regulation or special tax arrangements. The chief role of government in Italian conglomerates is that of shareholder and, therefore, absorber of losses, dispenser of subsidies, and appointer of managers for political reasons.

Again, this is not a new idea in Europe; long before the era of national airlines, shipping companies such as Cunard and the Italian Line were mixtures of private and government ownership. The Italian difference rests in the pervasiveness of the institution. Corporations had a formal role in government under fascism (and, needless to say, vice versa). At the end of the Second World War the state began to put such organizations together as a way of assisting the rebuilding of the nation; the first was called *Istituto per la Ricostruzione Industriale* (IRI), always referred to, in the Italian fashion, by the acronym, pronounced *eerie*. Government was able to provide great infusions of capital, which the private sector did not have available. Entrepreneurs with energy and imagination, such as Enrico Mattei,* thus were able to go to the government for the money for building huge enterprises. In Mattei's case, government capital was needed for a corporation dealing in petroleum and chemicals that would be big enough to permit Italy, which was just beginning to develop its first oil and gas resources, to have some kind of stake in the game dominated by Royal Dutch Shell, Exxon, and the like. The organization that Mattei built was called *L'Ente Nazionale Idrocarburi* (ENI), a title indicating its primary concern with petroleum; the many-legged fire-breathing dragon on *Agenzia Generale Italiana Petrolio* (AGIP) signs has been its most visible spoor for the visitor to Italy, but it ranges widely; it owns *Il Giorno* of Milan.

Much of the remarkable economic growth of the 1950s and 1960s was fueled in this fashion. In addition to direct government contributions, Italian banks made massive loans. Since the banks have also had heavy government participation, in effect, an attempt to call in loans made little sense. Besides, the disappearance of major businesses meant the loss of many jobs. Italian business and industry had for many years a tradition of overstaffing, a way of sopping up some of the country's perpetual unemployment. I remember a conversation with an American engineer in 1952 who had been an adviser to various Italian manufacturing companies in the years immediately after the war; when he would triumphantly present a proposal that would reduce costs by reducing the required work force, more often than not the plant's management would patiently point out that it would mean firing people, and where else were they to find work? By the late 1960s the powerful Italian labor unions had reinforced that custom, with the assistance of legislation, almost to the place where a business could be shut down only with the union's permission.

And thus, as large enterprises failed, or came to the edge, government in the form of one of the *Aziende di Stato* would take over and keep it going. In this fashion Montedison, and ENI, acquired a large chain of low-cost retail stores, much resembling K-Mart, called *Magazzini Standa*. In the mid-1970s the government also acquired two of the most delicious businesses anywhere, the vast candymaking and baking enterprises, *Motta*

---

*Not to be confused with the journalist of the same name, also referred to in this study.

and *Alemagna*. Those enormous stacks of the holiday bread, *panettone*, in pale blue paper in stores all over the world are now products of a government agency. There is little prospect that such enterprises can ever be made to pay, and there have been attempts to start minimizing the drain they represent. Most of the grand, gleaming stand-up coffee bars operated by Motta that once took up whole street corners in the major cities were closed, and so were many of the Standa stores. The process has moved slowly because of bitter trade union opposition.

Thus the presence of government throughout the country's economic life is constantly enlarged. By 1977 such enterprises controlled almost half of the turnover of Italy's industrial sector. The pattern of ownership was always arcane, completely understood by no one, and riddled with both mismanagement and corruption. One government conglomerate seems to have been developed primarily as a dumping ground for losers. It was called *Ente Autonomo Gestione per le Aziende Minerarie Metallurgiche* (EGAM), "Independent Management Group for Metallurgical Industries"; it collapsed in June, 1977, with charges and countercharges from all sides concerning incompetence and graft.

By the late 1970s, two of the four national "information papers," upon which this book concentrates, were officially an outright property of an agency of the state, ENI; they were *Il Giorno*, founded as an adjunct to Montedison, and *Il Messaggero*, acquired by Montedison from Rusconi and Alessandro Perrone in 1974. The informal reach of Montedison—which, at the time, meant Eugenio Cefis—was much broader. Cefis was a backer of *Gazzetta del Popolo*, a weak competitor of *La Stampa* in Turin. He was the chief backer of Indro Montanelli when that famous journalist was separated from *Corriere della Sera* and started seeking funds to found a paper of his own.[11] Cefis directed the placing of large amounts of advertising in the Roman daily *Il Tempo* because he liked its politics. He provided heavy covert support for the financial paper *Il Globo* for a time because other industrialists he perceived as his enemies controlled a competitive paper.

Cefis began to buy up papers because he wanted powerful voices on his side, discovered that it didn't work that way, and then decided that the most efficient way to make his weight felt was by providing money to others who wished to acquire papers. That realization came along coincidentally with the rise of Angelo Rizzoli as a builder of newspaper chains, and a far more successful one than Cefis. What Eugenio Cefis learned others had known all along; Italian journalists have made wry cracks for years about newspapers with "unknown fathers."

A statement by an anonymous journalist at the height of an ownership crisis at *Corriere della Sera* in 1974 sums up the dilemmas facing the Italian press, always financially marginal, with the approach of money men from the industrial-government complex.

> Italy is now at a watershed: there is the danger that the present situation, marked by abnormal ties between industry and the press, will spread to all areas of publishing and thus will emphasize the dependence of the press on economic groups. In increasing such a tendency there is risk (1) of reducing the credibility of the publication; (2) of encouraging negative public opinion and provoking obstructionism by political groups and trade unionists; (3) of spreading guerrilla warfare in the newsrooms of newspapers and to increase the bitterness of their disagreements, making necessary, as a result, an increasingly heavy hand to maintain control; (4) of being held responsible for journalistic behavior over which one does not have effective control.[12]

The statement was frequently attributed to Piero Ottone, then editor of *Corriere della Sera,* but he denied its authorship. Whoever the writer, he or she was prescient; those things did, indeed, begin to happen and are happening still.

There are two traditional sources of revenue for publications: circulation and advertising. In the United States, with a newspaper system based entirely upon profit making, the average daily gets about one-fourth of its revenue from the first of those elements, the sale of copies, and about three-fourths from advertising. Of the total advertising revenue, by far the largest share comes from local retail establishments—supermarkets, department stores, real estate dealers, and the like. Italian dailies as yet carry almost no advertising of this sort, but by 1980 there were signs of change. The number of supermarkets in Italy is growing, albeit slowly, and the efficient functioning of that merchandising system requires much advertising. Meanwhile the primary sources of local advertising revenue for Italian dailies are classified advertising, death and funeral announcements, and entertainment ads. The rest comes from national advertising. From all these sources most Italian dailies receive enough advertising to occupy 35 to 45 percent of their total space; *Corriere della Sera* from time to time has reached around 50 percent.

National advertising in Italy is placed through a system that is an open invitation to editorial and political manipulation, and is distinguished by the fact that an effective selling job is often only a minor consideration. All advertising comes through an intermediary organization called a *concessionàrio*. This agency signs a contract with a newspaper or broadcaster as its exclusive sales representative. The contract guarantees the publication or broadcaster a certain income over a specified period of time. The concessionàrio then sells space or time to the advertiser, making its profit, supposedly somewhere around 20 percent, by selling space or time at a higher price than it pays for it, in effect.

In rough outline, this sounds rather like the advertising rep system that is also common in the United States: most newspapers and broadcasting stations of any size in this country contract with a sales organization to sell their space or time in the national market and, in effect, pay them a commission. The difference in the case of Italian practice lies in the guarantees that the concessionàrio gives the medium. The figure sometimes bears no resemblance to the amount of advertising that actually will be carried; it simply represents a subsidy. If the owners of the concessionàrio firm want to keep a flagging publication alive, they simply provide enough "advertising" income to do it. This is what Eugenio Cefis did when he wanted to bolster *Il Tempo* of Rome.

Cefis was able to do so because he at that time directed Montedison, and Montedison, in turn, was the primary owner of a firm called *Società Pubblicità Italiana* (SPI), which was concessionàrio not only for *Il Tempo* but for thirty-two other papers, including *L'Unità*, the official paper of the Communist party, and the *Rome Daily American*. No details of the relationship with *L'Unità* have been available, but it carries a very modest amount of advertising.

There is another major concessionàrio dealing with newspapers, *Società Pubblicità Editoriale* (SPE), with a total of fourteen papers. Another called *Società Italiana per la Pubblicità* (SIPRA) has the potent weapon of complete control of advertising time on RAI, the state-owned radio and television broadcasting system. Moreover, SIPRA is actually owned by RAI and/or IRI, the overarching government conglomerate; ownership has been described in some accounts as 70 percent IRI, and 30 percent RAI, in others as 100 percent RAI, but since RAI is actually part of IRI (one must hold on tightly going around the curves in these matters), the distinction is essentially meaningless.

The monopoly of broadcast advertising is potent because there has always been a long waiting list for advertisers wanting to get on RAI-TV. The government keeps the total small; this not only helps preserve some of the BBC image to which RAI always seems to have aspired, but keeps advertisers from deserting print advertising altogether. SIPRA makes a convenient mechanism in that approach; it frequently specifies that the advertiser has to buy space in specified publications before it will sell him air time.

SIPRA's concern for a nonbroadcasting client caused controversy throughout most of the 1970s. Edilio Rusconi, the magazine publisher who made an attempt to buy *Il Messaggero* and for a short time owned half of it, in 1971 obtained from SIPRA—a property of RAI, an agency of government, it should be remembered—the biggest guarantee ever awarded at that point by a concessionàrio to a client, about $11.2 million a year. Under that contract, and with escalator clauses, SIPRA paid Rusconi about $34,117,650 over a period of four-and-a-half years.[13] The contract was then rewritten to provide about sixty million dollars over the next five years. Controversy arose because RAI was spending public money, and the arrangement amounted to the government, which can be read as the Christian Democrats, bolstering the fortunes of conservative voices in the media.[14]

The same kind of motivation seems to have impelled Montedison's backing of Indro Montanelli in beginning his paper, *Il Giornale Nuovo*, in June, 1974. Before Montanelli left *Corriere* he was searching for backing to launch a new daily. Although a ringing conservative, he was somewhat less of a political man than some Italian publishers, and first sought help from various other publishers and then industrialists. When these initiatives failed, a contract was negotiated with SPI, the concessionàrio closely tied to Montedison and Cefis, for 12 billion lire (something over $14 million) for a period of three years.

From whatever source, and to whatever amount, the income of Italian newspaper publishers is a long way from being enough. Giampaolo Pansa sees the summer of 1976 as the time of the collapse, the complete crash of the publication business in Italy.[15] (He calls it *Il Grande Crack*, a phrase frequently used to describe sudden economic failure.) The symptoms had been visible for a good many years and inspired a major attempt by the Italian national assembly to provide financial assistance; a special commission of inquiry was appointed to make recommendations, and funds totaling about $22,530,000 over a three-year period were voted for dailies alone. Despite that assistance, the figures by the beginning of 1977 were grim.

For example: *Corriere della Sera* enterprises, including several properties, lost about $14 million in 1975; $16,260,000 in 1976. *Il Messaggero* lost $2,235,000 in 1975; $4,235,000 in 1976. *Il Giorno*, taken by itself, has been the sickest paper financially in the country. In 1974, it lost $7,850,000; $10.5 million in 1975; $11.8 million in 1976. It should be remembered, however, that the paper is the property of ENI, and in the scale of that monster's corporate concerns, the paper is of minor importance and its losses of modest dimensions.

La Stampa and its evening edition, *Stampa Sera*, lost about $4.6 million in 1976. Figures from the previous year were not available.

Montanelli's *Il Giornale Nuovo* lost about $32,000 in 1975, its first year of operation; the figure was $63,500 in 1976 despite a solicitation for funds from readers that produced almost $115,000.[16]

Why did Italian daily newspapers begin to lose so heavily in the mid-1970s?

Many elements go into the answer, and we have already seen some of them. Italian newspapers have an inadequate and stifling distribution system that discourages circulation, rather than stimulates it. They have had only modest success in advertising, and furthermore, in most papers advertising began to drop off around 1972. Italian mercantile tradition has thus far closed to the industry the most lucrative of all advertising for newspapers, local retail. The newspapers continue some traditional but nonsensically expensive practices, such as the maintenance of foreign correspondents and competitive image-polishing. ("If *Corriere* sends a correspondent to Mexico," an editor once pointed out, "everybody has to send a correspondent to Mexico.") The cost of materials—ink, paper, and the like—rose spectacularly; the increase was 62 percent between 1973 and 1974 alone.

Most observers other than trade union leaders, however, point first to some figures that are fully as astonishing as those for newspaper losses. Italian media are almost laughably overstaffed.

At the beginning of 1960, there were employed on all Italian dailies together about ten thousand nonjournalist employees—printers, clerks, truck drivers, and the like—and about twenty-five hundred professional journalists. At the beginning of 1976 the same papers employed fifteen thousand nonjournalists and four thousand journalists. The total work force thus increased some 55 percent over a fifteen-year period and with absolutely no increase in productivity; newspaper circulation in 1960 and 1976 was almost exactly the same. All of those workers were, of course, members of unions; the increments in hiring were the result of negotiations over new contracts in the various categories, and give testimony to the enormous clout of trade unions in modern Italy. Most of that total cadre of about twenty thousand work less than a forty-hour week; their fringe benefits, all told, are superior to those of their American counterparts.

Corriere della Sera has roughly the same circulation as the *Detroit Free Press*. *Corriere* puts out a smaller paper, at least 150 to 200 pages less per week. The relative work forces compare thus:

	Corriere	*Free Press*
Editorial employees	309	120
Mechanical (printers, etc.)	2,079	450
Other (clerks, typists, etc.)	1,065	1,200

There are many variables that make any attempt at direct comparison between these two sets of figures unwise. The *Corriere* figures are from 1974, the *Free Press* figures from 1978; the *Free Press* figures have been almost constant since the early 1970s, the *Corriere* figures certainly have grown. On the other hand, almost all the content of *Corriere* is produced by the professional staff, other than a few wire service stories, where the *Free Press,* like all American papers, contains a great deal of material from feature syndicates and, of course, advertising agencies.

A comparison between two Italian dailies of about the same size might be more valid. When Indro Montanelli started *Il Giornale Nuovo* he committed himself to a professional staff big enough to do the job, but without overstaffing. He settled on a group of 59 professionals. At the same time *Il Messaggero,* a slightly larger paper both in circulation and in number of pages, but no larger in terms of the number of editorial columns to be filled, had 141 professional journalists. No comparison of the nonjournalist work force is possible, since Montanelli's paper is printed on contract by a company that also produces several other dailies.

At the time of his acquisition of *Corriere della Sera,* Angelo Rizzoli estimated that the enterprise was overstaffed by about 50 percent. That seems to have been a fairly common judgment among all observers. Such an estimate takes present contracts at face value, and does not take into account the staggering overtime required by a system in which a senior professional works thirty-six hours a week and receives almost two months of vacation and paid holidays a year.

Labor costs amount to more than 60 percent of the total operational costs in the Italian newspaper industry; in the United States the figure is less than half that. There seems, further, no possible road to a major reduction in that percentage in Italy. Demands for contract improvement on the part of journalists began to diminish as the critical state of affairs within the industry became apparent in the middle of the decade, but it is hardly realistic to assume any trade union's cooperation in actually cutting back its own reach or its members' compensation.

Why would anyone want to own a big Italian newspaper, and why would first Cefis and then Angelo Rizzoli spend billions in the attempt to add to their collection of losers?

A possible explanation might be that of the acquisition of mouthpieces; through the ownership of major papers it should be possible to exercise powerful influence upon public opinion. When the remarkable changes within the newsrooms of those same major papers, which are set out in the succeeding chapters, are taken into account, however, that explanation loses much of its persuasiveness, and raises a second question: why buy papers that were not only losing money, but over which control was highly imperfect?

The hope of eventual profit is the most likely explanation, despite the state of the Italian newspaper industry during the final years of the decade of the 1970s. Government subsidies to the press began in 1974; they remained relatively modest, but more elaborate plans were afoot that would involve the virtual abolition of taxes in the newspaper business, major government assistance in the acquisition of new equipment and the remodeling of the industry's obsolete plants, financial support for a variety of employee perquisites including severance pay during staff reduction, and millions of dollars paid as a continuing subsidy. If the government assumed enough of the burden, eventual private profit was assured. A special parliamentary commission went to work in the fall of 1976 to draft such legislation.

Subsidizing newspapers in secret while they maintain a facade of independence has usually been associated with Latin countries; the French have played the game, too, and no Italian publishers have ever been as venal as the French ones who accepted Nazi bribes before the outbreak of the Second World War. The notion of openly spending public money, however, to maintain a broad spectrum of newspapers was first accepted, and most willingly pursued, by the Scandinavians. Sweden took action in the early 1960s, when newspapers attached to political parties and labor unions went into sharp declines; money grants were provided to such sponsors to keep the publications alive. In the late 1970s the Swedish government set up a special commission, with a staff headed by social scientists, to investigate and report on the amount necessary to maintain the newspaper establishment as it then existed, with the clear intention of appropriating whatever might be required. (The total for 1980 was over $40 million.) There was no significant opposition from any party to the action.

Nor has there been significant opposition to the Italian initiatives, beginning in 1974, to aid the newspaper press. The U.S. Congress has never been called upon to consider such legislation; nearest to it is the venerable act establishing second-class mail, which amounts to a considerable subsidy to both newspapers and magazines. It is worth noting, however, that a proposal called the Newspaper Preservation Act, the effect of which was to free competitive newspapers from certain provisions of antitrust legislation, sailed quickly through Congress in 1970 with only scattered opposition. The fact seems to be that politicians, despite the endemic ritual of blaming the mass media for all kinds of defects in the way politics works, are not prepared to do anything that would mark them clearly as against the press, or even as laggard supporters.

Certainly there has been no evidence that the Italian Parliament, whatever its party composition, will do other than contribute increasingly large amounts to the support of Italian newspaper publishing. The primary problem has been the drafting of legislation that is satisfactory, not so much to the politicians, as to the factions within the newspaper industry.

From the beginning, three general issues have been the subjects of most of the negotiating. As a group, the owners have sought financial assistance for ongoing operations, the conversion of their aging physical plants to modern technology, and compensation for employees released in the reduction of staff. The journalists' trade union, FNSI, has put particular pressure on obtaining, as a part of the price of subsidization, public disclosure of all important financial data, including the identities of owners and the money received from advertising concessionàri. A coalition of trade unions and a few politically liberal publishers has pressed for provisions that will reward independent owners and in effect penalize chains controlling more than a stipulated share of circulation, such as Rizzoli.

Comprehensive legislation finally came close to passage in the fall of 1980, but bogged down. Meanwhile, the established subsidies set out earlier have continued and there has been increased assistance toward the purchase of newsprint by newly established papers.

Whatever the final arrangements for public assistance may be, it is unmistakably clear that only through such assistance can the Italian newspaper industry continue. Increasing numbers of Western countries are moving in the same direction. The implications of this tendency are touched upon later in this book.

One group of newspaper owner-publishers has not been included in this discussion, nor has there been any substantial analysis of their publications. Official party newspapers have been excluded because this study is primarily concerned with journalists and with journalism as a profession; this is not a survey of the Italian press. Although the journalists who produce party papers are members of the statutory Order of Journalists and usually of the professional trade union, the National Federation of the Italian Press, they share little of the professional aspirations or affluence of peers who work on conventional newspapers. More important, so far as I am concerned, is the fact that they have taken almost no part in the reform movement toward more staff control of newspaper policy. They cheered on the reformers and made frequent use of the catch phrases "completeness of information" and "freedom of information" so common in the 1970s, but always in connection with someone else's papers, not their own.

When my wife and I first went to Italy in the fall of 1952, the Communist daily *L'Unità* had a circulation of over half a million, published regional editions in Rome, Milan, Turin, Genoa, and Naples, and was generally one of the most visible sheets in the country. Part of that came from the distribution system, which enlisted party regulars as unpaid volunteers. It was a system that produced many leftovers.

It was also a newspaper with much to offer to the general reader. There were comics, including some familiar American strips (this at the worst of the cold war), elaborate and well-done sports pages; as I remember, the only women's section in an Italian daily, full of hints about cooking and housewifery; frequent feature stories with no particular political identity; and a comprehensive range of news from several sources, including all American news services. About the only standard ingredient it did not contain was elaborate display advertising. *L'Unità* has never abjured it; it simply gets very little, because the government, in indirect but very functional ways, as we have seen, decides where most advertising will go.

Added to the lack of advertising was the fact that an unknown but substantial number of copies were given away free; it was inevitable that the full-scale *L'Unità* had to go when costs began to rocket upward in the newspaper industry. *L'Unità* had been designed to provide an alternative to the conventional press, particularly to pull readers away from *Corriere della Sera* in Milan and *La Stampa* in Turin, cities with large concentrations of industrial workers and Communist party members. It did not succeed, and in 1962 sharp changes were made. The comics and the soft features were for the most part thrown out; to compensate, in an effort to retain readers, the length of the fustian political essays was reduced and an attempt was made at simpler and clearer writing. But as one history of the Italian press put it:

> *L'Unità* remains, even after 1962, for the great part of the militant Communists the second newspaper that one buys, especially on Sunday or in politically crucial periods; not a complete substitute—as the journalists who produced it or the leaders of the party had wished—for the dailies owned by FIAT or the Crespis or other entrepreneurs.[17]

The circulation figures are kept high in part by Stakhanovite methods based upon party discipline. Literally thousands of workers make themselves available to assist in distribution and selling, particularly for the Sunday issue. No figures are available on the actual income from sales of the paper. In current Italian practice, circulation figures quoted publicly represent the number of copies printed and distributed, not the copies sold. The second figure necessary to get an accurate picture, the number returned, is difficult to come by. This makes all newspaper circulation figures soft, and party papers are especially so. Countless copies are given away or simply pitched out. Reader enthusiasm under such circumstances is hard to appraise.

Regardless of the number of copies the volunteers who work for *L'Unità* sell, that is not the end of their contribution. They helped make up the paper's estimated 1976 deficit of five million dollars through Festivals for *L'Unità*—benefits generally featuring popular entertainers—and special-patron subscriptions. There was some grumbling about this, because much of the money contributed might have otherwise gone to the party's regional and local organizations, but it did make the paper's balance sheet look better.[18] Other devices have involved keeping journalists' salaries to a minimum and pressuring journalists from time to time to kick back a sizable chunk of their salaries to the party as a contribution.

No amount of qualification, however, can alter the fact that *L'Unità* is far better off than the remainder of the party papers. During the 1970s the party papers went into desperate decline, and after the middle of the decade there was recurrent speculation about their disappearance altogether. Circulations were diving: the Socialist *Avanti!* (meaning *Forward,* the classic name for Socialist papers in several languages) was down to 25,000 by mid-1976; the Christian Democrats' *Il Popolo* was down to 5,000; the far right *Il Secolo D'Italia* of the MSI printed 25,000, but, according to outside sources, gave most of them away. (The three also demonstrate some remarkable fantasies about circulation; only about a year earlier, *Avanti!* had claimed 130,000; *Il Popolo* 108,000; and *Il Secolo* 50,000).[19] Many were reduced in size to four pages.

In addition to the disappearance of circulation and, with it, the loss of more of the already modest advertising revenue, the party papers have always had special costs. Most have made a continuing attempt, as a matter of image, to get a few copies on newsstands in cities throughout the country; their distribution costs therefore run about 20 percent more than those of general newspapers. The salaries of party journalists, while sharply lower than those of the rest of the profession, are still within the minimums established by the national trade union contract; as things have gone from bad to worse, salaries increasingly have become a sticky problem. Most party papers are ludicrously overstaffed: the worst example was probably the DC *Il Popolo,* which, it was reported in 1976, had fifty journalists sometimes putting out a four-page paper with a circulation of five thousand.[20] Attempts to reduce staffing have brought vigorous opposition. The solution, trade union leaders have said, lies in expanding and producing better papers that will pay their own way, rather than cutting back on staffing.

Two of Italy's major parties greatly increased the support of their party organs in 1978–79; both the Socialists' *Avanti!* and the Christian

Democrats' *Il Popolo* were refurbished and their number of pages sharply increased to a minimum of sixteen. It seems probable, however, that this was less an expression of confidence in the future economic health of party papers than part of the search for an augmented party voice in a time of continuing political instability and uncertainty. *L'Unità* was also somewhat enlarged and broadened by the end of the decade, with the most visible change a cooling of its polemical ardor, which broadened its appeal as a newspaper but was, one suspects, a by-product of the Communists' cautious political position.

There seems little reason, in any case, to anticipate a revival of party papers as major media. Despite the substantial government subsidies now given political parties for campaigns,* the deficit run up by a daily newspaper is a devastating burden on most parties. A fourth of the total yearly funds of the Movimento Sociale Italiano has gone in recent times to propping up the moribund *Il Secolo*.

In the spring of 1978 there were nine party papers published in Italy. With the exception of the Liberals, each of the parties traditionally represented in Parliament—the Christian Democrats, Communists, Socialists, Social Democrats, Republicans, and neo-Fascists—supported a paper. Three far-left groups, all anti-PCI in one form or another, also published party sheets. Interestingly enough, Marco Pannella's Radical Party, which won four seats in the Chamber of Deputies in the elections of 1976 and attracted much attention from intellectuals and artists, had no newspaper. Perhaps it did not need one, since major publications such as *La Repubblica* and the weekly newsmagazines *L'Espresso* and *Panorama* gave it much attention, but during the electoral campaign of 1979 (see p. 210) the party spent its money on television and bought no print advertising, which suggests the leadership may have decided the day of print was past.

By the end of the 1970s none of these journals was a comprehensive newspaper of general interest. Although there are great differences in style and quality among them, all select their material in roughly the same way. All carry handouts and statements by party leaders. In addition, almost all concentrate upon stories in which the paper has a particular interest, either from the point of view of enhancing the party's position or the chance to damage the enemy. The pursuit of such objectives often

---

*Securities and Exchange Commission hearings in 1975 brought out that American oil companies also contributed to the support of Italian party publications. Over a period of two and a half years in 1969–72, the Gulf Oil Company gave a total of $627,000 to Christian Democrat publications and to the Socialist party's *Mondo Operario* and *Avanti!*

produces elaborate coverage of particular issues. *Il Manifesto,* the small, cheaply produced, but energetic paper of the radical *Partito Democratico di Unità Proletaria,* has done this so well that it built a considerable audience among nonparty members (although, it is safe to say, not among conservatives). It covered the complicated changing of the guard at *Corriere della Sera* in the fall of 1977, for example, with great thoroughness and was widely read for that story.

Most party papers are not so well done, and as a group their chief function is the informing of an elite (even though the word *elite* is a bit odd in reference to a newspaper such as *L'Unità,* with a circulation of almost half a million). For the most part, party papers in Italy are read by the politically active, either the party faithful or the opposition, as the most authoritative day-in-and-day-out reflection of the thinking of the party's leadership. The paper's editor generally is close to the party secretary and the leadership of the party's parliamentary delegation. As money became a desperate matter in the mid-1970s, disagreements between politicians and the journalists in their employ sometimes arose, but they were invariably about money or staffing or other trade union matters. The political line remains straight; only those who are dependable, flexible, and possessed of great political sensitivity get appointed to the job of running such papers. This is also true of eastern Europe, of course; the exegetical reading of *Pravda* and *Izvestia* has involved so many Americans in academia, government, and now business that it can be regarded as an established light industry.

The opposition reads the paper to keep informed about the thinking behind the opponents' moves and better prepared to anticipate the next one. When the U.S. Communist party was publishing the *Daily Worker* during the immediate postwar years there was a much repeated remark to the effect that the paper's buyers were chiefly FBI agents who, suitably disguised, bought it on New York newsstands or subscribed under cover addresses. It is a fair assumption that among the most devoted readers of *L'Unità* are some Christian Democrat functionaries, and that somewhere there are Communists who pore over the stodgy pages of the DC's *Il Popolo,* and even neo-Fascists who read *Il Manifesto* with care.

Friendly readers are a much larger group. They include those who seek reinforcement for their inclinations, or read out of a sense of obligatory ritual, or to obtain clues about what they should be thinking next. There are even some intellectuals who make a daily scan of several papers, simply to keep up with national political discourse, but they are few; not many of us are persistent in exposing ourselves to ideas with which we disagree.

Party papers are critical, in any case, to the operation of the political system in Italy and many other countries as well; regardless of circulation, each party paper reaches a section of the elite that runs the country. Changes in relative positions in the heirarchies of political parties often first become visible in the party press. So do intraparty quarrels. The schism between the Socialists and the Social Democrats that broke up the original postwar Italian left was spelled out more precisely in the papers than in any other form; so was the development of the atmosphere that made possible the "opening to the left," during which the Christian Democrats and Socialists attempted for a decade, with declining success, to run the country. When their leadership began to crumble, that also was visible in the party papers. During the tense election campaign of 1976, there were many who saw a reemergence of a Socialist–Christian Democrat alliance as the country's only hope; those who read *Avanti!* and *Il Popolo,* however, knew all along that it simply could not happen. And during the long months of jockeying between the Communists and the Christian Democrats following that inconclusive balloting, party papers provided both detail and insight not available elsewhere. American politics have functioned without official party papers since the early nineteenth century, but it is hard to imagine Italian politics without them.

If expense and public disinterest do wipe out the whole genre, something obviously has to replace them. The solution may lie in magazines. Italians are good magazine readers, and that is the direction of some of the political parties in the rest of Europe, where party papers also are dying or dead. The discourse will not be the same, however. Magazines have longer deadlines and less flexibility. Although they would serve very well for smaller parties where occasional flights of rhetoric are enough, they would seem inadequate for parties wielding, and negotiating for, considerable power.

Chapter 6

The Beginnings of Reform

In early winter of 1970 I went to Milan to visit *Corriere della Sera*. *Corriere* was at that time at the height of its prestige, although its political influence had been greatest early in the century. Outside Italy, it was frequently and tiresomely referred to as the *New York Times* of Italy. It had the largest circulation in Italy, one of the rare cases of a country's best paper also being its most popular; at that time, it even was making a profit. Belonging to its staff over the years had been some of the major names in Italian intellectual life.

I had by that time read it long enough to realize that most of its resemblances to the *Times* were to the inferior attributes of that paper. It was consistently overwritten and underedited. Perhaps it was not pompous, but at minimum it took itself with great seriousness. Its typography and makeup made it difficult to read. Politically, it was conservative in both a superficial and profound sense. At the superficial level, it backed the center-left coalition. In a much deeper way, its tone conveyed a sense of being both the guardian of the nation and the chief repository of the national virtues. In that sense it resembled both the *New York Times* in the period immediately following the Second World War and the London *Times* of the nineteenth century.

Corriere's editor in 1970 was a youngish, large, and solemn man named Giovanni Spadolini. He had come from academia, and still wrote scholarly pieces; some staff members called him *Il Professore* mockingly and, I presume, out of his hearing.

His functioning in those days could only be described as imperial; I have never seen such elaborate effort to create a presence anywhere else in the communication business. Because at that point I knew no one in journalism in Milan, I had asked the U.S. Information Service (USIS) to make the arrangements, and that may have had something to do with the splendor that was laid on, but the atmosphere of solemn deference was clearly standard. My train from Rome was late, and I found my USIS escort, a former Italian journalist, in an agony of embarrassment and open annoyance; Il Direttore was already waiting. We apologized our way into a vast and elegant office to find Spadolini in a frame of assistants and staff members. There was coffee in a silver pot with little cakes, and we sat with straight backs and made solemn small talk. He gave me reprints of a couple of his scholarly articles. The whole thing had about it the feel of some kind of state visit.

It thus was curious that it was there, in that monolithic principality that was the old *Corriere*, that I first understood that some kind of revolution was beginning in the business of journalism in Italy. During the next two days I spent time with several staff members, the most useful of whom was Luigi Manzini, one of three managing editors. He was the kind of professional I wanted most to talk to at *Corriere;* most time spent talking to editors-in-chief is wasted, of course. After a couple of sessions with Manzini, which in total came to almost four hours, I had exhausted the things I wanted to talk about; I thanked him and prepared to leave.

"Is that all, professor?" he asked. "You've finished?"

When I said that I had, he spread his hands in surprise.

"But you have not even mentioned the most important thing going on in European journalism," he said.

"What's that?"

"This, professor." He picked up a newspaper from his desk and waved it at me. *"This."*

It was a copy of *Le Monde,* the French daily, which most Italian journalists regard as the best paper in the world.* Manzini was referring to the beginnings of the European movement that has had many names, none of which has been enduring or satisfactory—"reporter power" and "the democratic newsroom," for example. There was, in fact, little resemblance between what happened at *Le Monde* and what later happened in Italian journalism, but *Le Monde* was the symbol.

A distinguished paper since its founding shortly after the end of the Second World War, *Le Monde* had been owned by stockholders representing a wide range of political commitments. Under the editorship of Hubert Beuve-Méry, it was neutralist during the cold war and increasingly critical of French activity in Southeast Asia. By 1949 some of the stockholders began to bring pressure to get rid of Beuve-Méry, and did it well enough that they forced his resignation in 1951.[1] Both the paper's staff and the readers were indignant, and both reacted with vigor. The staff threatened strikes, and the readers formed an energetic commit-

---

*This surprisingly common judgment may be related to language competence. Generally speaking, Italian journalists, other than editors on the foreign desk and foreign correspondents, are almost as poor at languages as their American counterparts. Most Italian journalists do not read publications in English, nor the Scandinavian languages, nor German. Almost any educated Italian, though, reads French with relative ease.

tee of supporters who rallied public opinion. After two months of wrangling, the ownership was restructured and the editorial staff acquired about 40 percent of the stock. Beuve-Méry returned to the editorship. To activist journalists all over Europe the affair always has been the shot heard round the world.

It was later in my stay at *Corriere* that I began to suspect that the state I was visiting was comparable to, say, the Austro-Hungarian Empire, or the White House of Calvin Coolidge. After the ceremonies with Spadolini were concluded, I was handed off with much courtesy to a young man charged with taking me to dinner. His job at *Corriere* was one uncommon in Italian journalism; he was attached to the public relations office. No other Italian daily at that time had anything like it, but it was a major enterprise at *Corriere*. Among other things it produced a thick, handsome house organ called *Prestigio*, with four-color covers bearing portraits of star journalists. It entertained and supplied the needs of constant visitors from all over the world who came to visit the *New York Times* of Italy; among the armload of publications and press releases that my host gave me was a history of the paper originally prepared for touring Japanese journalists, which therefore was in English. We went to one of those restaurants with character to which classy corporations send visitors toward whom they have kindly feelings, but whose sophistication they feel is dubious. A fat chef with medals on his tunic carved slices from a leg of suckling kid held in the air on a fork, and the young man from public relations and I talked about *Corriere*. He loved the paper, and had high hopes of becoming a foreign correspondent (that never worked out, alas).

Despite his enthusiasm for the company and his hopes for a future there, he was concerned about some recent ugly events. There had been an upsetting episode during the student outbreaks of 1968. In June a group of Milanese students had seized the *Corriere* building, fought off the police, and held up the distribution of the paper for several hours. While that could not be waved away completely, it was understandable because it was a student affair and part of a pattern of disturbances all across Europe at the same time that seemed to be aimed at targets of opportunity. But some other things had been going on that, while not so spectacular, might be even more ominous. It had become necessary to paint over the name on the trucks that delivered *Corriere* to newsstands; rocks had been thrown and drivers intimidated. The greatest paper in Italy had to be delivered anonymously, at least in certain popular *quartieri*. That not only disturbed the staff, he assured me, but shocked the owners.

I found that easy to believe. The relationship between *Corriere della*

Sera and the people of Milan for years had been something uncommon in the news business; a possessive feeling toward the paper was somehow a part of being Milanese. The Crespi family, on their part, were passionately devoted to the city. Spadolini, speaking of his tenure as editor of *Corriere*, gave testimony:

> I went to Rome six or seven times a year; that is to say, at a somewhat more frequent rate than Albertini [*Corriere*'s most famous editor], who went three or four times. And every time I went—and this does honor to the owners of *Corriere* and their Milanism—I always provoked a sense of irritation in the Crespis, who did not want the editor of their newspaper contaminated by the capital.[2]

The news of harassment by citizens that the staff of *Corriere* regarded as their people must have jarred them badly. There were worse times to come, including a bombing that caused considerable destruction, and even the invasion of the newsroom and the seizure of files by the police. The days of expensive entertaining of obscure visitors and Spadolini holding court were fast running out in 1970.

Other changes in the news business in Italy were already underway. They were to include, within a few years, the shift of all the major newspapers to the left in varying degree, to the extent that by the election of 1976 none of the national dailies entirely supported the Christian Democrats; the breaking of RAI's monopoly of broadcasting and the wild mushrooming of private television and radio stations; and, most important, a remarkable accretion of power over the policies and content of some publications by Journalists Committees.

The movement to acquire power is the primary concern in this chapter, but before looking at its chronology there are some elements of background that should be emphasized. They do not explain why the reform movement came about. There is a tangle of explanations, and the most obvious ones are, in all probability, the best ones; for example, the rise of new and vigorous people to leadership in important posts.

Paolo Murialdi and others have suggested that another explanation is the movement out of the profession, in the period of 1960–65, of "romantics," and the influx of more workmanlike professionals: "a felt need for concreteness, the desire for specialization, demonstrating a new professional commitment, less passionate, but more realistic."[3]

Undoubtedly there is something to this, although most foreign observers, at least, would find dubious the assertion that "almost all" of the old florid poseurs had disappeared from Italian journalism. It seems probable that with the new realistic professionalism came a developing confidence in the Italian journalist's view of himself, the conviction that he had important things to say to the country and that he was competent to say them.

The profession has always been a closed shop, and for most of the modern era it was one that kept its head down and looked inward. Journalists were underpaid for decades; during the Fascist period they were, of course, reduced to trained seals; for years after the war they were concerned with the mechanics of organization and internal politics. During the 1960s, however, with the Order firmly in place, things began to improve. Each new contract brought a brisk climb in salaries. A sizable number of the profession went into politics, some with spectacular success, and, because of the vital role in political communication of the Italian press, politicians of all varieties cultivated and supported newspapers.

The rest of the world was beginning to take things Italian seriously. Italian films had been influencing other filmmakers since the mid-1950s; Italian fashions and automobiles and even upper-class Italian degeneracy were models to the world. Mussolini had given Italians visions, but in the end made fools of them; now they were respectable again. Italy had something to say, and journalists saw themselves as primary spokesmen.

Most of all, the new journalists were secure and well off in a country where penury was a necessity for most people and the possibility of hunger never far off. Given that condition, it was only to be expected that the new professionals would eventually start taking themselves seriously as architects of a new kind of journalism.

At least that seems to me a reasonable explanation of the contrast between the moonlighting, often literally threadbare, journalists of the early 1950s and the affluent, often cocksure professionals I met when starting work on this enterprise in 1970. Once I asked a young, and predictably arrogant, officer of the Italian foreign service if, in effect, he felt the journalist's self-image had improved.

"Well, yes," he said, with a touch of a grimace. "Nowadays one's always hearing them announce, 'I am a journalist.'"

Having just been guilty of some psychologizing, I should like to deplore the practice before engaging in it further. It is dubious in accounting for individual behavior, and inevitably specious when applied to whole groups. That said, it might be added that there was, it appears, at least some sense of collective guilt, which gave further impetus to the reform movement.

Almost all historians and other analysts of the Italian press, including Murialdi, Castronovo and Tranfaglia, Grisolia, Borio, and the sociologist Bechelloni attach much importance to the influence of the civil disturbances among the young toward the end of the 1960s. The Italian media were particular targets of students, especially in Rome and Milan, and the fact that these youngsters hated them so much undoubtedly jarred many people in the profession deeply; it had the same impact as that of Milanese workers throwing rocks at the delivery trucks of "their" *Corriere.*

Whether or not it went further than that and made revolutionaries of previously contented beneficiaries of the corporative joys of the Order is another matter. Most of the writers mentioned above play with that idea, a bit winsomely, but press history in Italy, like everything else about the media, is invariably politicized, and most of these writers are well over to the left. It would be convenient to demonstrate that the burgeoning reform movement was on the leading edge of a whole new kind of politics. As time has gone on and much of the zeal for change has sputtered out, such an interpretation more and more seems wishful thinking. More likely than sudden doctrinaire incandescence seems the possibility that many journalists, faced with the evidence that they were not only mistrusted but hated, said to themselves, "What can we do to put out better papers and news broadcasts?"

Whatever new impulses were generated by the unquiet times, they accompanied generally increasing disillusionment with government by the Christian Democrats. Eventually the static ineffectiveness of the regime wore down the enthusiasm of even those most devoted to the system built by Alcide De Gasperi and his heirs. A young Roman journalist once reminded me "this country has had only two governments since the end of the *First* World War." By the end of the 1960s the government was, in the judgment of almost everybody, laced with graft and venality. The miracolo economico had run down, public services were inadequate, and urban life, in particular, was difficult in a hundred numbing little ways.

Worse, particularly from the point of view of most Italian journalists, government was tied to the Vatican. Light conversations with Italians might lead to the conclusion that their anticlerical attitudes are mostly a wry, continuing national joke, but they reach, in fact, far deeper than that. I did not make a systematic attempt to discuss the matter in talking to journalists, but it surfaced frequently, and I met only one journalist who was not anticlerical. He was the editor of *Il Tempo,* and his own Vatican reporter at that point was highly critical of the church in its efforts to influence secular affairs.

Obviously one can be a good, even pious, Catholic and still be anticlerical. But the notion of alliance between the political and financial apparatus of the church and government simply seems obsolete at best and eventually terribly damaging; perhaps no single action in the history of the Christian Democrats hurt them so much with middle-class, vocal

Italians as the untidy alliance with the neo-Fascists to defeat the abortion bill in 1975.

Not only was the government, in the eyes of many journalists, inept and corrupt, there were also many reasons for a guilty conscience within the news business for the service the media had given it. The first major scholar of the press in Italy, Ignazio Weiss, estimated that in 1960 76 percent of the dailies were controlled by the DC and church interests.[4] This included all of the national dailies (except, of course, the anticlerical papers such as *L'Unità* and *Avanti!*). More important than ownership, however, were the assiduous efforts of the most prestigious papers in the country to serve the DC cause. In his *La stampa italiana del dopoguerra*, Paolo Murialdi analyzed the process as it worked during the critical election of 1953.[5]

Evidence from administrative and regional elections had convinced the Christian Democrats well before the national balloting of that year that their success of 1948 would not be repeated and that achieving a workable majority would be difficult. They proposed a law that gave bonus seats to winners; a preannounced coalition of parties that won 50.5 percent of the vote would receive 65 percent of the seats in the Chamber of Deputies. There were howls of protest from all the minor parties and from the left; the proposal was nicknamed "the swindle law" by somebody, and the name stuck; after the election was over, even one-time proponents began to refer to *la legge truffa*.

Tied to that proposal was one that would establish new, sharp curbs upon freedom of the press in a variety of ways, the most offensive of which was the revival of an old device, the requirement that the first copy of each issue of a newspaper be presented to the authorities before general distribution. The newspapers of the country opposed it and attacks by the National Federation of the Press were so heartfelt that the president of the organization, the elderly, eminent Vittorio Emanuele Orlando, felt it appropriate to add a gesture of his own by resigning. Alcide De Gasperi, the prime minister, then announced that if Orlando would withdraw the resignation, De Gasperi would withdraw the proposal for a new law of the press.

With its own ox ungored after all, the press cheerfully turned to supporting the DC scheme for bonus parliamentary seats. According to Murialdi, all the big general newspapers and most of the magazines—including *Il Mondo,* at that time an "intellectual" weekly—gave support; they also gave little space to the opposition. "In news stories, in headlines, in the selection of photographs, they were far from the sense of evenhandedness which in similar cases one can find in other democratic countries."[6]

Support for the Christian Democrats during the campaign can only be described, on the basis of Murialdi's careful analysis, as shameless.

During the two months of the campaign, *Corriere, La Stampa,* and *Il Messaggero* did not publish a single photograph of opposition candidates, nor even of the minor party allies of the Christian Democrats. During the same period, however, they published nineteen photographs of De Gasperi; three of Pella, the minister of the treasury; and one each of the minister of internal affairs and the party secretary.

The final day of active campaigning in an Italian election is Friday. Saturday is the "day of silence" and voting begins on Sunday morning. The Friday afternoon or evening meeting of each party is its big effort, with a party leader as chief speaker and much music and pageantry. In Rome in 1953, the most important of these meetings were those of the Christian Democrats, with De Gasperi as the star, and the Communists, with Palmiro Togliatti. *Il Messaggero* gave the DC a seven-column headline, two photographs, and seventy-two inches of type on the front page. Togliatti and the Communists received ten inches of type on the second page, one line in a headline summarizing several stories, and no photographs. *Corriere* gave De Gasperi a five-column headline, a photograph, and a thirty-inch story on the front page. That was an event in another city, of course. The Milanese rallies associated with the biggest names were those of Mario Scelba, minister of internal affairs, for the Christian Democrats, and Pietro Nenni, longtime leader of the Socialists. The Scelba story got thirty column-inches and a three-column headline on page two; Nenni received six-and-a-half inches at the bottom of the same page and a two-column headline.[7]

It should be noted, perhaps, that the so-called swindle law proved to be of no use; the DC coalitions did not capture 50.5 percent of the seats, and the party was left in the by-now classic position of trying to rule as the largest minority.

The media not only served the government by providing a great deal of favorable attention; they also provided continuing cover-ups of government incompetence (or complicity) in potential scandals. Some cases, such as one discussed briefly below, eventually surfaced. Many journalists were always convinced that such episodes were common. That suspicious conviction has been behind the constant pressure for provisions in in-house contracts giving some authority to the staff in guaranteeing "completeness of news."

On December 12, 1969, Italy was shaken by a tragedy the threads of which are still visible throughout the political pattern. A bomb went off in the main lobby of the Banca dell'Agricoltura in Milan's Piazza Fontana. The place was crowded with customers; sixteen people were killed. The country already was in the grip of a fever about terrorism, and the question that came first to the fore was "Which side is to blame?" The formulation of the question is important; in politicized Italy, the question of which *individuals* were to blame was secondary. The party press divided predictably, with Communist, Socialist, and sympathetic papers accusing Fascists. The Movimento Sociale Italiano and at least some elements of the Christian Democrats accused the extreme left.

The case went on literally for years, inspired nine books, and was finally resolved after ten years with the conviction of two neo-Fascists. Throughout the investigations most of the giornali d'informazione followed the line laid down by the authorities and used the police as their primary sources.[8] The general assumption upon which the police operated was that the far left was responsible.

Within a day or two after the event, the news business was full of theories and presumably trustworthy inside information. Explanations ran all the way from those based upon the conviction that the Christian Democrats were secretly abetting a Fascist plot to those demonstrating that the Soviets were trying to reduce the country to chaos as a necessary preliminary to the Communists taking control. Positions in between included one that had a good deal of circulation, some of it in print, which held that the actual perpetrators were bumbling Fascists, that the police knew about the plot in advance, and deliberately let it go through on the presumption that public opinion would be so outraged that strong-arm government action would be accepted without protest by the public.

Within a few months after the Milan bombing, many journalists had a feeling that they had been had; or, to put it more accurately, that they had been a bit too eager to assist in their own deception.

There are good reasons rooted in the nature of the news business for the heavy use of official sources in complicated, potentially scandalous stories. The omission that grates afterward on the journalist's professional pride is the failure to ask questions or, even worse, the failure to follow up on what turned out to be genuinely important leads.

An attempted coup presumably planned by the top level of the Italian military in 1964 is a similar case. The story was a long time breaking. In the spring of 1967 General Giovanni De Lorenzo, who held the post equivalent to chairman of the Joint Chiefs of Staff in the United States, was suspended. Shortly afterward the center-left weekly newsmagazine *L'Espresso* began a series of articles that, according to that publication, showed that De Lorenzo was head of a plot mounted in 1964 by conservative politicians, businessmen, and the military. The plot called for the arrest of several hundred leftist politicians and trade union leaders in the name of the president of the republic (then Antonio Segni) with an eye to installing a government of "technicians" headed by the military. There was an obvious rallying point for those who disliked the story, for whatever reason: a paralytic stroke disabled Segni shortly after the story first appeared, and the new president, Giuseppe Saragat, bitterly attacked this impugning of his predecessor as one of the stroke's causes. Most of the press followed Saragat's lead.

"As always happened in earlier, similar circumstances," the authors of a recent history of the Italian press have pointed out, "there began a widespread campaign to organize a consensus and manipulate the news; the larger part of the major newspapers, in fact, accepted without the slightest reservation the embarrassed official denials. More than one went to lengths to carry the denials without carrying the explanatory background stories to which they referred.[*] Some dailies caught a glimpse of doubt and certain inconsistencies, but always within the context of a substantial acceptance of the tranquilizing picture offered by the public authorities. Once more the newspapers of the PCI [the Italian Communist party] and PSI [the Socialists] were the only ones to collect and circulate the accusations against De Lorenzo and his accomplices, and to participate in the action of denouncing the reactionary maneuver."9

The ghosts of fascism are still everywhere in Italy, as we have said before, and to be part of a regime that systematically ignored what might have been a rightist coup did nothing for the Italian journalist's pride. Long after the fact there seems to have been an attempt to make up for the neglect, although probably no editor thought of it in those terms; De Lorenzo and several others finally were brought to trial, and several papers assigned a correspondent to cover, in great detail in some cases, what was forecast to be a very long and very complicated business.

From a mixture of forces, then, came the thrust for reform in Italian journalism, nurtured by the confluence of circumstances. The most important element of all, however, was the rise of new trade union leadership in the profession. That process began near the close of the 1960s, but the pivotal point was the national meeting of the National Federation of the Italian Press at Salerno in 1970.

Until that meeting FNSI had concerned itself almost entirely with

---

*This is not a uniquely Italian fault. During the summer of 1972, when the *Washington Post* was carrying daily stories on Watergate, some important clients of the *Post*'s news service failed to carry them. When Woodward and Bernstein stumbled into their only substantial error, the White House tried to discredit the entire series, and the same papers gave that counteroffensive heavy play.

traditional trade union matters: wages, hours, work assignments. Activist journalists dismissed this kind of activity with condescension, but as a split developed at the Salerno meeting, a sizable part of the membership supported the traditional attitudes. Others began to push hard for a larger role in newsrooms and editorial offices, in particular a role not only in the official stance set out in editorials, but in such matters as the tone of headlines and the process of news selection.

The first organizational manifestation of this wing of the profession came in Milan, with the formation of a group that called itself the Committee for Freedom of the Press and for the Fight against Repression. It had about one hundred and fifty members. About a month later a much larger group, numbering about four hundred and fifty, organized the Rome division. Enzo Forcella, an eminent political journalist (and author of "The 1,500 Readers") was president. This group called itself the Democratic Journalists Movement. Individual groups organized in other cities, and a national meeting was held in March of 1970. At the meeting the Milanese group called for the resignation both of the president of the Order and of the president of FNSI and urged Journalists Committees to take more control of decision making within the paper. In the beginning the Roman group was more concerned with trade union matters; from Rome, however, came the first voices calling for abolition of the Order. And it was the first issue of the mimeographed newsletter of the Roman group that provided the most eloquent statement about objectives.

> Our Movement was begun to defend the dignity of the journalistic profession and to renew the sense of professionalism in reporting public affairs. It was born to fight the attacks on freedom of expression which are on the way and which already occur every day, whether from outside (through antiquated laws, archaic mentalities, or monopolistic concentration) or from inside our own professional world (through illiberal or corporative* rules, blackmailing authority, or the misuse of power). . . . We do not carry party membership cards nor political manifestos with our signatures on them, not because we regard such things lightly, but because we seek the common pattern which unites us in the Movement, and which reflects the sense of professional freedom.[10]

The next stage was an effort to take a larger formal role in FNSI's affairs, particularly in the most important regional organizations; slates of

---

*The Italian word is *corporativo*. As the text above indicates, in this context it is pejorative, implying authoritarian institutionalization. *Corporativo* is a common word in Italian political discourse, and its implications are always negative.

reform-minded candidates were presented in organizational elections of officers. It was a bad decision. Given a clear choice between two directions for the organization, the ordinary journalist seems to have found the choice easy.

In Rome the attack against the new group and its candidates in the Lazio-Umbria-Abruzzi-Molise section was led by Luigi Barzini, Jr. The insurgent slate was defeated, and Barzini was elected president of the regional association.

Barzini was, like some figures in the top levels of Italian cinema and music, a genuinely international figure who operated outside an ethnic context most of the time. His Italian critics sometimes wickedly referred to him as *l'Amerikano,* a comment not only on his acculturation, but also on his rightist politics. The brouhaha of trade union affairs, one might have guessed, was hardly the kind of thing to interest him in 1970, but he led the charge.

He bluntly explained why in an interview in 1973: "Because they were a bunch of Communists."

Most of them were not, in fact; there probably were more Socialists than representatives from any other party, but the difference between Communists and Socialists is as generally ignored by centrists and rightists in Italy as by most Americans. Barzini was expressing a common perception, that the reformers were political activists of the far left.

Yet the first national meeting in Milan included such non-Marxist oddities as the entire editorial staff of *La Voce Repubblicana,* the official paper of that center party, and saw the active participation of Carlo Donat Cattin, who was later to be a cabinet minister of the Christian Democrats.

Nevertheless I was told repeatedly in interviews with journalists after 1973 that the kind of people who got themselves elected to Journalists Committees, for example, were Communists and invariably the least competent journalists on whatever paper was being discussed; that political activism and general hell-raising was the refuge of inept professionals.

To an American academic, there was in such statements an interesting echo of a common assertion during the campus uproars of 1969–71; all the troubles, it was frequently said, were caused by bored or incompetent students. The extent to which that was true had, in my experience, a time dimension; on most campuses the first wave of activists were, in point of fact, among the most brilliant students in the university, but as the imitators and joiners came along the quality went down, and the final dribbles of dean-seizers, graffiti experts, and negotiators with administrative committees were simply tediously quarrelsome kids.

Certainly some of the most capable journalists in Italy identified with the reform movement during its early days: Angelo Del Boca and

Paolo Murialdi, both managing editors of *Il Giorno* and, oddly, both distinguished historians and critics of the Italian press (Murialdi was to become president of FNSI); Enzo Forcella; Furio Colombo, a fine political reporter at that time working for RAI; and many others.

After the defeat of its slate in the regional elections, the Rome group began to come apart. By 1971 it was finished along with the other localized organizations, but the spirit that had propelled the Rome group was at work at the national level.

FNSI had been headed for many years by Mario Missiroli, once the editor of *Corriere della Sera*. The national council elected at the Salerno meeting of 1970 had a slight majority of *innovatori*, journalists who felt that the profession should have a more important policy role. Missiroli was retiring because of his age and was replaced as national president by the noncontroversial Adriano Falvo. The new majority prevailed in the election of the new national secretary, however. He was a journalist at RAI named Luciano Ceschia. Ceschia came from Trieste, and had little of the sense of symbolic behavior and ceremonial stance. He simply dug in and went to work at remodeling the organization. His first task was the leadership of negotiations for the new national contract, which would cover the years 1971-72. The demands of FNSI represented a new conception of the role of the staff journalists, growing out of the Salerno meeting and the in-house contract negotiated at *Il Giorno*, which will be discussed later.

The draft language referred to a "more intense collaboration" between the Journalists Committees and management, particularly in reference to matters of firing and plant remodeling and relocation. It also referred to exposing any secret arrangements between publishers and editors, inquiry into advertising as a source of income, and the increasingly complex problem of concentration of ownership; it pointed to the need for reform of both RAI-TV and the Order of Journalists, and proposed a role for the profession in consideration of the then-new draft legislation establishing governmental subsidies for the press. It also called for Journalists Committees to formulate proposals concerning the organization of the various editorial departments within their various units, with an eye not only to the improvement of the paper, but also to providing "completeness of information," an obvious reference to a larger role in the definition and selection of news.[11]

The proposals were first made public in December of 1970, and newspaper publishers, accustomed to wrangling about hours, pay, and fringe benefits, balked at this sudden show of interest in transferring to the troops some of the prerogatives of command. A series of journalists' strikes during late winter brought eventual government intervention and a new contract reflecting the reformist spirit, however, as we shall see.

Although the original impetus came from the Salerno meeting and the National Council of FNSI that was elected there and which in turn elected Ceschia, it seems a reasonable assumption that the new secretary had much to do with making the initiative real.

Not all Italian journalists would give him that much credit. Some complained about his tendency to make long, hectoring speeches, and others regarded him as no more than a reasonably efficient bureaucrat. Ceschia was a man with a clear, deliberately narrowed vision of a job to be done, and a great deal of intensity about getting it done. He was also, as Italian journalists go, relatively apolitical, associated with the Moro branch of the Christian Democrats, a faction less capable than most of upsetting activists of either the left or right. The next step under his leadership was the development of tools to bring the new spirit in Italian journalism to bear.

American journalists are seldom concerned, in practical terms, with the political, societal, or personal character of the owners of the papers or broadcasting operations for which they work. They respond instead to their personal circumstances: appreciation from their superiors, particularly when it is expressed in promotions or pay increases, and a sense that they as individuals are respected and therefore trusted.

There are such professionals in Italy, too, but the early 1970s belonged to the other, much more visible kind, the journalist as political man. These activists felt they had been allies of a government dominated by a political faction that they considered ailing, inept, and corrupt. Therefore when they thought they saw a conspiratorial movement toward seizing control of the most important publications in the country on the part of conservative business interests tied closely to the Christian Democrats, they took it as a strategy designed to bolster incompetence and shut off dissent.

This was precisely the view of the staff of *Il Messaggero* when half the paper was sold to the conservative Edilio Rusconi in 1973 and an attempt made to install Luigi Barzini, Jr. as editor. They knew that Alessandro Perrone, the "honorary *puro*" who was both owner and editor of the paper, had been under constant public attack and intense pressure in personal terms since the paper's sharp move to the left.

Most of the staff wanted not only to support Perrone in his apparent intention to hang on (which proved to be short lived), but also to develop means to retain what they saw as the political gains they had already achieved. For a few weeks there were constant meetings, including not only journalists but printers, truckers, maintenance men, and the like. There was little disagreement or argument among the groups, according to some who were members; discussions dealt largely with organization and tactics. The Socialists on the staff took the lead. Support for Perrone was unanimous. More importantly, so was the growing demand for a shop contract that would guarantee not only the traditional trade union controls and benefits, but the right of the staff to set the paper's political line, taking away veto power not only from the publisher, but also from the editor (in case there was a change in either).

There were precedents for contracts within publishing companies that dealt with the relationships among staff, editor, and owners; in one form or another, they went back beyond the First World War in Italy. These contracts were traditionally devoted, however, to describing the working situation as it existed, generally specifying the complete authority of the editor. The first change in the direction of accretion of power by the newsroom staff came with a contract signed at *Il Giorno*, of Milan, in 1970.

Such a contract is sometimes known as a *contratto* (or *patto*) *aziendale*, which can be translated as "in-house agreement"; more commonly, and particularly with the rise of militancy in the early 1970s, it has been referred to as a *contratto integrativo*.

The English verb *integrate* means "to complete, to make whole," and that is the sense of the Italian adjective. Such a contract, that is, in no way replaced or altered the national contract under which all professional journalists worked; it presumably only filled in things that were not covered. There seem to have been few objections based on the idea that a contract of the sort that *Il Giorno* negotiated might be, in fact, in contradiction of article 6 of the national contract, which gives the responsabile the right to lay down the political line. That was the right the *Il Messaggero* staff also clearly had in mind.

For a time, and while Perrone and an ad hoc committee worked at building fences with politicians of the left, the Christian Democrats who led the government brought heavy pressure against them, largely in the form of what has come to be called "jawboning" in American politics. Amintore Fanfani, leader of the DC's conservative wing, was particularly displeased at his party's loss of the support of the leading paper in the capital. As winter turned into spring, political argument concentrated on the upcoming referendum on the repeal of Italy's new divorce law. Engineering the referendum was a DC-Vatican project, and *Il Messaggero* came down strongly against the repeal and for divorce.

By that time government indignation toward the paper had begun to cool, to the puzzlement of some of the paper's staff. Shortly before the voting, rumors began to circulate in Rome that Alessandro Perrone had sold his share of the paper to Montedison, a sprawling conglomerate led by a man named Eugenio Cefis.

At that point Eugenio Cefis was the favorite villain of the official left and of middle-class intellectuals, including the press. Montedison, his company, was part of ENI; it was involved in chemicals, variety stores, and other enterprises which included the ownership of *Il Giorno* of Milan. The company was also expanding rapidly; Cefis was acquisitive. He was known to have great interest in media properties, and was commonly described as planning to dominate all Italian journalism. He was also a conservative, a heavy contributor to the Christian Democrats, and reticent about talking to reporters. Books were written exposing his business methods. He appeared frequently on the covers of newsmagazines, generally scowling. He had a unique and, one assumes, involuntary drawing power for indignation.

The personnel of *Il Messaggero,* caught up in the exhilarating invention of whole new ways to run a newspaper, were jarred, to say the least, to learn that their paper had been sold to the current arch-villain of Italian corporate life. The morning after the sale was confirmed the banner headline read "The Free Voice of *Messaggero* is Smothered." The Assembly—that is, all members of the editorial staff and, in this case, the nonjournalist employees as well—was convoked, a continuing state of crisis declared, and a resolution passed.

> The Christian Democrats, inspired by Amintore Fanfani and by means of their financial tentacles within publishing (Eugenio Cefis for Montedison, Edilio Rusconi for RESI) have acquired from Alessandro Perrone and his sisters the remaining 50 percent of the stock of the paper. . . . It is another demonstration that aggression against surviving independent newspapers, the campaign against divorce, and the grab for power are part of a unique authoritarian scheme: the establishment of a regime in Italy.

For a "regime," of course, read "fascism"; the Assembly probably did not use the word because it is close to libelous in Italy, and Rusconi had sued Perrone and others when he had been described in that fashion the previous summer. The resolution concluded: "Let no one deceive himself that he can enter the offices of the paper without the consent of the staff and without signing the in-house agreement which constitutes irrenounceable guarantee of union rights and ideology."[12]

That last sentence amounted to a declaration of war, and a strike closed the paper down. The new proprietors remained remarkably cool. The new president of the board of directors was Raffaele Stracquadanio, who was head of another Montedison company, the chain of low-price variety stores called Magazzini Standa. (There was bitterness about this, too, among journalists; to put it in an American context, it was as if the head of K-Mart were put in charge of, say, the *St. Louis Post-Dispatch*.) When a staff committee pointed out to management that the strike had lasted a week, a spokesman blandly replied, "A week? At Standa we sustained a strike of six months."[13]

Throughout the negotiations the Montedison people were low-key, correct, and amiable. There were contacts with Cefis through intermediaries, and it soon became apparent that an in-house agreement might be possible. The single sticking point was Montedison's insistence on retaining the right of naming the new editor, as specified in the national contract. That was circumvented by the *Messaggero* staff accepting the formality as long as they were consulted and as long as the editor had little real power; the new pact that they had drawn up saw to that. Besides, Montedison was naming Italo Pietra to the job, an impeccable choice to the energetic Socialists leading the staff.

On May 24, 1974, the pact was signed and on May 28 *Il Messaggero* was again on the newsstands of Rome. The contract represented, at least so far as formal commitments were concerned, the crest of the movement through which Italian journalists attempted to take control of the content of the newspapers for which they worked.

It would be selling the *Messaggero* group short, it seems to me, to dismiss what they attempted as cynical. Nor was their motivation purely political, although it was shaped in the political context, like all Italian attempts at reform. Most journalists on important publications frequently wish those publications served higher purposes. *Il Messaggero*'s belligerent visionaries had established the farthest beachhead the reform movement was to reach.

Some details and ornamentation have been omitted from the following, but it essentially is a translation of the full text.

Prologue

The representatives of the Il Messaggero Publishing Company and the Journalists Committee, which has the explicit mandate of the Assembly of Journalists, agree to the following:

The publisher and the journalists of *Il Messaggero*, with the objective of contributing to the reinforcement of freedom of the press and of the news in Italy, solidly commit themselves:

a) to the maintenance and defense of the anticlerical, democratic, and anti-Fascist line of the newspaper;

b) to protect the organizational and professional efficiency of the company no less than its financial stability, recognizing that such conditions constitute the only guarantee of the independence and autonomy of *Il Messaggero*.

1) The publishing company commits itself to respect all the in-house trade union agreements now in force.

2) The publishing company guarantees the jobs, salary levels, and the present structure of the news departments dealing with both local and external affairs. Changes in such structure will be carried out under the conditions of this contract and particularly of paragraphs 6 and 7 [below].

3) It is required that nomination to, or changes in, the posts of editor or coeditor be subject to preliminary consultation with the Journalists Committee. The owners may not begin such proposed changes before hearing the Committee's opinion. The Committee is charged with expressing its opinion within five days of the notification from the publisher.

4) The publisher is charged with naming one or more Associate Editors who must be selected from among the certified professionals on the news staff. Such nominations must have the approval of the Journalists Committee.

[Note: after the installation of this contract, *Il Messaggero* always had two associate editors, both of whom were, practically speaking, chosen by the Journalists Committee. In daily operations, power rested in the hands of these associate editors; through a variety of devices, including article 5, immediately below, the editor was almost stripped of any unilateral authority.]

5) The agreements between the publisher and the editor regarding the conduct of the paper's affairs shall correspond to the provisions of the national journalists contract and the standards of membership in the profession of journalism and must be communicated in advance to the Journalists Committee in order that the Committee may carry out the functions required of it by the national contract.

The editor exercises the function of direction as described in the national contract, in collaboration with the newsroom staff, by means of the organizational structure, and with recognition of mutual prerogatives.

Autonomy in carrying out the work of each department is recognized within that framework, and autonomy of initiative and function are guaranteed the Journalists Committee and the Assembly.

6) It is required that hiring and firing involve preliminary consulta-

tion with the Journalists Committee. The judgment of the Committee is binding in cases of dismissal.

In regard to matters affecting professional status and contractual matters, the company particularly affirms its commitment not to carry out any acts that might be counter to the anticlerical, democratic, and anti-Fascist line, and the Committee reserves to itself the right to verify the observance of this charge.

7) It is required that transfers and changes in professional requirements and duties be submitted for preliminary consultation with the Journalists Committee, which will take into account the opinion of the interested parties.

8) Modification and editing of any article or news dispatch must carry—provided that it is reasonably possible—the consent of the author, whose right to withdraw his by-line is hereby recognized.

The Journalists Committee may express its judgments on the completeness, accuracy, and omissions in any general interest news and may request of the editor completion or correction for the next issue. In case agreement between the editor and the Committee is lacking concerning the completeness of news, the Committee reserves the right to convoke a meeting of the Assembly.

Again, a note: the calling of a meeting of full staff is a classic trade union device in the news business in Italy. At best it delays getting the paper out on time, and the group can always decide to stay in session for hours, or simply to walk out altogether.

The three articles that conclude the pact are essentially administrative, dealing with the definition of a quorum (half the professionals and apprentices on the staff, plus one), and covering matters in which the Journalists Committee is obligated to call a meeting of the full Assembly before acting, for example, the approval of a new editor or associate editor, any hiring or firing, and transfers or changes in job descriptions.

The contract was signed by the Journalists Committee and the president of the Il Messaggero Publishing Company, the Montedison subsidiary that formally owned the paper.

In broad outline, the story of the development of a liberal in-house contract at *Corriere della Sera* quite closely parallels that of the same process at *Il Messaggero;* they took place at almost exactly the same time. Uncertainty about *Corriere*'s ownership and the knowledge that the paper was losing both readers and a great deal of money (the company, including its magazine properties, had lost a total of about $11 million in 1973) produced disquieted staff members; indications of the movement of most of the stock into the hands of two conservative industrialists, Agnelli and

Moratti, did nothing to restore calm. When the working arrangement became clear, however, with control of paper in the hands of Giulia Maria Crespi, there was some easing of concern (with the exception of a few journalists, such as Indro Montanelli, already doing preliminary work for a new paper of his own). The editor, Piero Ottone, had been installing some major changes as well. Some were largely mechanical; he had broken up the pastone romano and moved the fragments inside, for the most part; front page stories were shorter, the writing tighter and clearer throughout.

Other changes were political. This was most visible in the front-page editorials, but a skewing to the left was apparent in such things as headlines and the choice of news. Not only Socialists but Communists moved into major roles in the editorial departments.

As Italian journalists go, Ottone was not much of a political man, and it seems probable that the most important factor in the decision to move the paper in such directions was the search for more circulation. Milan has more trade union members and intellectuals than any city in Italy; there was evidence that their interests and commitments had wandered far from the old *Corriere*. Perrone had made the same movement in the attempt to increase *Il Messaggero*'s sales. Whatever the combination of reasons, there was much going on at *Corriere* during 1973–74. A journalist friend on *Il Giorno*, *Corriere*'s local competitor, once said to me during that period, "I'd rather be working on that paper right now than on any paper in the world. In the world!"

That atmosphere did not endure long, however. Giulia Maria Crespi's partners became restless about the losses and the fact that nothing was apparently being done to reverse them. That led to a management proposal to cut back expenses by limiting the paper to ten pages and raising the per copy price; the *Corriere* Assembly, including both journalists and printers, rejected the proposal, saying that financial profit or loss was not the issue at all. "The paper provides a political profit which should appear in the balance sheets of cement manufacturers, petroleum merchants, sugar refiners, and automobile industrialists who support deficits in exchange for other services to the company."[14]

That rhetoric, with its implications of complicity between the company and the paper's management, produced a backlash within the staff, petitions and counter-petitions, and general acrimony. Montanelli announced his plans to establish a new paper in Milan, and several of the biggest names on *Corriere* resigned to go with him. *Corriere* was clearly going to be sold; Moratti and Agnelli were openly trying to get out. At the end of March, editor Ottone met with the Assembly and proposed a structural reorganization of the paper, including three new associate editors. This meant realignment of assignments and some decentralization of power. On their part, the staff presented a proposal for an in-house agreement providing some changes of their own. Although there were some negotiations during the next few weeks and the crisis at *Corriere* was not fully resolved until the middle of July when the new Rizzoli ownership took over, the essential provisions of the *patto integrativo* remained unaltered. In important ways they resemble those set out in the *Il Messaggero* contract.

In the *Corriere* pact, changes in news articles were permitted only with the consent of the writers; headlines were to be altered only with the consent of the desk men who wrote them. The Journalists Committee could challenge the accuracy and completeness of news stories or articles and call for correction and improvement, inserting, if necessary, additional material that had appeared not in *Corriere* but elsewhere, in wire service dispatches or other newspapers. Emphasis was also placed upon the autonomy of individual editorial departments and their supervising editors; a quarterly meeting of the management and the Journalists Committee was established for the specific purpose of reviewing departments.

Some observers felt that this document would be unacceptable to Ottone and would force his resignation. They misjudged him.

"One reads the document and may judge that it reduces the position of the editor," he said. "I personally don't think so. Things are set down here which . . . every editor who has a conscience applies. To put these things in writing reinforces the freedom and the independence of a daily paper."[15]

Not all Italian dailies have an in-house agreement. Rome's second daily, the substantial *Il Tempo,* has never had one; some smaller papers have none, some have a document for purposes of form only.

The contract drawn up at *Il Secolo XIX* of Genoa gave considerable power to the staff, but differed from *Il Messaggero*'s and *Corriere*'s in two major respects: it had no provisions regarding alterations of articles, and it carried the name of the editor; it was a contract between one specific man and his staff. When Alessandro Perrone and his sisters sold their half of *Il Messaggero* to the Cefis interests, they retained full ownership of the Genoa paper, which was the first owned by the family. Perrone became both editor and publisher, and shortly afterward the in-house contract was signed. As a political guideline it used precisely the same words as *Il Messaggero*'s pact: *anticlerical, democratic, and anti-Fascist*. It gave Perrone a vote of confidence and accepted his promises to maintain the line and involve the staff in major decisions. It also contained, like several other contracts, a provision requiring the paper to carry official statements from shop unions when requested to do so.

The in-house contracts gave journalists the tools of influence in the major publications in Italy; the Journalists Committees were delegated to use them. Like the contract, the committee device is an old one. The first national contract to describe such a committee's organization and function was that drawn up in 1947. For twenty-three years, however, such committees amounted to little; they were charged chiefly with monitoring the precise execution of the contract, a straight trade union function, and with making suggestions for the improvement of the paper.

The *Il Giorno* contract mentioned earlier as the model for the first national contract setting a larger staff role also set the pattern for the emerging role of the Journalists Committee. It specified the "consultative presence" of the committee in matters relating to:

1. the structure and organization of jobs;
2. evaluations of professional competence, reassignments, and hiring;
3. rates of pay for all staff;
4. the problem of part-time collaborators; and
5. the political stance of the newspaper.[16]

All but the last of these are familiar trade union concerns; although they went somewhat further than the responsibilities assigned previously to such committees, they still represented nothing that a vigorous shop steward would not be concerned about. The land mine is in the last provision: consultation on the political line inevitably leads to a role in making it, and, though "consulting" can be a meaningless ceremony, such is not the case when the consultants have the power to shut the place down by going on strike.

That *Il Giorno* contract was effective in January, 1970, and the then-new leadership of the National Federation of the Italian Press set to work to acquire for the rest of the journalists in Italy what the staff of *Il Giorno* had acquired for themselves. Article 34 of the national contract that came into force in February, 1971, was an elegant blurring of the old role of union watchdog and the new one of intellectual, social, and political collaboration. It began:

> In companies which publish daily newspapers, magazines, and in the news services of the daily press which have at least ten editorial employees, there is hereby established a Journalists Committee [comitato di redazione], which is charged with the protection of the moral and material rights proceeding from the present contract and the provisions of the law. . . .

Paragraphs *a* through *e* set out the responsibilities of the committee. The first is administrative, the maintenance of liaison with the regional association of journalists; the second is the watchdog provision, calling for monitoring of the "exact application" of the contract and pertinent social legislation; the third is a rather bland injunction to "attempt to conciliate individual or collective controversies which may arise among the parties." The fourth is the most important.

d) express their opinions and formulate proposals concerning the shaping of the news product with the object of improving the newspaper and assuring completeness of information.

The final words are a literal translation from the Italian *completezza dell'informazione*. They have a much larger meaning, however, in context. The key word is *completezza; informazione* in this usage more or less means "news." Since 1971 the Journalists Committees of the national dailies probably have fought more battles under that banner than under any other. It is code language that might be translated, with reasonable accuracy, as "both sides of the story," and which, in practice, has come to mean "presentation of the nonestablishment side of the story."

As a practical matter, to be told that something must be printed or broadcast regardless of its news value is, to most editors, an evil as oppressive as being ordered not to print something which *does* have news value. In the abstract, at least, the point is not the news itself, but the business of being coerced. The next chapter deals with some specific cases.

Since the contract of 1971, the section dealing with the powers and responsibilities of the Journalists Committee in the national contract has more than trebled in size, but the changes have largely been interpretive; the substance remains the same.

By midsummer of 1974, then, the professional journalists who worked for Italy's largest dailies had acquired the means of influencing much of the conduct of the paper's affairs. They had a role weightier in that regard than journalists anywhere else in the world. They had owners who were prepared to be far more accommodating than the journalists thought possible at that time. Everything was ready for *la riforma,* the term that provoked so many soaring words in so many meetings, so many press releases, so many articles and books about the press.

Understanding the moment, some journalists went to work to seize it.

Chapter 7

Reformers at Work

This chapter deals with "involved" journalists, and what they did with the new tools for participation that they had hammered out for themselves.

We should remember, however, that while all this was going on there were thousands of Italian journalists of a different sort working on papers of a different kind. On a trip to Verona in 1977, for example, I looked into the situation at the local daily, *L'Arena*. *L'Arena* had a circulation of forty thousand and was devoted almost entirely to local news, since the major national newspapers were available on local newsstands. The Christian Democratic organization owned a small part of its stock, but most was in the hands of local businessmen; it did not run deficits, and had produced a profit of about forty thousand dollars the previous year.

A conversation with a member of *L'Arena*'s Journalists Committee indicated that the committee met infrequently and then only for routine union affairs. ("We're not political, really," he explained, with what seemed like a little embarrassment.) On occasion they had had meetings of the Assembly, but since these had not drawn an attendance of more than four or five—of a staff of twenty-two—they had pretty much stopped doing *that*. He felt that being a journalist was about the best job in the world, and Verona a great place to practice it, since it was close to skiing, fishing, swimming, and, of course, Venice.

There have always been more professionals of that sort in Italian journalism than activists, and most newsrooms outside Milan and Rome essentially were tranquil during the 1970s. Even within those cities, there were politically conservative papers in which Journalists Committees were largely inactive. An acquaintance on *Il Tempo* of Rome wrote in response to an inquiry: "Our Journalists Committee neither has nor seeks the powers of *Il Messaggero*'s. They certainly represent the rights of the staff but—on the whole—they think this can best be achieved by working with the management rather than against it."[1]

The fact that there were no substantial quarrels with management of *Il Tempo*, even about trade union matters, did not mean the complete absence of any newsroom intrigue. The spring after that letter was written

I was assured by another staff member that the Communists on the staff—there were a few—had organized a shadow Journalists Committee that was stirring up trouble and campaigning hard in preparation for the next newsroom election, ready to take over at the first opportunity. The opportunity never came, and *Il Tempo* continued to be the voice of the old Roman bourgeoisie and aristocracy.

In Milan, Indro Montanelli's *Il Giornale Nuovo* apparently lacked even small personal intrigue. To an extent unique in modern Italian journalism, *Il Giornale* was in its early years the reflection of one all-powerful man; the most important members of the staff followed Montanelli in the break with *Corriere della Sera* and the group remained relatively small and homogeneous. When I asked one of the staff about the functions of the Journalists Committee, he spread his hands and smiled.

"Look, this is Montanelli's paper," he said. "And we wouldn't want it any other way."

Nevertheless *Il Giornale* carefully observed the provisions of the national contract; the new Journalists Committee had just been elected at the time we talked, and the staff member gave me a copy of the announced results. I did not ask if Montanelli had made any suggestions about candidates, but the unanimity on the three chosen was remarkable.

More Journalists Committees have been concerned about strictly trade union matters than about partisan politics or the polemical direction of the publication. Furthermore, as the reporter power movement cooled, even the most reform-minded committees moved more and more in the direction of monitoring the application of the national contract, a development that will be considered later in this chapter. It is enough to note here that the contract is sufficiently specific that arguments about its interpretation tend to fall into angels-on-the-head-of-a-pin sophistry, rather than large matters of either partisan politics or the role of the staff in the paper's policy. Such concerns have been the primary things discussed in the Italian bureaus of the wire services, for example, and the offices of the Italian agency L'ANSA, and most smaller papers such as *L'Arena*. It has also been true, of course, of specialized newspapers devoted to sports or business.

It has also been true of *La Stampa* of Turin, while the other three traditional national dailies were filled with uproar. The circumstances were unique at *La Stampa*, however, and the way the system has worked demonstrates the extent of differences among newsrooms and the importance of personal style in editors. When Arrigo Levi was offered the post of editor of *La Stampa* after the resignation of Alberto Ronchey in the spring of 1973, Levi accepted on the condition that the full staff approve. He made his position clear; he intended to be in charge, to be the boss. In a sense, it amounted to a warning that the Journalists Committee and the Assembly had a minor function so far as he was concerned. The discussion with the staff was both long and intense; a columnist on another paper was outraged that Levi permitted it. The man had permitted himself, said Enrico Mattei of *Il Tempo,* to be "subjected to a humiliation without precedent in the history of Italian journalism."[2]

Humiliated or not, Levi obtained an all but unanimous vote of approval. The great Vittorio Gorresio, a man with an un-Italian flair for self-deprecation, puckishly abstained.

"But it wasn't an act of no confidence in Arrigo," he said later. "I just did it to play the fool."

Levi not only received his approval, but acquired on paper his authority to control the content of the publication. He proceeded to do so, and the Journalists Committee contented itself with details. During the conversation in the spring of 1977 that is referred to several times in this book, Levi showed his weary irritation at the topic that had dominated his meetings with the committee for a year. A reporter had filed a story from Genoa that someone on the desk had cut sharply. The reporter's by-line was not removed, however. She had protested vigorously to the committee, which backed her complaint in meetings with Levi. The matter had been discussed for months, the end was not in sight, and the ultimate lunatic touch was provided by the fact that the desk man who had done the original cutting was a member of the Journalists Committee, which was pressing unanimously for justice for the reporter.

The circumstances at *La Stampa* and Levi's action in negotiating for autonomy were uncommon, but the role of the Journalists Committee is not. Most have been more concerned with improving life on the job than with bringing the revolution to Italian journalism. Yet it is also true that the people and the forces that are most influential in the profession were the malcontents; the bringers of change were the handful who provided an altogether disproportionate piece of the significant history of the news business.

It was these people who were elected to the Journalists Committees in the yeasty days of 1972–74, and these quickly developed as the real locus of power in the reformist movement. The full Assembly was by nature a clumsy device. Even on small papers, getting a quorum was likely to be a problem, as the experience of *L'Arena* indicates. In theory, the Journalists Committee was to do the detailed negotiation and the daily monitoring, repairing to the Assembly for policy decisions. The extent to which the system actually worked varied from paper to paper. The Assembly at *Il Messaggero* was very active for several years, and seems to have been the most active in the industry. Assembly meetings were called frequently; on some occasions Assembly meetings were called between editions. (*Il Messaggero* claimed a total of thirty-four editions in the early 1970s,[3] but most of these consisted of the same newspaper with a column or two of local news supplied by telephone from a part-time correspondent in the area at which the edition was aimed; basically there are two editions, a first one that goes to press about 9:30 P.M. and then is rejigged for the region and a single late Roman edition. Italian morning dailies tend to print their last edition later than American counterparts; 1:30 A.M. is common, and holding until 3:00 A.M. is not difficult.)

Corriere della Sera's Assembly seems to have functioned according to the book for the most part; it was active during the most tumultuous phases of the ownership crisis, but after that, and under Piero Ottone's skillful and subtle management, its role attenuated. It exercised no significant amount of power by the time of the editorship crisis of 1978.

A different tradition developed at *Il Giorno*. In practice, most of the staff role in making decisions at that paper was carried out by the Journalists Committee working with a body called the *consulta*. As we have seen, *Il Giorno* was the innovator in establishing the model for in-house contracts, and its consulta device was written into the 1975 national contract. It is a body made up of representatives of each of the news operations departments—foreign, city news, and so on—of which *Il Giorno* has twelve. The basic notion was to provide participation for parts of the news staff not represented on the three-member Journalists Committee, and may have grown out of the hotly contested elections for those posts. The consulta works closely with the newsroom committee and meets at specified intervals with the editor. *Il Giorno*'s Assembly functioned largely in ratifying the decisions of the smaller groups.

Since the Assembly is the body that officially promulgates most big decisions, however, it is the group tagged with the pejorative overtones of another of those mind-bending Italian neologisms: *assemblearismo*. It refers, in one sense, to any irresponsible action taken by anybody under the rank of editor; in another, it seems to mean a vague threat to the established order from antigovernment newspapers, and is favored by conservative editorial writers, particularly those from the right wing of the Christian Democrats.

It would appear hazardous to essay many generalizations about the journalists who were elected to Journalists Committees in the early 1970s beyond the fact that they were interested in bringing about some changes. An eminent editorial executive who retired to consultation and the casual supervision of two specialized magazines had no difficulty in formulating such generalizations, however. Mario Oriani spent twenty years on *Corriere della Sera* and then several as editor of some *Corriere*-owned magazines.

As part of a generally pessimistic view of Italian journalism, he shrugged off the rhetoric and saw the changes as simply another trade union offensive to get more power. That was particularly true, as he saw it, of elected Journalists Committees.

"They're union leaders, or union hacks. They're all leftists; they're organized and know how to push themselves forward. Most good journalists are simply bored with the whole business and are perfectly willing to let them go ahead."[4]

I brought the question of what kind of people the activists were into most of my conversations with journalists in both 1973 and 1975. Several agreed, to some extent, with Oriani's summary judgment. That group included a couple of first-rate American journalists who had lived in Italy, and worked with the Italian press, for twenty years; by 1975 their disenchantment was total. They saw the reform movement as cynically self-serving and judged Italian journalism the worst it had been within their memory. Some others, such as Barzini, simply dismissed newsroom activists as Communists, and incompetent journalists at best.

The unifying perception of this group of unbelieving and disaffected was that this was simply another trade union ploy in a country where trade unions have great power and where they constantly seek to institutionalize their own role in politics. It seems to me, however, that such a conclusion excessively discounts a number of initiatives that I would describe as more high-minded than hard-nosed tactical unionism. One makes a decision about that, I suppose, on the basis of the dimensions of one's cynicism about such things as the transformation of important ideas into slogans.

A number of words and phrases became stylish in the discourse of the reform-minded among Italian journalists. The word *oggettivo* had been used in reference to newspapers, outside as well as inside the business. Our first landlord in Italy was a traveling salesman for Buitoni spaghetti and Perugina chocolate, but a serious reader; when I asked him about his chief criticism of Italian papers he immediately replied, "The lack of objectivity."

In the torrents of debate and writing about journalism in the 1970s there were occasional references to *oggettività*, but the word was slipping out of clinical use. A set of phrases based upon the word *informazione* began to appear. *Informazione* is also a familiar and well-established word in Italian, of course, but it had not been applied, so far as I know, in a special way to journalism until about 1970. Then one began to hear about *la riforma dell'informazione* and *i problemi dell'informazione,* and then two phrases that became a kind of battle cry: *completezza dell'informazione* and *libertà dell'informazione.*

The word *informazione* apparently had a cachet that made it sound a touch classy. In Italian it has an overtone of producing the state of informed-ness, the kind of thing implied in the English phrase *he was an informed man* or *a well-informed presentation. Informazione* simply implies heavier, deeper stuff than *notizia,* which is about the equivalent of the English "latest news."

Usage of *informazione* may have filtered in from the international communications research community, which has spread it over the world from its beginnings in the United States. The phrase "information theory"—which has nothing to do with media at all, but still is a part of communication study—has been used in this country for several decades.

The current U.S. phrase *freedom of information* would seem to be the equivalent of the Italian *libertà dell'informazione,* but such is not the case. The American reference is not to journalism at all, except that journalists have made use of the Freedom of Information Act, which permits the public to get at certain information previously held secret by the government. When Italian journalists talk about *libertà dell'informazione* they mean something more or less equivalent to "freedom of the press," the right to write what they please despite pressure from authority or financial interest.

In practice, completezza dell'informazione appears in the national contract not only as a general philosophical objective, but in the stipulation that the Journalists Committee has a right to space for their side of the story in the coverage of trade union matters. In-house contracts often also represent the printers as well as the journalists on a particular newspaper; a quarrel between Ottone and the printers of *Corriere della Sera* about a report of union activities led to the strike that is detailed later in this chapter.

In the United States the chief users of normative catch-phrases in the news business have been owners and publishers, not payroll journalists. The most common is "freedom of the press"; there are financial advantages to be gained through the unique protection of the First Amendment, and it has been invoked on issues ranging from antitrust actions to child labor laws. Italian management almost never talks about such things. Most journalists, however, are members of a trade union whose leadership talks constantly about such things and negotiates contracts that attempt to establish or guarantee them. Rhetoric much of the evangelism may be, but it was impossible in the early 1970s to talk with Italian journalists at any length without beginning to feel that among some of them there was a new sensitivity to the possibility of bringing about change on *their* terms, of improving the standards and reputation of the profession, the quality of information available to the Italian citizen, and the functioning of the Italian state.

Perhaps the easiest way to picture the range of activities of Journalists Committees and Assemblies at work is to lay out some examples under obvious headings: the hiring and firing of bosses, partisan politics, professional concerns, and trade union activities.

The incident that provided the first impetus for the European "reporter power" movement concerned who was to be in charge. In that case, the staff of *Le Monde* organized to halt the expulsion of the paper's editor. As we have seen, the staff of *Il Messaggero* helped stand off the expulsion of Alessandro Perrone in a somewhat similar situation.

Negotiators of both the national work contract and the various in-house contracts of particular companies have tried repeatedly to get formal provisions giving the staff full rights of approval or veto of new editors and associate editors. As the 1970s ended, the efforts had failed; the editor continued to be the owner's man. A staff that disapproves obviously has some powers of its own, however.

The firing of Italo Pietra as editor of *Il Giorno* proved to be an opportunity for building more leverage on the part of one of the more restive newspaper staffs in the country. There seems to have been little regret about the departure of Pietra; he had been in the job twelve years, the paper was in decline, and he himself felt that, because of the changed political situation, it was time to go. Nevertheless he was for all practical purposes fired, and without notice to the Journalists Committee. They protested formally and went to work to get the appropriate sections of their in-house contract strengthened. The staff leadership at *Il Giorno* wanted some rewriting of their contract before approving a new editor. ENI, the state-controlled conglomerate that was publisher of the paper finally agreed to "inform the Journalists Committee of changes in the direttore responsabile, or in the associate or coeditor, to provide for the news staff in all cases the timely expression of meaningful, though non-binding, opinion."[5]

None of this was aimed at Gaetano Afeltra, who was to be named the paper's new editor; although his tenure was eventually to develop into an exercise in nonstop contention, in the beginning he was unanimously welcomed as a fine professional and a confessed Socialist.

Il Mondo is a venerable name in Italian journalism. It was founded as a weekly magazine shortly after the end of the Second World War, and from the beginning aimed for a serious, well-educated audience. Over the first few years it attracted such contributors as Benedetto Croce, Gaetano

Salvemini, and Luigi Einaudi. Vittorio Gorresio once described it as "intransigently anti-Communist in the name of liberty, intransigently anti-Fascist in the name of intelligence, intransigently anticlerical in the name of reason."[6]

That publication died in 1966. The title appeared on some experiments in both format and content, finally settling into place as one of Italy's several weekly magazines oriented toward news and comment; by that time it was the property of the *Corriere della Sera* organization. In the summer of 1975, management nominated Antonio Ghirelli as *Il Mondo*'s new editor.

Ghirelli was a Neapolitan who had been associated almost exclusively with sports dailies; he also had something of a reputation as a savior of failing enterprises. Those things, perhaps, inspired the staff members of *Il Mondo* to think about some specifications defining his authority. They negotiated a new in-house contract, based to some extent upon the document already adopted by *Corriere della Sera,* but with additional safeguards on the exercise of authority from the top. Ghirelli signed it on July 2, 1975.

It specified the political line: "at the side of the workers' movement. . . . unequivocally to the left, anticlerical and anti-Fascist, and with an intransigent independence from the centers of economic and political power in order to guarantee freedom of the press and full professional autonomy."

Il Mondo, the document points out, is divided into sections, and is the product of professionals who have as much role in making plans as in executing them. The editor is defined as something of a first among equals who leads the rest of the staff in not only producing the magazine, but in guaranteeing everyone's rights.

The heads of the various sections of the magazine were given extraordinary powers: they, along with the staff members under them, had complete authority over content, including the choice of photographs. Any proposed changes in the arrangement of departments within the magazine or in work assignments were to be submitted in advance to the Journalists Committee for consultation. Covers were to be decided in consultation with staff members. Writers of headings and titles were to be consulted before any changes; no signed article could be significantly altered without the consent of the writer, and necessary cuts made either by the author or someone in his section. The right of the Journalists Committee to call for correction, in the following issue, of "incompleteness, inexactitude, or omissions" was also set out.

A standard protocol for newly nominated editors had developed by the time Franco Di Bella replaced Piero Ottone as chief at *Corriere della Sera.* It was an adaptation of the procedure in the Levi case; the nominee appeared before the Assembly and laid out his plans for the publication. Discussion followed and finally a vote of confidence by secret ballot was taken.

In the case of the Ottone–Di Bella change there was a good deal of dissent. Many of the paper's staff members believed that Ottone had been pushed aside at the demand of conservative Christian Democrats who were supplying, or arranging for, much-needed new capital; Di Bella was felt by some to be an unremarkable journalist at best; papers on the left identified him as being a party to the embarrassing Zicari affair (see p. 76). His appointment was approved by the Assembly of journalists, with ninety-two yes votes, twenty noes, and sixty-two abstentions. "Few votes for Di Bella," said *Paese Sera*'s headline.[7]

Even if a majority of votes had gone against the nominee, however, he could still have assumed the post. There have been no examples of the staff of a publication getting an editor fired; as we shall see, the newsroom at *Il Giorno* tried for years to torpedo Gaetano Afeltra, with no effect.

Nevertheless, and despite the lack of legal weapons, the feelings of the professional staff clearly have major influence on the choice of editor and his administration of the paper. The business of getting out a publication or a news broadcast against deadline is mechanically so complex that it can be sabotaged by little more than ill will. Both printers and journalists in Italy have developed a wide range of skills in producing inefficiency; the most commonly used is the sudden discovery of the need for a staff meeting. The greatest mark of staff influence in choosing news administrators is visible when one looks at the men nominated as editors almost since the beginning of the reform period. Publishers have obviously chosen people they guess will be acceptable, in some cases against what must have been their own political sentiments.

The primary purpose of the first leaders of the reform movement was the development of ways to influence and eventually control the political line of the media for which they worked. Even the sketchiest description for U.S. publishers or editors of what has gone on brings blanched faces and spilled drinks. "When that comes in the door," said a U.S. wire service bureau chief, "I go out the window." He took a long breath. "Head first."

Many Italians, in and out of the profession, have felt the same way. Guido Gonella had been not only a journalist, but president of the Order of Journalists, when he told an interviewer for the weekly *Il Settimianale*:

> After having been oppressed by dictatorship and then suffocated by economic overlords, freedom of the press may fall victim to the despotism of Journalists Committees. Freed from oppression from outside, the journalist can fall under arbitrary internal authority

representing a fictitious newsroom majority, frequently arrogant, and in no way respectful of the opinion of the minority. . . ."[8]

Gonella was also a leader of the Christian Democrats, which may explain some of his fervor; among the most bitter critics of the reform movement were several members of the DC-journalist bloc in Parliament.

There is no way of knowing precisely how widespread may have been staff infighting over political directions in content. There is no central place where such information is compiled; a real brouhaha may get to the regional offices of the National Federation, at which point it generally makes the papers, but other conflicts do not. The anecdotes that follow, therefore, are a sampling, but not a sample (in research terms). Most appeared in the public record—Italian newsmagazines, newspapers, some of the histories of the contemporary newspaper, such as Murialdi's and Pansa's. The others were picked up during interviews with Italian journalists or people who, for whatever reason, are journalist watchers in that country.

Gonella's angry outburst, quoted above, came in specific reference to the case of a headline in *Corriere della Sera* in the spring of 1975, during a political crisis in Portugal. Italians had been watching with great interest the struggle between Communists and Socialists for power in that country; in many ways the situation paralleled their own (the strength of the Italian Socialist Party at that time was greatly overestimated), with the whipsaw tensions that always go with attempts at alliance on the far left. It was also the period during which, in common talk, *Corriere* was identified as being at the apogee of its leftward swing. References to the "red *Corriere*" were common.

On May 20, 1975, the paper published a front-page story about violence in the offices of the Portugese socialist daily *Republica*. *Corriere*'s first edition headline read: "Communists Occupy the Socialist Newspaper." In the second and subsequent editions the headline read differently: "Tension in Lisbon between PC and Socialists." The "play" of the article on both the first and the jump pages was also attenuated. The story thus came off as much more neutral in tone and of much less importance.

"All this doing and undoing," according to one *Corriere* staff member, "was due to a disagreement between some people on the foreign desk and the foreign editor, Renzo Carnevali."[9] Controversy arose immediately, of course. Editor Piero Ottone, who had spent much of his time up to that point making soothing noises, found nothing remarkable about the episode when he talked to a reporter from *Panorama*. "It was based on technical considerations, not censorship, not politics; without pressure, threats, or intervention by outsiders or unions." (In several newspapers, and especially *Corriere*, the printers were more radical than the journalists, and not at all reluctant to move in on newsroom decisions; this will be discussed later.) "The episode, from this point of view, to me seems unexceptionable."

Foreign editor Carnevali nevertheless took exception. "It was real, authentic political censorship," he told the same interviewer, "carried out by desk men and not by the section editor [i.e., himself] who has the responsibility for determining that headlines are more or less balanced."[10]

The news departments of RAI, the state-operated broadcasting system, were relatively little involved in partisan controversy after the restructuring of the service. The Christian Democrats had control of Telegiornale 1; the left—with Socialists in command, but ample PCI participation—directed TG2. Both have contended that they deal in unflavored truth, of course, but in practice steadily reflect a predictable bias. The audience of each hears what it expects to hear, and, although the two services have quarreled frequently about allotment of budget and space, there have been few controversies about news coverage.

Some remarks by Jimmy Carter about Communist participation in the Italian government produced an exception. The U.S. position during the delicate jockeying to hold together a functioning Italian government in 1976 was difficult; Carter could not appear to be deserting the traditional anti-Communist posture, but at the same time had to avoid the appearance of American intervention. In an interview broadcast by TG2 during the summer of 1976 he said that he would not regard eventual Communist participation as "catastrophe." That much was broadcast. The words immediately following—"but that would not be my preference"—was not. *Corriere della Sera* spotted it and, always eager to gore the broadcasters who have taken away so much of both the potential audience and the potential advertiser revenue, raised the alarm. Angry questions on the floor of the Chamber of Deputies followed immediately.

Since Parliament directly finances most of RAI's operations, any great expression of concern in that body produces a quick response. The direction of TG2 explained that the omission had been a "technical mistake" in the taping of the original transmission from the United States. It later rebroadcast the interview in its entirety.

Even if TG2 had given a deliberate twist to the news, it was a mild and uncommon episode compared to what went on in some newspaper newsrooms. The treatment of the gang fights of the early and mid-1970s were indicative. The persons who seriously injured or sometimes killed members of the radical left were generally identified as Fascists or neo-Fascists; those who stormed and blew up Fascist headquarters or party offices were generally referred to as "students" or "unknown assailants."

Journalists Committees looked for "tendentiousness" in headlines and, particularly in the case of *Il Messaggero* and *Corriere della Sera* in the 1973–75 era, frequently found it. It almost invariably was indentified as being favorable to the right and, as in the Carnevali case, headlines were sometimes rewritten between editions. Up through the national elections of 1976, those two papers and *Il Giorno* can only be described as giving a continuing impression of loading the news against the political right and toward the left. That is a personal and impressionistic judgment, but it is shared by observers with good credentials for making judgments.

Claire Sterling has lived in Rome several decades. She is a distinguished journalist who has contributed to many important U.S. publications, including the *Washington Post,* the *International Herald-Tribune,* and the *Atlantic Monthly.* She became thoroughly disillusioned at what she saw as the irresponsible excesses of the reform movement and a blind warp to the left in news coverage.

In a piece for the *International Herald-Tribune* for May 29, 1978, she spoke bitterly of the Italian press's glorification of a terrorist named Petra Krause, soon to come to trial. After setting out various events in Krause's career—the burning of a factory in Milan, the killings of German diplomats, the engineering of a raid on a Swiss depot that produced large quantities of arms that were promptly distributed throughout Europe—Sterling concluded:

> To this day, not a single Italian daily paper, left-wing or otherwise, has told the public who Petra Krause really is. . . . How is it that even after these two nightmare months of the Moro case, not a single daily paper here has done so? Is it conceivable that Petra Krause might still find a cheering crowd waiting when she walks into that Naples courthouse next month?
>
> Behind these questions lie customs and attitudes without which Moro's murder might never have happened: a pervading reluctance to believe that murderous terrorism could come from anywhere but the fascist right; an instinctive conviction that any cop here or anywhere is bound to be a brute, victimizing any hapless creature in his clutches; a passive acceptance of sloganeering in the place of hard reporting, by people who have too long suffered from too much of one and too little of the other; and an all too-human unwillingness to think that anybody who is against the establishment could be all bad.

There are Italian journalists who would admit bias and defend it energetically, beginning with the unarguable fact that most of the press, including those same papers, had been loaded heavily to the right for decades. In the United States there used to be talk about "compensatory discrimination" in hiring until somebody came up with the euphemistic "affirmative action." The Italian journalist leaning staunchly to port as he wrote headlines might defend himself with the same phrase.

In addition to what was visible in the columns of the papers, there was, predictably, a continuing effort to keep other things out. Although there are constant references to fascism in Italian journalism—always pejorative, of course—there traditionally has been very little coverage of what are seen as neo-Fascist politics or people. The major dailies all refused to carry MSI advertising during the campaign of 1976. In most cases the policy seems to have been adopted through action of the staff, but Levi at *La Stampa* simply imposed it. "I didn't need any committees to tell me that," he said.[11]

Accounts of MSI party activities have rarely appeared in the press, nor have the names of the party's leaders, except as part of epithets. There has been constant effort to avoid any glorification of the old regime. Sometimes the suppression descends to the level of the petty and spiteful. If a conservative columnist in *Il Tempo* may be believed,[12] a low point was reached by one paper in its handling of the announcement of the death of an elderly military hero, Frederico Morozzo della Rocca. Italian dailies carry paid funeral notices, which generally consist of two or three column-inches of elaborately sentimental prose, ornamented with small black crosses and sometimes a photograph of the deceased, for which there is an extra charge. Morozzo della Rocca was past ninety years old, and the original copy for the announcement said that his last thoughts, beyond his family and his country, were of the king. The reference to the king was not permitted.

The Journalists Committee of *Corriere della Sera* not only wanted to prohibit that paper's carrying political advertising by the MSI during the electoral campaign of 1976, a prohibition which the publishers accepted, but also sought to secure a balance of advertising by limiting the amount of space sold to any one party or individual. The publishers did not accept that condition, and a *scioperino* (the Italian word for "strike" is *sciopero*) resulted. During the argument, the Journalists Committee issued a communiqué explaining their position.

> Today *Corriere della Sera* is published late, and with some departments incomplete, because the journalists convened an Assembly meeting, along with the printers, to consider a sudden change in the publisher's attitudes toward the problem of election advertising.
> In an earlier meeting the Journalists Committee, the printers'

council, and the publishers' representative—as in the last elections—agreed to the following.

The prohibition of neo-Fascist advertising is set out through the common device of restricting it to "constitutional" parties, then

> 2) to the end of preserving the image of the newspaper, the company and the union would have searched together for a means to avoid excessive imbalance in the advertising visibility among the various parties. . . .
>
> In yesterday's meeting, however, management presented plans for advertising which they were not willing to discuss with the Journalists Committee and the printers' council; plans which, in our judgment, present obvious imbalances.
>
> This attitude is even more disturbing when tied to the campaign carried out by Rizzoli to concentrate its ownership of newspapers without discussion with the trade union movement.

The communiqué concluded by reaffirming the "necessity of protecting the pluralistic and democratic image" of *Corriere* and the right of the work force to discuss with the publishers those things that involve "the image and the [political] line of the newspaper."[13]

Both the publishers and editor Ottone refused to change their positions, and there were no further difficulties over the matter. That fact, and the rather self-serving rhetorical tone of the statement, perhaps indicate that the Journalists Committee was concerned with its own image as much as with the paper's. A good many statements from such groups during this peak period of activism have the same quality.

The staff of *Annabella,* a weekly magazine, also published by Rizzoli in Milan, also quarreled in high level terms with management during the 1976 campaign. *Annabella* normally concerns itself with fashion and homemaking. But, as a statement of the Assembly pointed out, this was a different matter.

> The staff of *Annabella,* in an extraordinary Assembly on June 15, 1976, took note that in issue number 25 of the magazine, on sale during the week preceding the election, appears a surprising invitation to vote DC, in contrast to the line previously taken; and with reference to articles 6 and 34 of the national labor contract, expresses its disapproval and concerned disassociation from such content. The professional staff believe that a woman's weekly must not back any specific party because no party supports all the concerns of women, much less the DC which always is opposed to divorce, abortion, and other fundamental rights of women. The staff of *Annabella* further

deplores the editor's moving away from the explicit commitment, made two weeks ago, to objectivity in campaign news.[14]

In 1970 the Italian Parliament passed a bill legalizing divorce. Almost immediately upon losing the fight against that legislation, the Catholic church and the Christian Democrats began a drive to annul it through a national referendum, which was held in 1974. Needless to say, the issue provoked bitter and intense argument. (Along with the abortion issue, it did much to increase the growing estrangement of the middle and upper class from the DCs).

Corriere della Sera, La Stampa, and *Il Messaggero* all were prodivorce, and hence urged a no vote in the referendum. *Corriere* and *La Stampa* provided occasional coverage for spokesmen of the other side, but made their own position clear and urged it vigorously. *Il Messaggero,* then at the height of its strenuous radicalism, on election day ran a front page with the word "No" in five-and-a-half-inch letters and a streamer headline above it which read "Against the Fascist-Clerical Attempt to Suppress Democracy and the Autonomy of the State."

Il Giorno was at that point having problems unrelated, at least in any direct sense, to politics. Gaetano Afeltra, after having been generally welcomed as editor two years before, by this time had been at odds with his Journalists Committee for months; the paper's circulation and advertising were dropping, morale was miserable, and the atmosphere one of suspicion. A truce was worked out in which Afeltra and the staff agreed that *Il Giorno* would not accept political advertising on the divorce issue, and would take no editorial stand, but instead would present impartial coverage of the campaign; Afeltra described it as being limited to "official acts." Predictably, that arrangement did not suffice; within a few days the editor killed a story for tendentiousness, the Journalists Committee thought it balanced, and the paper did not publish the next day. Neither did it publish the following day, because Afeltra refused to run the communiqué issued by the Journalists Committee. For the rest of the campaign the paper picked its way through the mine field, technically neutral, but in the opinion of an observer who analyzed headlines and photographs definitely leaning toward the Christian Democratic position.[15]

Girolamo Modesti, then editor of *Il Resto del Carlino,* found himself amid controversy not because he refused to publish something on the divorce issue, but because he published everything.

Il Resto is one of Italy's oldest and best known papers, and is generally regarded as the best of the country's regional publications. It published its first issue in 1885. Like most Italian newspapers, its political history has been multicolored. Its founders were members of the *Circolo Democratico* of Bologna. It went Fascist early (1923) and without compulsion. After the war the workers who printed it were given the property. They published it for a time as a cooperative, under the title *Giornale dell'Emilia*.

From the postwar cooperative *Il Resto* moved again to industrial ownership, and since 1966 it has belonged to Attilio Monti, who also owns *La Nazione* of Florence and other publications; he is a sugar baron and committed member of the right wing of the DC. That fact has not prevented *Il Resto* from continuing to be a vital part of the life of a city sometimes called "Red Bologna." Socialists began sweeping elections there as early as 1913; during fascism and Nazi occupation there grew up a strong Communist underground organization that took charge of the city at the end of the war and has been reelected ever since.

Il Resto generally has not been much involved in controversy because its primary commitment has been to Bologna and the country around it. There is a parallel with Milan; *Il Resto* is to Bologna what *Corriere* has been to that city, and the relationship may be more intense because Bologna is smaller and more homogeneously middle class; it lacks the huge blocs of immigrants from the south that mark Milan and Turin.

Since *Il Resto* is not a newspaper whose political character makes a dominant impression, it was somewhat surprising when a quarrel between the editor and the Journalists Committee surfaced on May 1, 1974, twelve days before the divorce referendum. On page two of that issue appeared a letter signed by ninety members of the staff. It stated their support for the law permitting divorce, saying that they felt they owed the readers a public statement of their beliefs, particularly since there were strong pressures from "outside"—an obvious reference to the Vatican—trying to convert the issue from one of personal "liberty" to one of "ideology."

Published alongside was another document signed by nineteen of the staff deploring the initiative of the Journalists Committee that produced the first letter. A flurry of argumentative statements followed. Modesti, the editor of *Il Resto,* decided to publish them all, invoking his belief in "objectivity and impartiality," but adding that "we're abstaining from partisan involvement, unlike almost all Italian newspapers, which are lined up on the side of divorce under the command of the PCI" [Italian Communist party].[16]

As the campaign went on, the Journalists Committee monitored the content of the paper. On the fifth of May, a week before the vote, they released a stinging communiqué. Despite pious announcements of objectivity and impartiality, the communiqué began, there actually had been a systematic loading in favor of the Vatican-DC side.

> ... between the 21st of March and today there were published in the national news section of the paper, largely on the front page, 63 headlines on divorce, of which only 6 reflected a prodivorce position, with a good 50, to the contrary, put at the disposal of the propagandists for abrogation [of the law] (those remaining were neutral).
> ... in the last 25 days, out of 38 "letters to the editor" relating to divorce, those favorable to retaining the Baslini-Fortuna law numbered exactly 8.[17]

The report went on to list other examples, including a remarkable predilection for running photographs of Amintore Fanfani almost to the exclusion of other politicians.

In reply to that, Modesti said in the same report that the matter was purely internal and of no significance to the reader, suggested that other dailies be measured on the same scale of objectivity, and explained the frequent appearances of Fanfani's photograph were justified by his role as the "major antidivorce leader and also the major leader of the major party, the pivotal party which gave the thrust to Italian democracy and upon which it is based."

Several aspects of this encounter are worth noting carefully. The first is the fact that the exchanges all appeared in the paper itself. Publication of statements relating to union affairs issued by the Journalists Committee is required by the national contract, but quibbling about definitions is standard. Modesti did not niggle; he displayed the exchanges prominently. Since he was a tough-minded, combative conservative working for a publisher with the same characteristics, that seems to indicate acceptance, however reluctant, of the right of the staff to argue publicly with ownership.

That right has not been established in the United States, it might be observed. It is a cliché that the politics of most American working journalists are different from those of the people who employ them; there have been informal polls of the reporters covering the campaigns of both candidates in presidential years, for example, and the Democratic candidate invariably has been the journalists' favorite, although the Republican candidate has received a substantially larger number of official editorial endorsements in the modern era with a single exception.* In most cases

---

*A majority of the U.S. newspapers that made endorsements in 1964 supported Lyndon Johnson in his campaign against Barry Goldwater.

the staff simply shrugs off this disagreement. Most are still ambivalent about an active political role, and practically all accept the idea that it is the owner's paper and his right to use it, at least formally, to forward his causes.

Occasionally that premise is challenged. In March, 1971, a group of employees of the Field newspapers in Chicago, the *Daily News* and the *Sun-Times,* objected to the papers' endorsement of Richard Daley for another term as mayor of the city. A total of 174 signed petitions opposing the endorsement. They first asked for editorial space to endorse Daley's opponent and, when that was refused by the publisher, Marshall Field IV, asked for publication of a letter to the editor. That was also turned down. Field did agree to the publication of an advertisement, paid for by the journalists and originally scheduled for both publications. The editor of the *Sun-Times,* however, made it clear that journalists signing the ad would be restricted in their handling of political assignments during the campaign, and the paid statement finally ran in the *Daily News* alone.

It is worth noting that the professional employees of the Field papers, long considered towers of liberalism in the United States, had far more difficulty and less success than the journalists of *Il Resto del Carlino.* That is not to say that U.S. publishers considered liberal are secret or conspiratorial conservatives; rather, it sets out strikingly the difference between the two cultures concerning the reporter's right to be politically active in opposition to the requirement that he appear, at least, a political neuter.

In any case, it is beyond belief that any major American newspaper would publish the kind of itemized, documented attack upon its own fairness that *Il Resto* carried. It also is beyond belief that newspaper owners and editors in Italy are more devoted to freedom of expression for everybody than their U.S. counterparts. The debate carried on in the pages of *Il Resto* was testimony to the solid gains achieved by the reform movement and the rise of Journalists Committees.

At the same time it demonstrates that the way the newly acquired power works has varied widely from one publication to another. In one sense the most remarkable thing about the committee's analysis of biased journalism is the obvious fact that the editor was able to control the content of the paper despite the opposition of most of his staff. That was not true of the major national dailies; headlines that leaned the wrong direction in the judgment of the Journalists Committee on *Corriere* or *Il Giorno* or above all *Il Messaggero* were rewritten. The color of such papers essentially was established by the staff, while *Il Resto*'s remained under control of the management.

Public attacks upon editors by their own staffs were a common phenomenon of the era. Not all could be classified under the heading of political action; sometimes they represented personal antagonisms and petty gripes, but even in these cases rhetorical window dressing generally gave the complaint a tone of high principle. As in most other aspects of the reform movement, there were differences among publications.

Piero Ottone of *Corriere della Sera* and Arrigo Levi of *La Stampa*, for example, were seldom criticized in the communiqués from their Journalists Committees. Ottone as an editor was a master at staff relations, rarely putting his foot down and sometimes agreeing with staff protests or, indeed, anticipating them. On occasion, for example, he called for more democracy in the newsroom than the staff seemed to be requesting. Levi insisted upon both the authority to run the paper and on a vote of confidence from the staff before accepting the job, as we have seen, which may have been some help, but he also had a talent for what used to be called human relations. Meetings with the *La Stampa* Journalists Committee sometimes had a distinctly grumpy tone on both sides, but issues remained too trivial for public uproar. Both papers benefited from the high professional competence of almost everyone, journalists and editors alike, involved in the operations of the country's two best dailies.

Matters were quite different on other giornali d'informazione. After his original warm reception, Gaetano Afeltra and most of the staff of *Il Giorno* increasingly became estranged, and after Perrone left *Il Messaggero* his successors found themselves in constant quarrels with their associate editors (chosen, it should be remembered, by the paper's Assembly), the Journalists Committee, and the combined force of journalists and printers. Those situations produced some bitter, highly public displays.

Consider the case of Afeltra. Within three months after his installation as editor of *Il Giorno* in June, 1972, he had a strike on his hands; a month later he received a lengthy letter from the Journalists Committee that accused him of moving away from the style and spirit in which the paper had been founded: short news stories, tightly written; good headlines; no "third page"; and attractive graphic design and photography. The committee asserted that the paper was in deep trouble with its readers and that the staff "has something to say about the type of paper, its function, and its market." It closed with a suggestion that a dialogue begin while it was still possible for it to be conducted calmly.[18] Afeltra never replied.

That letter was not made public until several years later, and it had only the faintest of political overtones. The attack that appeared at the end of Afeltra's first year as editor, however, was public and highly political.

Because it reveals so much about the political involvement of some Italian journalists it deserves a careful look.

Afeltra, it should be remembered, had identified himself as a heartfelt Socialist at the time of his appointment to the job, an announcement that had much to do with his warm welcome. Now, a year later, eleven prominent members of the staff who identified themselves as Socialists, including one of the managing editors, attacked him publicly for his lack of political concern.

After pointing out a series of changes in the paper—more commentary by outside experts, less by staff members; a more neutral line in trade union matters; more "human interest" material—the document condemned him for

> the thrust, constantly and in spite of the resistance of the staff (two strikes, numerous protests, written and verbal [*sic*]) to achieve a politically uncommitted newspaper; "reinforcing," in every sense, a process of depoliticizing that has spread through the format, the makeup of news sections, and that has led to the abolition of the "Internal and Foreign Politics" page and the return of the old-fashioned "From Inside and Abroad" section that throws together Nixon and the eruption of a Central American volcano. . . .
>
> It is basically a newspaper of evasion. A newspaper always among those most aligned with "centrality." Even *Corriere* now is further to the left. At the distance of a year, we thus find ourselves with a paper often directed at those uninterested in politics[*], of little influence, withdrawn from the function for which it was created. At the same time costs have gone up and financial losses, already heavy, have increased precipitously.[19]

Six months later there was another attack, this one expressing the same concern but with highly specific reference. *Il Giorno*'s committee of consultation (the *consulta*) felt that the coverage of the squabbling then going on over ownership and editorship of *Il Messaggero* was not sufficiently serious.

In a telegram sent to the staff of *Il Messaggero* they protested that two articles that had appeared in *Il Giorno* "tended to present the case of *Il Messaggero* and *Il Secolo XIX* [Perrone's paper in Genoa] as personal joust-

---

*The word that I have tried to convey with the phrase "those uninterested in politics" is *qualunquista*. It refers to a movement that began after the First World War and has seen periodic revivals since. *L'uomo qualunque* means "the common man" and, by extension, has come to refer to those who have no interest in political and societal concerns. Not surprisingly, it has sometimes appeared on the ballot in Italian elections—candidates of the party representing those who have no interest in political parties.

ing between quarrelsome knights-errant and not as a strategic battle by journalists and printers for freedom of the press."

They disassociated themselves from such an approach, contending that the new part-owner of *Il Messaggero,* Edilio Rusconi, was clearly a reactionary and therefore against the interests of the Italian working class.

A day later the committee of consultation hit their own editor, Afeltra, again, criticizing his abilities as an administrator as well as "cuts, censorship, manipulation, etc.," which had the effect of draining the paper's "political and formative [of public opinion, presumably] capabilities. . . ."[20]

Sometimes, instead of political rhetoric, the committee's communications switched to mockery. A series of investigations by magistrates and special investigators in the spring of 1974 brought evidence that Cefis's company, Montedison, had been making secret, substantial contributions to all Italian political parties, except for the Communists. This was the scandal of the "black funds" (*fondi neri*). The story broke first in the pages of *L'Espresso,* but *Corriere, La Stampa,* and *Il Messaggero* picked it up and gave it substantial attention. *Il Giorno* handled it with caution, concentrating on the government crisis to which it was tied while making almost no mention of the secret spending by the corporation that was its proprietor. After a few days of this the Journalists Committee sent Afeltra a letter.

> Dear editor, We have been requested by the staff in Milan and Rome to present a matter we all consider important: the question of the *Unione Petrolifera* [the trade association of refiners] and the investigation by the courts. We are conscious of the extreme delicacy of this subject. Nevertheless it is a common opinion that the minimization of the news in this morning's paper risks the growth of a completely unfounded suspicion: that is, that ENI finds itself involved up to the neck in this story and might have, therefore, great interest in hiding it in its own newspaper. None of us think that the scandal must be emphasized. But we feel that the opposite attitude could be dangerous.[21]

By 1975 the conflict between the editor and his staff was open and ugly. After the regional elections of June, 1975, the Journalists Committee of *Il Giorno* set it out in bitter terms in a statement submitted to the paper's Assembly.

> *Il Giorno* can and must rebel, with all its strength, against becoming the fiefdom of the secretary of a political party, as it did during this campaign. . . . [The reference was to Fanfani]

> When it comes to political direction, we assert that *Il Giorno* is the cultural patrimony exclusively of the employees of *Il Giorno*. . . . [Afeltra] can no longer follow one road while the staff have for years followed another; without this essential clarifying premise it will never be possible to achieve a genuine collaboration between top management and the staff.[22]

Meanwhile the paper steadily declined in circulation and prestige while its losses grew almost exponentially. It had always had serious problems trying to solicit advertising against the competition of *Corriere della Sera;* even in its prime, when it had something more than half of *Corriere*'s circulation, *Il Giorno* was receiving only a tenth of the advertising. By the mid-1970s a kind of atrophy, both physical and intellectual, was visible. ENI, the conglomerate that has always owned *Il Giorno,* had been required to pour increasing millions of dollars per year into its subsidization. Most of its big names had gone elsewhere, and in the conversations that I had with a few staff members, they seemed depressed and frequently petulant. During recent visits I have found myself remembering, sadly, a conversation I had when I first began work on this project in 1970. It was with one of Italy's best social scientists, a researcher of international rank whose work touched tangentially on the Italian press. He was alive with enthusiasm for *Il Giorno*.

"It's the best newspaper in Italy," he said. "Nothing else even comes close to it."

It would hardly have been necessary to ask him what he thought by the end of the decade. There still are no detailed studies of newspaper readership in Italy, but the left-leaning intellectuals and professionals have, I suspect, moved to papers such as *La Repubblica.* The members of industrial and craft unions, originally attracted to *Il Giorno*'s Socialist orientation, for a time found, as one of the Journalists Committee's complaints said, that the once elitist *Corriere* was further to the left. Less pragmatically directed readers who were attracted to it because of its early élan, its joyous aggressiveness in trying to outdo the *Corriere* colossos, eventually found it sometimes dispirited and sometimes hysterical.

Yet ENI and Montedison kept putting in money, and Afeltra continued as editor. Furthermore, despite the furious antagonism of some of his staff, he managed to put his mark on the paper in the same way that Modesti imposed his own brand of "objectivity" on the rebellious journalists of *Il Resto del Carlino* during the divorce law campaign. During that same period, according to one interested observer, of eighteen front-page headlines in *Il Giorno* referring to party leaders, thirteen referred to Amintore Fanfani; two to Francesco De Martino, then secretary of the Socialist party; and one each to Enrico Berlinguer (PCI), Flaminio Piccoli (DC), and Pietro Nenni (PSI).[23]

After the departure of Alessandro Perrone, the activist group at *Il Messaggero* seems to have found grounds for tension with every editor, beginning with Italo Pietra. Pietra, it will be remembered, was named to the editorship by his friend Eugenio Cefis, the president of Montedison. At the time it was seen as a brilliant stroke, given the hostility of most of the *Il Messaggero* staff toward the new owners; Pietra was unmistakably a Socialist hero. De Martino, the PSI secretary, was involved in negotiating the appointment as well as quietly clearing it with Fanfani, who had decided, after the Rusconi-Barzini *opera buffa,* that the DC were going to have to live with a left-leaning *Il Messaggero*.[24]

Despite these certifications of suitability, however, tension between Pietra and the leadership of *Il Messaggero*'s staff quickly began to develop.

For one thing, Pietra was unquestionably Cefis's man, and Cefis was at that point still regarded by much of the liberal press as a prime villain, the hatchet man of a Christian Democratic attempt to gain control of the nation's press. (The fact that he was, rather, an ambitious businessman interested primarily in money, highly flexible in politics, and attentive to them chiefly when business advantage was involved, was to emerge slowly over the next few years.) Pietra defended Cefis when his newspaper attacked him.

The relationship was also complicated by Pietra's distance from the actual news operation in the paper. In this he was unlike people such as his predecessor, Perrone, and such established professionals as Ottone and Levi. Pietra was much less able to do anything about content and usually was reduced to jawboning after the fact. There was much jawboning at *Il Messaggero*.

Meanwhile the leadership of the Christian Democrats was making clear to Cefis and Montedison that they were losing their tempers; in early 1975, with regional elections approaching, DC attacks upon several newspapers grew furious, with *Il Messaggero* first among the targets. (The newsmagazine *L'Espresso* drew the most dazzling epithet, however; to express its annoyance, the DC's official *Il Popolo* coined the word *radicalautomobilisticodivorzista.*)

When Pietra attempted to take direct action to soften his paper's more strident attacks upon the government, the associate editors and Journalists Committee reacted with asperity.

"In this farce," Giampaolo Pansa pointed out, "Pietra was increasingly weaker and increasingly alone."[25]

On June 10, 1975, Pietra was censured by a majority of *Il Messaggero*'s Assembly for having vetoed a feature about Amintore Fanfani, then leader of the Christian Democrats. Shortly thereafter he was informed by Cefis that he had to leave the editorship; on June 18 he formally resigned.

The Assembly promptly produced a document which, under the headline "Attack on *Messaggero*—Italo Pietra Forced to Resign," made it clear that they considered that "his dismissal constitutes an attack on the anticlerical, democratic, and anti-Fascist line which is the patrimony of the newspaper" and declared a "state of agitation." The paper also carried support for that position from De Martino and Berlinguer. The staff leadership furthermore demanded explanation of the firing, but received nothing from Montedison other than a vague observation that Pietra was too old.

Politics was only one ingredient in the turbid relationships between management and staff at *Il Giorno* and *Il Messaggero*. There are some other factors that might be considered demonstrations of concern about the profession of journalist and the professionalism of individuals, and still others that are traditional labor contract matters.

Even these are generally intertwined; the journalists union pressed steadily from the late 1960s, in its negotiations with publishers, for incorporation of what it saw as the principles or conditions of good journalism into specific contract terms. This converts disagreements over, say, what constitutes fair coverage of a news story to a matter of observing the contract, very much as if there had been an infraction of the hours-per-week provisions.

Another *Corriere* case provides an example. There was an echo of the Carnevali affair in it; Ottone, his sweet reasonableness apparently depleted, was to talk a good deal like his resigned foreign editor before it was over.

On November 12, 1976, *Corriere* published an article on a meeting in Arese of delegates from Alfa Romeo employee locals. The headline indicated friction between the rank and file and the leadership, and the body of the story indicated that there had been disagreement about the wage raise requested in the new contract. Both *Corriere*'s Journalists Committee and the printers' roughly parallel *consiglio di fabbrica* ("shop council") protested on the grounds of lack of "completeness of information," which contributed to the image of a weak and divided union. The final resolution adopted by the auto workers' assembly had been passed almost unanimously. That information was not included, probably because the conclusion of the meeting had been closed to the press. Ottone was in Rome; reached by telephone, he immediately agreed to the original reporter's writing a follow-up story and to the publication of the text of the resolution finally passed by the Alfa Romeo workers. That was not enough for the two committees, which instead prepared an article of their own, including bitter criticism of the original. Ottone flatly refused to publish it, even after some modification.

"We make such criticisms in private, not in public," Ottone said. "There's a risk of the Journalists Committee becoming a court. . . . publishing that act of censure would confirm the existence inside the paper of a body parallel to the management which would evaluate the work of the journalist."

The standoff led to a strike that kept the paper off the stands for a day. When it reappeared the next day, the second page carried statements in explanation of the strike from both the management and the Journalists Committee.[26]

The zesty spirit of the "democratic newsroom" was in decline by the autumn of 1976, as was the support for it within the profession. The reaction to the committee's heavy hand at *Corriere* showed that more support—or tolerance—had been swept away. *La Repubblica* called it an attempt upon freedom of the press; *Avanti!*, still angry, compared it to *Corriere*'s handling of the earlier story on Communist occupation of the Socialist daily in Lisbon. The furor among what many of *Corriere*'s staff normally considered their ideological allies obviously hurt, and there were some clumsy attempts at further explanation that were close to apologetic.

In another case, interesting but little noticed, the staff of a party newspaper forced the resignation of an editor on the grounds of his professional inadequacy. For reasons that have already been pointed out, Journalists Committees on party newspapers are very tractable on matters other than contract provisions for wages, hours, and assignments. The statute requires that each paper has a committee, but frequently they have little function.

In 1977, for example, I asked a member of the staff of *L'Unità* about that organ's committee. He assured me that there was one, but with some embarrassment admitted that he could not identify the members. He volunteered to write a note of introduction for me, however, to someone who could tell me all about it. A copy was sent around to our hotel; I then called the offices of the paper to set a date to present it and conduct an interview. I never managed to get one set; it eventually appeared that the addressee was out of town more or less indefinitely. This did not necessarily reflect any embarrassment about the state of the Journalists Committee, of course; perhaps the man simply thought talking to professors, or Americans, a waste of time. In any case, I have never come across any evidence of rebellion on the part of any staff group on the Communist daily.

The Journalists Committee of *Il Lavoro* was not so passive. *Il Lavoro* is a Socialist daily, founded in Genoa in 1903. It was, inevitably, seized by the government of former Socialist Benito Mussolini in 1940, turned over to a Fascist labor organization, then reestablished after the war as the property of the Genoa division of the PSI. Neither its circulation nor its influence have ever been large, but it has survived.

In 1976 its editor, formally designated as its *direttore politico,* was a Socialist politician named Paolo Vittorelli. Its associate editor and the paper's responsabile was Giovanni Fenu. The division of authority between the two was not clear, nor was decision making within the paper a predictable process.

The Journalists Committee formally requested De Martino, national secretary of the Socialist party, to "move to the naming of a single direttore responsabile, without political commitments and clearly with a journalistic background."[27] It was not necessary for them to push; Vittorelli almost immediately resigned, admitting a certain amount of bitterness but citing his heavy, and increasing, obligations to the PSI at both the national and local level. Fenu, the actual responsabile, also resigned; he had been something of a figurehead, picked for the spot because he was a professional member of the Order. The division of authority between him and Vittorelli obviously had never been clear. Shortly afterward a single responsabile was appointed, eliminating the post of political director.

The significance of the episode lay in the fact that the staff of a party-owned paper (although it classifies itself as a giornale d'informazione) felt a greater loyalty to the efficient functioning of the process of getting out the paper than to political rhetoric. That could not always be said of the staffs of the national dailies.

A larger number of conflicts have grown out of the mix of professional and contract considerations that deal with the professional rights of the individual journalists. Since the mid-1970s allegations of violation of those rights have been common. They generally grow out of the editorial judgment to cut a news story without the writer's permission or in some fashion other than the one the writer authorized.

The tradition in the English-language press, it was pointed out earlier, is all to the contrary. Almost everyone who writes for money in the United States or the United Kingdom, save for certain media stars, assumes an editorial right to chop and even rearrange, although sometimes there are complaints from reporters about their by-lines being left on stories so completely altered that they no longer say what the reporter intended at all.

The no-cutting tradition in Italy, like most journalistic conventions in any country, probably derives to some extent from mechanical considerations. The narrative style was traditional for many years in Italian newswriting. Even major breaking news stories frequently began with setting the scene, then proceeded to introduce characters who perhaps were not even identified as a means of building suspense, but whose actions reached a denouement, after which a quick paragraph of exposition finished the piece. After a thousand purple words, the reader finally discovered that the man shot dead on the station platform was the town's leading banker, and that the lady with the pearl-handled revolver was his mistress.

It is practically impossible to cut such an account in half without losing meaning. Ease in cutting, on the other hand, was one of the primary considerations in the development of American news style; everything important is in the first paragraph; the later ones contain detail and elaboration. Cutting thus can begin at any point after the first paragraph, and those making up the page can do it when faced with the problem of too much material.

Since the end of the Second World War, the narrative tradition has been diminishing in Italian newspapers. Front pages have moved closer to the wire service mode, and both the selection and presentation of local news increasingly has taken the "hard," succinct style. There has been sharp editing and cutting on the local news pages of *La Stampa,* of Turin, for several years, for example.

Both the national labor contract and the specific in-house agreements are designed to protect or extend the virtues of an Italian journalism whose style is aging. The intersecting trends probably mean that there will be even more quarrelsome little cases in the immediate future growing out of the processing of news copy.

It also seems inevitable that controversies and negotiations over more conventional aspects of the contract will increase. In some offices a special staff committee is in charge of monitoring compliance, but in most the Journalists Committee also has that responsibility. By the late 1970s the majority of committees chose to spend most of their time in monitoring compliance, rather than in partisan political activity, for reasons we shall examine in the next chapter.

In addition to representing the interests of individual employees, Journalists Committees generally lead the way in expanding and consolidating the position of the union. There is a traditional union commitment to increase the number of job holders, of course, and to the improving of working conditions. The following is typical: in March of 1976, the Journalists Committee of *Giornaleradio 1* (GR1) fired off an angry letter to RAI's president and director-general

> to denounce publicly the organization's negligence and to call the staff to take action if immediate, adequate steps are not taken.
>
> . . . The Journalists Committee of GR1 contests the total failure of the enterprise to provide the indispensable, minimum number of journalists. At this time there are no fewer than twenty staff members who work the entire day for four days a week, well beyond the contractual commitment. Added to the lack of supplies and some kinds of equipment this becomes a serious discrimination against GR1. . . . It is an insupportable situation which, within 48 hours, will make it impossible to put broadcasts on the air.[28]

The classic tendency illustrated by the statement simply collides head-on with the necessary major changes in technology, particularly in the case of the newspaper business. Publishers who are interested in the possibility of profit will seek ways to make operations cheaper: to go, for example, to cold type composition instead of the traditional linecasting machines, to offset presses that use less space and smaller crews, and to reducing editorial staff. It seems probable, in any case, that as political controversy cools in the Italian media, labor-management uproar will increase.

Chapter 8

"The Return to Prudence"

The quotation marks around the title of this chapter are there because the phrase was originally used by Giampaolo Pansa to describe the changes that began to move through Italian journalism in late 1975.[1] Pansa had a long professional career on *La Stampa, Il Giorno,* and *Corriere;* his has been an authoritative voice. Little expertise was required to make the same assessment of that period, however. The changes were visible to anyone who carefully read Italian newspapers.

The most striking change was between the springtime of 1975 and early June of 1976, culminating in a critical national election. The newspapers in particular, it seemed to me, had a curious quality of restraint about them; the violent rhetoric I remembered from other elections seemed largely absent. It is always difficult to know how much of one's own vision is imposed on whatever the reality might be in such situations, of course, but a sense of great caution, of a concern about national fragility, seemed pervasive. I asked again of all my journalistic acquaintances the stock question I'd been asking for years: "What are the Journalists Committees up to?" Now that question usually provoked the reply "Nothing," accompanied by a look that signified "now that I come to think of it."

Almost all Italian elections have been called critical by someone or, at least retrospectively, a watershed. The voting of 1976 was the first national political expression of a new, grimmer Italy, following a year when, for the first time since the Second World War, the annual gross national product declined; it was the first election in which there was a background of urban terror for the display of what had usually been gaudy factionalism. Many Italians were holding their breath; it may have been the first election since the Second World War in which there was no spirit of carnival, of zest for one of the country's favorite sports. Even the posters were drab and functional; in the past, Italian walls during a campaign invariably had provided a remarkable show of great graphics and Latin wit.

It was the beginning of an improbable government by consensus, sparked, in part, by the universal sense of concern; it also marked the end of much role playing. For that reason the fact that the period also marked the end, for most purposes, of the passion for reform in journalism may not be entirely coincidental.

To say that the reform movement had lost its drive by June, 1976, is not to say that it had left no legacy. There was a pronounced antigovernment tone in some of the country's largest general newspapers.

This had not been the case for more than twenty-five years. During that period the Communist daily *L'Unità* had the country's third highest circulation, behind *Corriere* and *La Stampa,* while the Christian Democrats' *Il Popolo* was a skimpy throwaway sheet. The contrast between the two sometimes led to speculation as to why the DC did not put more talent and money into producing something more competitive. The explanation was conveyed in a wry remark, common among Italian journalists, to the effect that the Christian Democrats did not need a newspaper to speak for them; the national dailies were their mouthpieces.

By the time of the campaign of 1976 that explanation no longer served. The most important newspapers that unequivocally spoke for the DC were *La Nazione* of Florence, Montanelli's *Il Giornale Nuovo,* and *Il Tempo* of Rome, all essentially regional newspapers. *Il Messaggero* and *Corriere della Sera* were somewhat more radical than De Martino socialism; most of all they were antigovernment and anti-DC. *La Stampa,* while not entirely hostile to the nation's political establishment, was hardly recognizable as the voice of FIAT. Its move to the left, together with a general upgrading under the editorship of Arrigo Levi, had been just far enough to leave it somewhere in the middle. *Il Messaggero*'s streamer headline the morning voting began read "A Vote to Change"; the page one editorial was headed "We Must Save the Country." *La Stampa*'s streamer read "Forty Million Citizens Vote; the Whole World Watches Italy." The editorial was headed "The Ways of Democracy"; its substance was that some changes were to be hoped for, but that in any case the country would muddle through.

That was as close to a progovernment stance as could be found in any of the big four during the campaign. Generally, coverage of government was characterized by continuing emphasis upon various aspects of the Lockheed bribe scandal, although it could be argued that this was simply a part of the regular flow of the news. The story centered on the activities of a parliamentary commission that could, in effect, bring in indictments; it adjourned on June 16, four days before the election, and on an eleven to nine vote decided to order no arrests; most papers made much of the narrowness of the vote and the curious minority coalition of Communists, Socialists, and MSI far-rightists.

Speculative stories about the possible involvement of such DC leaders as Rumor and Leone continued, however; so did accounts of a strike of bank employees and one scheduled by farm workers for the period immediately after the election. Stories concerning the gloomy fears of DC leaders about the results of the election were common; *Corriere della Sera* carried one headlined "DC is Pessimistic About Postelection" shortly before the voting.

The amount of attention given to the Socialists seemed disproportionately large, considering both that party's recent history and its appeal to the public as measured by the election results. Several factors may contribute to the explanation. The center-left coalition had recently governed the country, and its revival seemed to many the only hope for a stable postelection government, even though the PSI during the campaign renounced the idea in favor of a broadly based "emergency" government.

Nevertheless the tendency to cover the last few days of the campaign in terms of a "big three" among parties seems to have reflected more than a little the political commitments of the journalists of the leading general newspapers. *Il Messaggero* was openly pro-PSI, and the direction of *Corriere* was also strongly leftward; only *La Stampa* conveyed a general impression of a neutral line.

On the eve of the voting, for example, *Il Messaggero* devoted all of page three to three interviews: Andreotti of the DC, Mancini of the PSI, and Pajetta of the PCI. No other parties received serious attention. *Corriere* ran comprehensive interviews with Berlinguer of the PCI, De Martino of the PSI, and Zaccagnini of the DC; its final front-page editorial made no specific endorsements, but castigated the Christian Democrats and spoke highly of both the Socialists and the Communists. *Il Giorno* ran a profile on De Martino the same day as its formal interview with Zaccagnini, and the Socialist received the larger play.

The feeling that Italy was involved in one of the most critical periods of its modern history was widespread even before the campaign began on May 10. For two years there had been outbreaks of violence between the fringes at either end of the political fabric, including street killings, political assassinations, and bombings. The general assumption was that the campaign would be violent, and there was an inarticulate but very real sense of the precipice.

The newspapers handled this issue cautiously, seldom referring to the possibility of severe disturbances, but with steady emphasis upon the seriousness of what was going on. When June 20 arrived there was a good deal of relieved congratulation in the press. *Il Giorno* proudly quoted Minister of the Interior Cossiga in his praise of the police: "You have performed a service not to this or that political sector, but to the whole country." *La Stampa* spoke in headlines of the completion "without incident" of a "tense" campaign. Each of the major papers made repeated references to the number of foreign journalists in Italy for the balloting, by far the largest group ever; *La Stampa* said "the whole world watches Italy," and *Corriere*'s Washington correspondent wrote in detail about the way the *New York Times, Wall Street Journal,* and *Washington Post* were covering "changing Italy." *La Nazione* of Florence spoke of the most important election in years, and spoke with pride of the lack of an atmosphere of fear.

There was little coverage of the *Movimento Sociale Italiano–Destra Nazionale* (its official name since a merger with the Monarchist party in 1972), and none that could be considered favorable. The vigilance of Journalists Committees toward what they considered tendentiousness in favor of the right became particularly acute.

Generally, the committees assumed a role that was more linear than strategic during the campaign. There was no need for elaborate consideration of broad objectives in the offices of the big dailies; these had been hammered out in the negotiations for the in-house contract and in the daily production of the paper. The only decisions to be made were short range.

One particularly striking illustration of the role of a Journalists Committee was, not surprisingly, at *Il Messaggero*. The Socialist party bought a full-page advertisement that included a list of people whom they considered the most dangerous figures in Italy. One of the men named was Eugenio Cefis, who at that point headed the company that owned *Il Messaggero*. The editor wanted the name of Cefis omitted; the Journalists Committee refused, and made their decision stick.

In 1976 there was, for the first time, considerable use of polling and pollster projections by the media in Italy. Both newspapers and magazines commissioned their own polls, generally from DOXA, an affiliate of the Gallup organization, or a competitor called *Demoskopea*. These tended to indicate major losses by the DC, major gains by the PCI, and relatively small changes in the minor parties. Because of the long voting period (all day Sunday and until noon on Monday) and the complexity of the ballot (Romans in the election of 1976, for example, voted for four different sets of officials, each on a separate ballot), results have traditionally come in very slowly. Each of RAI's news services also hired a pollster—TG1 had DOXA, TG2 Demoskopea—and each was making projections of the final results by early Monday evening. The major dailies also carried stories based on projections with their first editions late Monday night.

All of these erred, but modestly. Since both the regional elections of 1975 and the prevote polls had indicated heavy losses for the DC, during the first hours there was a tendency to overestimate the extent of the DC recovery and to underestimate the gains of the PCI. The party papers gave it their own emphasis; *Il Popolo* screamed "Victory to the DC!" and appended some highly misleading figures; even *L'Unità,* while hailing in a torrent of red ink the "impetuous advance" of the PCI, recognized in the second line of the streamer the recovery of the Christian Democrats.

In fact, the Christian Democrats lost 4 seats in the Chamber of Deputies and finished with 262 seats (38.8 percent of the vote). The Communists won an additional 49 seats and finished with 228 seats (34.4 percent). Despite all the media attention laid on them, the Socialists lost 4 seats in the Chamber and had a bit less than 10 percent of the vote. The Social Democrats (PSDI) had 3.4 percent. The rightist MSI had only 6.1 percent; they lost 21 of their 56 seats. The Republicans received 3 percent; the comparable Liberals less than 2 percent. Both lost seats. None of the leftist splinter parties received as much as 2 percent.[2]

There were only two real political parties left in Italy. "The Most Difficult Parliament of the Republic," *Corriere della Sera* said in a headline.

Since the end of the Second World War, Italian politics has essentially been a matter of an antiestablishment, secular left led by intellectuals and philosophical revolutionaries of the classic European pattern set against a right that represents the heirarchical structure of the society and that is led by an elite with money, status, and the power that grows out of that combination. In this alignment during the past thirty years there was no real center; the center, as represented by the Christian Democrats, in the minds of many has been essentially rightist. For many reasons, including tradition and a love of politics for its own sake, a variety of political parties, the differences among which are often subtle, has stayed alive at the superficial level in Italy. As institutions, the media of mass communication have reinforced this fractionation; political parties have spent heavily to keep official newspapers alive, and the Italian journalist, proud of his or her identity as a political creature, has reinforced the variety through elaborate attention to the arcane dynamics of both intra- and inter-party relations. This has resulted in a political journalism outside the understanding of most of the voters. The most pervasive of all the media, radio and television, in the past have been so shorn of obvious political involvement that they seemed not involved in party politics at all.

A confluence of several trends made the election of 1976 different. Continued economic crisis and civil unrest helped create an atmosphere of deep concern for the country's future; the media, and especially newspapers and magazines, reinforced it. Court decisions produced first some reforms in the state-controlled broadcasting system and then limited its monopoly to national broadcasts and permitted the rapid and completely unregulated growth of local broadcasting.

All this did much to dilute the elitism of Italian party politics. Politicians, suddenly aware of addressing huge numbers of people, with hundreds of thousands of them possible converts, began to turn their attention to projecting a favorable personal image on behalf of their parties and offending no one. (Only sure losers are ever willing to be really offensive in the media.)

The total effect of all these factors was to produce an election resembling, much more than in the Italian past, the familiar pattern of politics in countries such as the United States, Germany, the United Kingdom, and Japan. It may also have helped set afoot the process of some depoliticization of the Italian press.

By the spring of 1977, something like a retrograde movement from the far edges of the reform movement in journalism was visible. This was especially true in *Corriere*. The paper had undergone numerous changes in addition to its political line during the period of activist leadership. The inside political talk of the pastone romano was cut sharply, sometimes broken into several short pieces, and generally consigned to the second page. Headlines became aggressive, highly politicized, and frequently slanted with a heavy hand. There was more emphasis on crime news, less on the traditional stories of international and governmental affairs.

To pick an issue literally at random, the front page of *Corriere* for March 11, 1973, featured a flashy six-column display of a crime story. In the city of Vicenza, near Milan, three bandits had held up a jewelry store and escaped, taking two salesgirls as hostages; pursued by the police at high speed, they had run off the road, and all were killed. A slightly out of focus photograph occupied almost a fourth of the page.

It was the kind of story the old *Corriere* would have carried, and probably on the first page, but beneath the fold in more or less summary form.

That kind of treatment was instead given to a story that once would have led the paper; March 11, 1973, was also the date of important French national elections. There was a two-column picture of a puffy, dying Pompidou and a brief underline with the intelligence that the story was on page twenty-eight. The *fondo* (the day's editorial) was in the usual position in columns one and two; it was headed "Government Parasites." The Milanese news section contained, on two pages, sixteen news items, six of which were about crime or criminals; these occupied about three-fourths of the total space. All in all, it was a paper far removed from that edited by Professor Spadolini.

By the spring of 1977 the swing back toward the traditional was unmistakable, both in content and in style. A friend in Milan who is an old journalist diagrammed it for me with his hands on top of his desk.

"Let's say Spadolini's *Corriere* was here," he said, establishing an imaginary center line with the edge of his right hand. "Ottone's *Corriere* moved to here—and then here—" his left hand kept moving away, toward the edge "—and here, let's say."

Shaking his head in wonder, he began to pull the extended hand back. "And he brought it here—and then here—and now it's just about here." He indicated a position a modest two inches left of the center point.

Some newsmen had a cynical explanation of what Ottone had been up to during that swing, as we shall see, but in any case it happened. *Corriere* being what it is to Italian journalism, it was a striking sign that the spirit of reform had cooled.

There were other signs of change that seemed to be part of an alteration of spirit. Some were indirect, but easy enough to read. Indro Montanelli's *Il Giornale Nuovo*, for example, was riding a circulation growth unseen since the end of the Second World War. The paper's circulation had been around 150,000 in the fall of 1974. In June of 1976, shortly after the elections, it reached, according to Montanelli, over 400,000. (It is probably prudent to restate the caveat from earlier pages about Italian circulation claims.)

Part of the increase was attributable to an insightful move designed to capitalize upon the episcopal dullness of RAI-TV's news broadcasts. Montanelli made an arrangement with Telemalta, a company with a transmitter on the island of Malta that puts a strong signal into northern Italy, through which he paid for the privilege of providing the evening news program as a special service of *Il Giornale Nuovo*. Montanelli himself was the newscaster several nights a week. The tie-in was credited with raising the paper's circulation somewhere around 25 percent.[3]

Relatively few of these readers seem to have been lured away from *Corriere della Sera*. Montanelli had hoped, and Ottone had feared, that the new paper's chief audience would consist of disaffected *Corriere* readers; what Montanelli seems to have done instead was to draw from throughout the northern half of the country a literate, affluent group that had been waiting for something like his paper for a long time. After the shattering earthquakes in Friuli in the spring of 1976 most of the country's major newspapers launched drives to raise aid money. In a few weeks *Il Giornale Nuovo* raised about $3.5 million, far more than any other paper.

This kind of loyalty led some observers to announce that Montanelli was building a new, rightist political party. There was little evidence of that. During the 1976 election Montanelli advised readers to "hold your nose and vote Christian Democrat." A couple of staff members ran for Parliament, but as members of regular parties: one as an "independent" Liberal, the other on an anticlerical Liberal–Republican–Social Democrat ticket. Montanelli also suggested to the voters the names of forty candidates from varying constituencies, giving them a remarkably backhanded endorsement.

> We know none of these men, but you're invited to choose them because we know enough about the old ones. But it's not enough to help in the campaign. We must lend a hand to change what's inside the parties, and this we can do only by signing up and becoming militants. All of us feel an irrepressible repugnance toward those bordellos which are the political parties. But if we want to change them, we have to go inside.[4]

Of the forty candidates that Montanelli endorsed—if it could be called endorsement—thirty-seven were elected.

Il Giornale Nuovo was a conservative newspaper, of course. But if its success* had some influence in changing the atmosphere of Italian journalism, that influence lay in something in addition to the obvious chastening effect on militant liberals of a conservative newspaper becoming the hottest sheet around. For a long time there has been worried talk among Italian journalists about the widening gulf between their work and the reader for whom it at least *should* have been intended. The topic was debated earnestly in meeting after meeting, and editors such as Perrone showed frequent concern about it.

Il Giornale Nuovo has been a paper to which people did listen, to which they obviously felt a personal tie. It also was a very old-fashioned paper. Its typography and layout were staid, its writing clean and frequently marked with a touch of the literary (Montanelli regularly railed against the decline of standards in journalistic writing), its personality that of the single man who completely dominated its staff. Whether one liked him or not, he unmistakably had style, wit, and high professional competence. The paper did not scream at its readers, did not threaten them; instead it spoke with the dry, artful cynicism that is the essence of Italian style. To many it made the lunging about of *Il Messaggero* and an earlier *Corriere* seem the work of impassioned bumpkins.

Toward the end of 1976 there was an episode that demonstrated the

---

*Success, that is, in terms of circulation and apparent political influence. Financially, it was from the beginning a disaster; at the peak of its success in late 1976 it was issuing appeals to its readers for additional support to avoid going under.

failing powers of the "democratic newsroom," or at least that a newspaper's staff, however well organized and committed, could be easily bypassed. The newspaper involved was *Il Mattino* of Naples.

One of the many elements of a highly developed society that the Italian south has always lacked is a first-rate regional newspaper. The most likely modern candidate was *Il Mattino* of Naples. It had been a strong paper in the early part of the century; after the Second World War, however, its course moved steadily downhill. It belonged to Achille Lauro, head of the Monarchist party, and the country around Naples was always the center of Monarchist sentiment in modern Italy; it was a freestanding kingdom, of course, for many years before the country's unification. The ownership moved from Lauro to a partnership of which the important members were the Bank of Naples and the Christian Democratic party, and by the 1970s the paper was no more than a poorly produced voice of a conservative segment of the DC.

In 1976 Angelo Rizzoli set out to acquire *Il Mattino,* leading the newsmagazine *Panorama,* which has a passion for coy headlines, to entitle its story *"L'Angelo del Mattino"* (*mattino* means "morning"). More importantly, the move sent some of the paper's staff and its Journalists Committee into action. Rizzoli's eventual acquisition of 51 percent of the paper's stock gave him control, presumably; 40 percent remained in the hands of the Christian Democratic party. The editor at the time was Orazio Mazzoni. Rizzoli, and apparently most of the staff, wanted a change. Since Rizzoli wanted in particular to change the paper's stolid total commitment to the DC, he proposed as the new editor one of the managing editors of *Corriere,* Michele Tito, a competent and well-known professional with inclinations toward the left.

That much was public knowledge. What happened afterward was a matter of rumor. The most common story was that the DCs had flatly vetoed Tito and instead offered Rizzoli a choice from a slate of four they could approve. Rizzoli found only one of these acceptable, and he was unavailable. The old regime was thus returned and Mazzoni reappointed.

The paper's employees rebelled. Almost unanimously a joint assembly of journalists and printers rejected the description of the political line set out by the owners, and the journalists, again almost unanimously, refused to confirm Mazzoni. The gesture was pure theater, however; the new management had closed down the paper three weeks before and fired the entire work force. It was announced that the structure of the paper was to be changed.

Giampaolo Pansa, in his account of the affair, summarized what finally happened with a quote. "Naples," said one of the printers, "always gives in to hunger."

All of the employees were eventually rehired. Mazzoni was still editor, and, whatever his competence, a candid one. He had said earlier that Rizzoli would have to be "crazy" to rename him to the post. He later praised Rizzoli for his "courage" in doing so and added: "I am a person outside the current trend, and I therefore pose many difficulties."

His first fondo when the paper resumed publication was headed "As We Were Saying. . .".

An assistant managing editor said of the whole thing, "It's a shameful blot on Italian journalism."[5]

What had happened to the power that the working journalists of the best papers in Italy were once able to wield in the interest of what they considered more honest and credible journalism?

Answers to that question, as the next few pages will illustrate, are as unsatisfying as they are numerous.

We can begin with the most cynical view, a distinctly minority one, but held by some persuasive people. It holds that there never was a reform movement except in the rhetoric of some journalists; that the things that went on in *Corriere* and *Il Messaggero,* in particular, were plots of owners who wanted to sell and who capitalized upon the natural proclivities of staff members for noisy rhetoric to raise the circulation of their papers and thus their price. Once the properties were sold, the analysis continues, the new owners started the process of bringing the papers back into line; the papers have ended back in the same groove from which they started.

The first putative illustration to come to mind, of course, is *Corriere della Sera,* which has indeed gone through such a cycle. That makes Piero Ottone a prize manipulator.

When I commented to that effect to an Italian journalist who believed that the reform movement never happened, he nodded in agreement. "And Fiengo, of course, worked with him," he said. "All the way. It was all carefully planned."

Raffaele Fiengo was the most conspicuous member of the *Corriere* Journalists Committee during the period of peak staff militance. He was generally regarded as a major operative in the changes in that paper. The theory that he was a tool of management was, to say the least, extraordinary.

The most significant thing about the statement, however, was the offhand way in which my journalist acquaintance delivered it. He did not note my surprise and convey by overtone (Italians are better at overtones than any people alive) that I was a naive foreigner; nor did he in any way convey a claim that he had thought very much about the matter. He seemed to be saying, rather, something like "What other explanation could there be?" If there was any conviction at all in his attitude, it was that the *prima facie* explanation could not be correct.

There are compelling explanations why an Italian of his education (superb) and experience (major newspapers and magazines, RAI-TV) thinks—perhaps cannot avoid thinking—that way. I am convinced that he is incorrect, however. I do not know what might have been in the minds of the Perrones and the Crespis, but I do know what was in the minds of some of the journalists who played activist roles. Even if it was a piece of theater, the important thing is that they did not perceive it as such. Some of them thought they were, in their own way, revolutionaries who were to remake the character of Italian journalism. They took themselves seriously.

And what they did was taken seriously by such journalist-historians as Murialdi, Pansa, Del Boca, and Borio, and academicians such as Castronovo, Barile, Cheli, and Bechelloni.[6] Certainly, the leadership of the Christian Democrats, as well as naive industrial giants such as Eugenio Cefis, took the reform movement seriously; so did much (probably most) of the Order of Journalists, including Luigi Barzini, Jr., and Indro Montanelli; so did the careful watchers of the Italian press among American journalists long resident in that country. These, and others, who were opponents or at least severe critics of the manifestations of "reporter power" in the 1970s were either remarkably well-orchestrated actors or themselves equally deceived.

If the reform movement was a game, then what Pansa called "the return to prudence" is easily explained; the people in charge simply turned the game off. If the movement was, instead, a modest revolution that accomplished some objectives, failed others, and in any case lost its fire by the end of the 1970s, the explanations are complicated.

Paolo Murialdi, the journalist-historian who became president of the National Federation of the Italian Press about the time of the reform movement's beginning,* thinks the central factor was a developing economic threat. Murialdi had a unique involvement with the reform period. In addition to his work as a journalist and trade union official he published a highly detailed history, *La stampa italiana del dopoguerra 1943–1972*. That book thus covers the early years of the movement. In 1975 he wrote, with Nicola Tranfaglia, what amounted to an update as a chapter in Castronovo and Tranfaglia's *La Stampa italiana del neocapitalismo*. In 1976 Murialdi, along with a few others, established a serious new quarterly called *Problemi dell'informazione*. He also became its

---
*He left that office in 1981.

editor and a major contributor. It might be roughly described as the voice of the intellectuals among the reformists. In addition to these things, of course, he was at the head of his union while it steadily built what has to be the best contract in the profession in the world.

Murialdi summed up his analysis thus:

> The revelation that the gains won by journalists were fragile because of the economic situation generally and particularly within the field, with some publishers who no longer appeared disposed to sustain at whatever cost the losses of certain newspapers, diffused a certain fear of losing the contractual position already won and running the risk of reducing the number of jobs, something that already has happened in a small way. . . .
>
> Given this fear, it happens—and there is a risk that the phenomenon will grow and consolidate—that professional journalists may tend to return to their corporate shell [and] the Journalists Committees turn to housekeeping chores, neglecting the broad objectives of the group.[7]

Journalists had every reason to become concerned about their jobs. As the 1970s rolled on, the deficits of all the major papers escalated at fearsome rates. The figures mentioned earlier are worth repeating. In 1975, *Corriere* lost $2,250,000; in 1976, it lost $3 million. *Corriere dell'Informazione,* the afternoon edition, was a much heavier loser; all told, the *Corriere* group, including magazines and specialized publications, lost $14 million in 1975; in 1976, the figure was $16,260,000.

The corporate organization that publishes *La Stampa* and two other publications broke even, according to its own statements, in 1972. In 1973 it lost $1.4 million; in 1974, $4,260,000; in 1975, $6,670,000. Losses in 1976 were technically somewhat lower, but only because of the "sale" of the printing facilities (incorporated separately but totally owned) to the principal owner, the FIAT company. The big loser in this group was, again, the evening paper, *Stampa Sera. La Stampa* proper lost a relatively modest $61,000, and was probably the only major paper in the country close to breaking even.

Sickest of all was *Il Giorno;* a loss of $7,850,000 was run up in 1974. In 1975, it was $10.5 million; in 1976, $11.8 million.

Two new publications that were generally considered successes, particularly in editorial prestige, got off and running—downhill. Montanelli's *Il Giornale Nuovo* lost only $31,750 in 1975, its first year. (It should be remembered that Montanelli had substantial advertising guarantees.) In 1976 it lost $63,500. The figure was misleading, however; as noted earlier, the paper made a plea to its readers for financial help, and the $1,130,000 that came in was classified under "miscellaneous receipts" and subtracted from losses.

Finally, Eugenio Scalfari's *La Repubblica* lost almost $3 million during 1976, its first year of operation.

The story is the same for the rest of the major papers; the figures differ, the trend is the same.[8]

The sense of the English word *prudence* is "the ability to discern the most suitable, politic, or profitable course of action"[9]; the Italian *prudenza* conveys almost precisely the same thing: *capacità di ben giudicare e di scegliere il meglio in ogni circostanza.*[10] This seems to be what Italian journalists, not through official action as an organized group, but simply as an inevitable consensus, chose to utilize in an increasingly crisis-ridden Italy as the 1970s began to wind down. Too many good things were at stake, and even the most committed hater of corporate capitalism could see that the money men were in trouble. There was little inclination, under the circumstances, toward martyrdom.

Several other factors were also involved. There were marked changes in the way the news media in Italy operated over the period, most of them directly related to activity within the profession and most with an eventual decompressing effect.

For example, FNSI succeeded in negotiating into the recurrent national contracts an increasing number of objectives enunciated by the reform minded toward the end of the 1960s. The position of Journalists Committees and Assemblies was carefully defined, established, and protected by law. Additional protection was set up, at least so far as contracts can do such things, for the professional "pride and dignity" of the individual. In the establishments where activism was strong there were in-house contracts that refined and extended the national contract in such matters as the journalists' control over their own work. In the 1977–78 contract negotiations, FNSI obtained compulsory disclosure about ownership: who owns how much, and with what commitments. Throughout the period, of course, wages and fringes and perquisites continued to climb reassuringly.

As this pattern developed there was increasingly only one fuel to fire the engines of reform, an almost abstracted, completely normative political commitment. That commitment works far better if politics is entangled with hunger or some other circumstances that touch daily life, and by this time journalists were among the best-situated people in Italy.

The reform movement also lost force through the attenuation of personalized villains, of archetypal Bad Guys whom all right-thinking people could attack. Feeling at war with one's bosses gives a certain sustaining muscle tone to many individuals. An Afeltra, nominally a Socialist but a demonstrable hewer of wood and carrier of water for the Christian Democrats, is easy to oppose; furthermore, he had never been more than an adequate journalist. A Spadolini, although not a pedestrian political conniver, was clearly more of a public figure than a journalist (and, once fired, entered into that career with gusto).

Spadolini's replacement as editor of *Corriere,* Piero Ottone, was something altogether different; a good professional apparently unconcerned about his public image, with a solid background in a good but undistinguished regional paper, *Il Secolo XIX* of Genoa. He was somewhat impatient with the conventional politics and politicians, and much more likely to listen to his staff than to the secretary of whatever political party. He gave no indication of ever wanting to be anywhere else than in journalism.

Arrigo Levi, Ronchey's successor at *La Stampa,* had never been an editor, but he, too, had been identified only with the profession; even the rather peremptory way he laid down his conditions for assuming the editorship sounded like a newspaperman, not someone moving into a symbolic role.

At *Il Messaggero,* Italo Pietra's successor, Luigi Fossati, was known chiefly for his work as a foreign correspondent in Moscow and London; he was approved unanimously by the staff after refusing to lay out a description of a political line for the future. He chose to talk instead about the importance of everybody working together to save the paper.

A few months later two news executives of *Corriere,* Alberto Sensini and Franco Di Bella, became the editors of two important regional papers, respectively, *La Nazione* and *Il Resto del Carlino.* Sensini had been Rome bureau chief; Di Bella, in effect, the news editor of *Corriere.* Neither had any particular standing outside the profession. A few months later there were bitter complaints when Di Bella was called back to succeed Ottone as editor of *Corriere,* but they had to do with his professional competence and ethics rather than with any symbolic role.

It has been noted here several times that for years there has been a good deal of talk among Italian journalists—much more than among American journalists—about the need for more professional competence; professional standards have been invoked as the ultimate articles of faith. The cynical might note that as this rhetorical concern rose in volume the actual profession in Italy contented itself with nest feathering and playing partisan political games. The rise of a new kind of editor, men named to the job by owners who, in part, were responding to the atmosphere created by the reform movement, may prove to be the most important thing to come out of the decade.

If professionalized, rather than politicized, editors had something to do with the dampening of the more gaudy manifestations of the spirit of reform, so did the exposure of the true nature of the people who chose those editors, another classic set of villains, the Italian media barons. The most dependably provocative image of these shadowy figures is that of conspirators whose interest is not in media, but in power.

The idea that there is an inaccessible elite who really order everything in a given society obviously is very attractive. There are dozens of books that have identified various groups at work in a given country and, almost invariably, with global aspirations. Media owners are among the favorites. Some analyses are essentially skeleton rattling (Lundberg on Hearst); some akin to standard Marxian approaches (Schiller on the media and American imperialism); some the vicious billingsgate of bigots (U.S. media are controlled by Jews).

Whichever group may be identified as conspirators, however, there are two standard elements; what they are up to is covert conspiracy, and their ultimate objective is political power so darkly ominous that it can barely be described.

To many middle-class Italian intellectuals of the 1970s, including a great many journalists, the conspiracy was among financiers (with media owners most directly involved, of course), the Catholic church, and Christian Democrats. Social researchers have spoken of the kernel of truth in stereotypes, and there have indeed been an infinity of ties among those three entities (see pp. 123-24). It does not follow, however, that every kind of entrepreneurial activity can be explained in terms of that conspiracy.

Eugenio Cefis was the most hated and fiercely attacked man in the news business in the 1973-75 period. He turned out to be an aspiring (and unsuccessful) empire builder who had no real interest in newspapers at all. His most energetic activities were directed to expand control of Montedison, basically a chemical company, to control of ENI, its parent conglomerate. He poured money into keeping *Il Giorno* afloat in the naive belief, apparently, that if one owned a newspaper it would say nice things and forward one's cause. He complained publicly when this did not happen, and decided to buy the most important paper of all, *Corriere della Sera,* for the same misguided reason, but the effort failed. Like many other Italian big businessmen of the time, he suddenly discovered public relations and decided it was a magic art. The first operatives hired by him for the public relations division of Montedison were a Christian Democrat, a Republican (conservative, but stoutly anticlerical), and a Socialist.[11] Cefis cheerily described the new department's function as the maintenance of "the facial plastic of this old lady while we operate the body."[12]

He apparently cultivated politicians because they, and other noisy people, had to be placated, once saying "I bought *Il Messaggero* to please Fanfani and De Martino," that is, the head of the conservative wing of the DCs *and* the secretary of the Socialist party. Both seem to have had something close to veto powers during the negotiations. Cefis told the directors of Montedison that he bought the paper to get a good press in the capital and to cut down advertising costs.

I remember well a conversation with one of Cefis's most intense opponents shortly after the sale; he was convinced that Cefis was only the tool of Fanfani. But that paper's most savage attacks on the DCs came after Montedison, with Cefis as president, took over, and Fanfani attacked Cefis as bitterly in reply. Cefis often indicated that he personally preferred a government slightly to the left of center, because he thought it would be best for business.

Whatever the plans or Eugenio Cefis's motivations, they all came to nothing in the end. He never really ran ENI, he lost Montedison, and he began to drop out of sight by 1975. In April, 1977, he was found guilty of shady financial practices, sentenced to jail, fined, and barred for ten years from future activity in the company. The man who, by himself, generated enough steam to keep some reformers going was no longer any help.

The Rizzoli push, headed by young Angelo, never inspired the deep fears of the Cefis maneuvers. The pattern of Angelo Rizzoli's financial relationships, including some with Cefis, has never been completely untangled. From the point of view of those concerned with the rise of monopoly, Rizzoli was a far greater threat to the independence of the Italian press than Cefis ever was.

It was hard, however, to get agitated about Rizzoli as one reaching for the strings that move the country. From the beginning he openly cultivated any politician likely to affect his business affairs. When he began moves to take over *Il Mattino,* one of the first people he consulted was the Communist mayor of Naples. When the first maneuvers got underway in Parliament for the massive government subsidization in which lay his chain's only hope for profit, Rizzoli stayed, according to common report, in continuing informal touch with the PCI. He worked with equal flexibility with every major current of Italian politics, with the exception of the far right.

Furthermore, he made no attempt to influence his paper's content. When he finally obtained control of *Corriere* from Giulia Maria Crespi, Rizzoli made a triumphant ritual of arrival as new owner, announced that this was a moment to which the Rizzoli family had aspired for years, and proceeded to leave the paper in the hands of Ottone and his staff.

Rizzoli had naturally, as a part of his personality, the thing Cefis was never able to buy with all the money spent on public relations men and buying newspapers: Rizzoli was an amiable man who said the right things. Even such newsmagazines as *Panorama,* reflexively hostile to any burgeoning monopolist and particularly watchful about the press, generally wrote about him with bemused respect.

It required of the average journalist a genuine effort of will to mount a barricade against Rizzoli, and with Cefis gone, Rizzoli was by far the most important figure among the owners.

It may even have become harder to crusade against the government, which meant the Christian Democrats. For many years the scandals within government remained hidden, in part because the vast net of corruption included mechanisms for concealing it, in part because the digging for exposés was not part of the Italian journalistic tradition. "If people only knew what's going on . . ." was a conventional lamentation.

As the ineptitude and ineffectiveness of government mounted during the decade, even the most profligate usage of payoffs was not enough to contain it all. The new, small-circulation journals on the left, such as *Il Manifesto,* and weekly news magazines such as *Panorama* and *L'Espresso* began to find sensation a highly marketable commodity, and the big dailies followed the path. By the time of the 1976 election, the Antelope Cobbler scandal and the parliamentary maneuvers related to its investigation (or noninvestigation) had touched almost every member of the Christian Democratic leadership. (Antelope Cobbler was Lockheed's code name for an unidentified principal contact in a bribery scandal.)

It was pointed out earlier in this chapter, however, that the national newspapers took a curious stance as voting day approached in 1976. None went, as the saying goes, for the jugular; their analyses were cautious enough that someone like Pansa, for example, could conclude that most national newspapers were pro-DC.

I have indicated my belief that this attitude toward the election of 1976 grew in large part out of a new kind of concern for the country. There is a mirror image of the bitter remark quoted earlier in this book to the effect that Italy has had only two governments since 1921: fascism and the Christian Democrats. At the same time it is true that the DC regime was not imposed by a march on Rome, nor was it maintained at the cost of enforced consensus. In its own muddled, inept, perpetually corrupt ways, it represented Italy, the choices of Italy's people: a mix of the psychological security—and simplicity—of Catholicism; of the joys of the flesh of capitalistic consumerism; and, most important, the marvelous exhilaration of the hope for unique individual fulfillment. The confusion that has been Italian government since 1945 represented not a political party, but the inability to put all these things together in ways that worked. Never mind that it was impossible from the outset, that other societies have always settled for less. With the government at the edge of collapse, knowing Italians suddenly caught their breath in a new awareness of what they stood to lose, and role playing was no longer simple. This was especially true for that well-educated, perceptive, expert user of the system that had been so good to him, the Italian journalist.

Chapter 9

The Profession in Italy and America: Some Comparisons and Speculations

Is there anything for professional journalism elsewhere in the world to learn from Italian journalism, especially from its history since 1970? A superficial glance might suggest an answer in the negative. The overall quality of Italian journalism is not high by the usual standards, and some of its important institutional characteristics, such as the licensing of professionals, make it unlike other press systems in the Western world.

Yet the Italian experience seems to imply more upon careful examination. The primary reason is the fact that, although media systems vary widely, journalists in most nonauthoritarian countries are alike in important ways; ideas and actions that originate in one group of professionals may suggest something about the future for those elsewhere.

There have been few studies of journalists as people and professionals, but three published in the 1970s are illustrative: one in the United States, another in Great Britain, another in Italy. They are not closely comparable; it would be impossible, for example, to make statistical comparisons across the set. They have in common, however, the circumstance that all three collected a good deal of demographic information: family background, amount and kind of education, and the like, and going further, the journalist's perception of his job, his relations with his superiors, his ethical standards, and his normative judgments about the profession.

One of these profiles, perhaps the most disciplined study ever made of journalists, was carried out by John W. C. Johnstone, a sociologist at the University of Illinois in Chicago, and two associates.[1] The data were collected from a carefully structured sample of professionals in newspapers, newsmagazines, and radio and television news departments in the United States. The interviews, most of them around two hours long, were conducted in 1971. Of the three surveys discussed here, this is the only one that can be projected (because of its careful sampling) as an adequate representation of the entire profession in a particular country.

A British sociologist, Jeremy Tunstall of the City University of London, did an equally workmanlike but somewhat more limited study of British specialist journalists, collecting his data through mail questionnaires in 1968.[2] No sampling was involved; he simply sent a copy of the questionnaire to every British journalist identifiable, by his definition, as a specialist. The fields represented were foreign news, parliamentary correspondence, education, labor, fashion, football, crime, motoring, and aviation. He received 207 replies, with a rather remarkable response rate of 70 percent.

The third in the set was carried out in late 1976 in Italy and was considerably more slapdash. It was not intended to be academic social research, which some Italians do very well indeed, but rather was the project of a body described only as "a group of Milanese journalists." They confined their inquiries to journalists in Milan. The survey began with personal interviews, but after a time it was decided that respondents were "too embarrassed" (an understandable analysis, judging from the schedule of questions), and the data collection switched to mail questionnaires. These were directed to professionals over a wide range of media in the neighborhood: *Corriere* and *Il Giorno,* of course, and *Il Sole; 24 Ore* (a financial daily); *La Repubblica* (the Milan bureau); *Il Manifesto,* the lively, sometimes slightly hysterical publication of a far-left splinter party; Montanelli's *Il Giornale Nuovo; La Notte,* one of the city's sensationalized evening papers; *La Gazzetta dello Sport* (one of four Italian dailies in that category); and five magazines: *Panorama,* a newsmagazine; *Grazia,* a traditional women's publication; *Due Più,* vaguely concerned with better living for young couples, and generally featuring conjugal nudity on its covers; *Annabella,* another women's magazine; and the Italian edition of *Vogue.* The group produced 116 responses, and an account of the findings appeared in *Prima Comunicazione,* a magazine about journalism and the media also published in Milan. The authors, Mariapia Gianotti and Claudio Castellani, eschewed any nonsense about science.

> We are not functionaries of Demoskopea [a professional polling organization]. That which we present therefore is not a rigorous sociological inquiry but a journalist survey conducted by means of a questionnaire. The study is of course based on statistical data, but not from a scientifically established sample. But we believe the results are convincing. Or probably so.[3]

All told, it may be one of the liveliest and most entertaining pieces of research ever published. Not only did the investigators dispense with the investigative methods of social science; they also dispensed with conventional approaches to presentation and summary. They were openly dismayed by most of the things they found out about their colleagues: "The results . . . are hardly uplifting. There exists a big, if not majority, bloc of contented or indifferent journalists in the present situation." They refer to certain responses as "stereotyped formula, a sort of political catechism." They speak of one respondent as "blasé and ignorant." And in a summary of findings about staff activism, they conclude: "The fact is that there is in Milan, by strict definition, a 'progressive' majority which, however, as we have seen, in daily practice ends up being the docile and resigned instrument of traditional editorial structure."[4]

We shall return later to the discussion of, and partial disagreement with, that and other conclusions in the Italian study, but a look at the three surveys as a group seems appropriate first. Their differences in design and, especially, the groups from which they were drawn seem so great that no parallels could be expected. It therefore is the more surprising to find an array of common elements, constants in a mass of differences, that suggest there are certain characteristics of professional journalists that cut across most subgroups and most societies in Western Europe and North America.

There is, for example, the tendency for journalists to come from the same social class. In the Johnstone study of U.S. news professionals, just short of half, 48.8 percent, had fathers who were in what Johnstone identifies as the "professional-managerial" class; another 13 percent were other white-collar workers. Thirty-eight percent came from blue-collar backgrounds. Tunstall does not provide a tabular breakdown of his British specialist journalists, but he does say that only a third are from the manual trades; the fathers of the remainder are "heavily weighted toward administrative, educational, and service occupations."[5] His football specialists were most likely to be of blue-collar origin.

Italian journalists working in Milan were loaded even more heavily toward the top of the social scale than the United Kingdom–United States group. Congruent with the general air of detachment with which those data were presented, the article was headed "Above All, Daddy's Boys." This title was idiomatic for upper-class children who get their position through family influence: "children of generals, diplomats, industrialists, managers."[6] Somewhat more soberly, the actual data classify 58 percent of the group as *borghese* ("bourgeois"), another 30 percent as *piccolo borghese* ("petit bourgeois"), such as secondary school teachers and shopkeepers. Only 12 percent of the Milan group came from the blue-collar group, probably a reflection of the thickness of the walls that still sharply separate the layers of Italian society.

These three inquiries help confirm what research in the United States began to establish a good many years ago—that journalists do not enter the profession because it is an expeditious channel for upward mobility (many even move down in social status), nor even for money (although this may be a substantial factor in Italy, given journalists' salaries compared to most other salaried professions).

There was a somewhat broader spread in educational levels. The Americans and the Milanese have the most; 58 percent of Johnstone's U.S. sample have college degrees. "Less than half" of the Italians (no specific data were provided, but that seems to imply "but close to") had a college degree. The Italians interviewed by this writer over the years were, as indicated earlier, almost without exception university trained. That group was, of course, in no sense of the word representative of anything beyond my conviction that they would have something useful to say, and the superficial discrepancy is probably accounted for by two things: I for the most part talked with those near the top of the profession, and in inquiring about education, I did not inquire specifically about a degree. "I studied economics at the University of Turin," therefore, might well refer to a year or two only. The published data from Milan did not include these, but an additional 28 percent of the American sample had "some" college.

The British, reflecting an old tradition that is finally beginning to crumble and under which most students did not even have a chance at university education, had the least. Only 30 percent of Tunstall's specialist reporters had a university degree, and "most" had left school at seventeen, upon finishing secondary school. The British data were collected three years before the U.S. material and eight years before the Italian.

The Italians and the Americans were also much alike in salary levels, apparently. The proud Italian contention that I frequently encountered was that Italian journalists were second only to Americans in income, and the data from Milan supports that, in my judgment. There are no hard numbers for Italian salaries, of course, but an oblique question on the subject drew a set of responses remarkable enough to be set out here in full. The replies to the question "What do you consider the economic condition of the journalist?" went like this:

Good	52%
Sufficient	20
Remarkably high	14
Very good	10
Poor	4[7]

It is improbable that Americans, with their average salaries around twelve thousand dollars in 1971, with 3 percent making more than thirty thousand dollars, would answer that question with such dazzling sunniness.

The United Kingdom journalists, again in line with an old and appalling tradition, were well behind. Official British National Board for Prices and Incomes data for 1969 indicated that of journalists stationed in London—presumably, the better-paying posts in the national dailies and wire services—a full 75 percent received forty-five pounds a week in 1968, the equivalent of about $108.[8] Almost half the reporters, as distinguished from various news administrators, made between thirty and forty pounds a week (from about $73 to $97). Again, the British and American data were collected some time before the Italian, but the relative positions did not change.

The most significant resemblance across the lines of all three studies was the fact that the majority of journalists liked their jobs and seemed to have little concern for improvement. It was precisely this condition that shocked the activist-minded commentators of the Milan survey. Not all the surveys attempted to frame a direct question on the subject, but all contain, in their responses, clear evidence. Tunstall, for example, apparently did not inquire directly about job satisfaction, but his British specialists found very little with which to quarrel in their situations. Seventy-one percent of them, asked if their own organization's total news output was "too serious," "about right," or "not serious enough," chose "about right." He also found that most had little awareness of, or concern about, their audiences. For example, political specialists were satisfied if 10 percent of their papers' readers read *them*, and few had pretensions to any kind of influence; they also overestimated the size of the audience.[9] Johnstone's Americans, for the most part, liked their jobs; more than 60 percent said they hoped to be working in the same organization five years in the future, and, on another dimension, "almost seven in eight . . . gave positive rather than negative responses to a direct question on job satisfaction."[10] In fact, journalists were well above average in job satisfaction, and far fewer than the national average of the labor force (12.9 percent versus 17 percent) who expressed dissatisfaction. Tunstall and Johnstone, both sociologists, did provide constructs of tension and unhappiness on the job. Johnstone sees large differences between what he calls "participant" and "nonparticipant" journalists, that is, those who think the presentation of news can and should be "neutral" and "objective," and those who seek a more direct social purpose. Tunstall speaks of tensions between "news gatherers" and "processors," growing out of structural differences, but neither seems to have found data that they feel are meaningful beyond being detectable.

In quizzing their colleagues, the Milanese journalists poked about in several directions. They found that more than 80 percent of those who had chosen the profession "spontaneously" were happy with the choice, a condition undoubtedly related to the satisfaction with salaries cited earlier. In reply to a question about reasons for choosing the field, most proffered vague observations about being a witness to history or journalism's being a dynamic profession. Less than a fourth said they would change jobs at that point, even if they could do so without financial loss.[11]

In rough outline, the journalist-respondent, whether American, British, or Italian, is male; he is from a middle-class background, or better; he likes his job; and, although he gives high-minded reasons for choosing the profession, finds little to criticize about it and has few suggestions for its improvement.

It seems to me that there is one dominant reason for such uniformity. The practice of journalism, particularly deadline journalism, requires submission to a harsh, particularly complex personal discipline. It requires the unquestioning acceptance of the sacrifice of much personal identity to the newsgathering and processing apparatus. Yet the successful professional journalist is brighter than most of his or her fellow citizens, better educated, better informed, and generally a good deal more sophisticated. He or she was first attracted to the profession because it seemed important work, or because of an interest in doing "creative" things. These all are qualities that emphasize the sense of one's own uncommon identity. The newsroom, in a variety of ways from the subtle to the heavy-handed, wars directly on those sensibilities. The successful journalist is someone who can accede to the newsroom while holding on to his perception of himself.

The people who can do it come out being pretty much alike.

Before looking at the data from the Milan survey in detail, the caveat about its flaws needs repeating. Not only does it not represent a carefully drawn sample, the published version in *Prima Comunicazione* does not even indicate how many questionnaires were sent out. If one was sent to each member of the editorial staff of the publications listed, the 110 returned would be a modest fraction, given the size of Italian staffs. There is an obvious possibility of nonresponsive bias, that is, the people who chose to answer the questionnaire were self-selected; it would be useful to know the characteristics of the group that chose to ignore it.

There is a remarkable range of jobs represented, from political pundits on *Il Mànifesto* to artisans of soft-core pornography for *Due Più*. Although they all are members of the Order, people at either end of the spectrum barely recognize those at the other as being in the same profession at all. The presentation of responses is broken down into two groups, one representing dailies, the other magazines, which is a modest help; even so, the differences within the magazine group are still very great. *Panorama* and *Vogue* are produced by quite different kinds of people. For example, almost 25 percent of the respondents working on daily newspapers were members of a political party and only about 5 percent of the magazine staff respondents were members, although the newspaper respondents include representatives of a newspaper devoted exclusively to sports, and the magazine group a highly politicized news weekly.

Taken together, that means that about 82 percent of the Milanese respondents are not political party members. That may seem contradictory to the repeated references in these pages to the high degree of politicization among Italian journalists. Belonging to a political party in Italy, however, is a more formal condition than in the United States. Official members pay dues and have a party card; most of the parties conduct membership drives periodically. Once officially signed up, one's commitment to the party is presumably complete and active. Perhaps the closest equivalent in the United States is to the low-level party worker, a precinct captain, for example. The Italian whose inclinations are to the left is very likely to want to choose, in a given election, among candidates from the Communists, the Socialists, or even the Republican party, and a formal commitment to one would cramp his options. The act of belonging says nothing about one's generalized political fervor.

The presence of such fervor is demonstrated by the responses to another question: "Do you hold that the protagonist in a situation can also be a good reporter?" To that only 35.8 percent flatly said no. Thirty-two percent said yes and another 17 percent said "sometimes." There was a relatively high number of nonresponses (15 percent), but in any case just about half of the Milanese respondents felt that the role of a central actor in at least some "situations" need not interfere with reporting them well. There is no research, at least none known to this writer, in which the same question was asked of journalists in English-speaking countries, but it is a safe generalization that the percentages who believe that would not be in double figures.

The published data do not indicate, in the case of this question, the differences between magazine and newspaper journalists, and it seems probable that only newspaper reporters were asked the question; the question uses the word *cronaca* ("local news").

That view of the virtues of involvement might, to some extent, be an echo of the new sensitivity—or at least the rhetoric—of the reform movement. However, it should be remembered that the data were collected in 1976, with most of the thrust of that movement gone, for reasons discussed earlier. The disappointment apparent in the bitter commentaries by Gianotti and Castellani on the results of the survey, although they make no direct reference to the earlier period, seems an expression of their conviction that little had changed after all.

Yet some elements in the Milan survey give solid reinforcement to the assessments by people such as Paolo Murialdi. Three questions dealt with hypothetical situations that test what might be described as professional ethical standards.

In the first, the surveyors went right to the nerve on a subject normally too painful to discuss. The first question: "If you came to know with absolute certainty that one of your colleagues was corrupt, what would you do?" The answers:

I would discuss it with the editor	15.0%
I would discreetly advise my other colleagues	7.5
I would discuss it with the Journalists Committee	33.7
I would inform the Order of Journalists so they could make an official inquiry	10.0
I would try not to give anything away, speaking in confidence with the colleague involved	21.2
No response	6.2[12]

There is no way of knowing, of course, how much cynicism was in those replies. Even so, and once again discounting much on the ground that this particular group may well represent nothing except themselves, I find the fact that the largest single group of responses was "I'd go to the Journalists Committee" says much. When you add to that another 10 percent who said they would go directly to the Order of Journalists, there seems to be a widespread sense of looking first to the structured procedures of the profession. Those procedures had not even existed in any real way twenty years earlier.

Two more questions, closely articulated, produced something like the same result. The first asked:

> In your opinion, should the journalist have the right to express his own thoughts in the articles he writes, or should he limit himself to a simple exposition of the facts?[13]

The response was a stout 65.5 percent for facts and comment mingled; interestingly enough, the magazine staff members were more conservative than the newspaper employees, 71 percent of whom asserted the right to expression of their own opinions in the news. (Johnstone, in his study of U.S. journalists, spent considerable time in the analysis of "participant" and "nonparticipant" attitudes, with reference to the journalists' feelings about the issue of providing interpretation in the news story; the situations are not exactly parallel, but his responses showed between 60 and 80 percent, depending on the issues, on the side of "participation.")[14]

The group among the Milanese that believed in their right to express their "own thoughts" were then asked: "If you were to express your own personal opinions and these were then censored by the editor, what would you do?" The responses were:

Accept the decision, because that is the editor's right	30%
Would not accept the decision	70

The 70 percent who said they would not accept such a decision were then asked what specific action they would take. The responses were:

Discuss it with my colleagues individually	7.1%
Raise the question at a meeting of the Assembly	16.0
Submit the case to the judgment of the Journalists Committee	59.5
Talk with the editor about it	16.6[15]

Their confidence in Journalists Committees is hardly unbounded, it should be noted. Immediately following the question about editorial censorship on the questionnaire came the following: "Do you believe that staff meetings:"

Constitute a genuine situation for the formation of policy	22.4%
Constitute purely a formality, because the content and Direction of the paper are in fact established by the editor	68.9

About 10 percent, apparently, failed to respond.

Again, this might be taken to indicate that most of the ideological impetus of the reform movement, to whatever extent it may once have existed, was largely dissipated. The majority of the best-paid and most competent Italian journalists, the Milanese, apparently did not feel that journalists could take over control of their own publications as a social and political force. Despite the outcries of alarm from every quarter about great papers bent to the will of irresponsible Journalists Committees, it was not really possible. The reform movement had not achieved that.

It did achieve a strengthening of the journalist's role as an individual within a profession. The drive for reform had not only defined and made clear a great many problems, it had provided, largely through activities of the national trade union, ways to attack some of them.

The fact that Italian and American journalists are alike in some fundamental ways makes their differences more important, and some of the differences are things that they might learn to advantage from each other.

Perhaps the most important thing Italian journalism could learn from the vocation in the United States is a deeper sense of professionalism and a larger reputation for it. As the Italian journalist moves closer to seeing himself as a member of a free-standing, independent institution rather than as an essential, but still subordinate, part of something else—the political order, for example—the better journalism in that country will become and the better it will serve Italy.

The first loyalty of U.S. journalists as a group is to journalism. That tradition has grown from several roots, among which are the neutrality required to attract a wide range of advertisers, the competitiveness of businesses concerned first with making money, and the pervasive spread of news agencies with their necessarily spare and unflavored basic news product. Although none of these factors suggests uncommon nobility of spirit on the part of the American journalist, they have helped shape the journalists' image in American popular culture.

The journalist has been a frequent hero in American adventure stories for years. Older viewers of the "Lou Grant" program on television in 1980 watched motion pictures in the 1940s in which actors such as James Cagney, Cary Grant, and Tyrone Power played reporters who were smarter than the police, more honest than judges, and who when drunk became whimsically charming rather than noisome. Every sentient American child for almost fifty years has known Superman's real-world profession. In the late 1970s Robert Woodward and Carl Bernstein became the perfect amalgam, real people easily mythologized.

The popular culture of no other country in the world has journalists as stock heroes. It is a perception that would not be possible if the profession were not seen as independent. (There have been no public relations operatives cast yet as media heroes.) Consider the others in the American gallery: the cowboy, the private investigator, the frontiersman, the gangster—all of them figures who, first of all, wear no man's yoke. Even the policeman-hero is commonly portrayed as a rebel against, or at least a circumventer of, his superiors.

Many critics, including some within the media, do not regard either the business or the profession as independent, and the typical citizen may complain about the papers, about their inaccuracies and prejudicial handling of whatever matters are close to his heart; he or she might deny loudly that they are to be trusted. But in fact most citizens do trust the media's essential institutional integrity. According to public opinion polls, respect for the news media went down during the 1960s and early 1970s, although not quite so much as that for schools, legislative bodies, lawyers, judges, and doctors. It rose dramatically toward the end of the Watergate affair and then began settling back again, while retaining a considerable increment of good will. Shortly after a Supreme Court decision declared that the press had no constitutional right to protect sources and that a reporter's rights in no way differed from those of an ordinary citizen, a Gallup poll showed that 68 percent of a national sample felt to the contrary. The figure rose steadily from 1972 through the end of the decade.[16]

It would be easy to read too much into such figures. Public attitudes in such issues are lightly held, and both opinion surveys and past history have indicated that most of the special status of freedom of expression in our legal system could be stripped away without mass protest. What the Gallup survey does show is that, asked a question they have thought relatively little about, a majority of Americans more or less reflexively indicated their basic trust in the institution.

There are no precisely comparable data on Italian readers, but there are some clues. The most meaningful evidence, perhaps, is the way Italians stay away from reading newspapers at all. Beyond that, there are some other indicators. In late 1976 and early 1977 a commercial survey research firm, Makno, was commissioned by RAI's TG2 (the second news service) to study a wide range of reader perceptions of, and attitudes toward, newspapers. Unlike the cheery amateurishness of the Milan survey of journalists quoted earlier, the Makno procedures were carefully worked out and the findings based upon personal interviews.

No questions asking about the right to confidentiality of sources or more directly about trust in the media were put to the sample. One question called for choosing from a group of choices to complete a sentence that began with "I believe that journalists in Italy . . .

a) do not have the importance they deserve.	12%
b) have about the importance they deserve.	21
c) are a privileged and arrogant group that needs discipline.	14
d) inflate and distort news, misleading public opinion.	29
e) are determined, in their reporting, to guide political choices.	29
f) are serious, honest people, but are not free to write the truth.	32[17]

Obviously other researchers might quarrel with the particular choices, but the overall impression is clear: there is little confidence, at least, in the reliability of newspapers. The three choices with the largest percentages each indicate that the papers are not to be trusted.

These figures become more significant when the circumstances under which the data were collected are taken into account. Interviewers were stationed at newsstands and, at random, questioned buyers of newspapers after the transaction was completed. The information thus is gathered from the 10 to 12 percent of the Italian population that still reads newspapers, whatever the level of their unhappiness with them.

The fact that Americans trust the media as institutions—and, by and large, journalists as individuals—is the key to an uncommon societal role for them in the United States. It means this country has an extra social institution, which has a unique relationship to the others; it monitors and reports on them as an independent agency. It is a means of evaluating their activity. Through that function the media have a critical role in making the system work.

There is another face to the business of independent professionalism, however, which reflects its undesirable characteristics. Someone once compared American newspaper publishers to a herd of longhorn bulls; if there is an attack on any one member of the group, they all form a circle, rumps in and horns out. That stance might be expected of many businessmen, but in the news business it is more than that; it is almost equally true of editors and even reporters. The profession is clannishly protective.

The American Society of Newspaper Editors in its early years drew up and solemnly adopted a code of ethics which included a provision for expulsion of errant members. The sins of only one member have been found, over more than fifty years, sufficient to bring him to the point of a formal investigation,[18] and that effort ended in permitting a face-saving resignation from the organization. The dominant tone of the discussion among the members was "Who am I to lodge hard charges against a brother?"

This attitude meant, for a long time, that there was no significant criticism of American media in the media, unlike countries such as Italy in which attacks upon other publications have always been an editorial staple. The only visible critics of print and broadcast journalism in the United States were outsiders, generally academics, and they were accounted for within the field by invocation of the stereotype of vague and impractical theorizers. The most impressive attempt was made by the so-called Hutchins Commission, which produced in 1947 a report called *A Free and Responsible Press,* full of insight and solid thinking. Although it was financed by a publisher, Henry Luce, most of its members were social scientists and its chairman was Robert M. Hutchins, then chancellor of the University of Chicago. Hutchins was an acerbically witty man who, whether he intended it or not, always conveyed a sense of contempt for both media owners and journalists. Although a few of the country's best editors and reporters took the report seriously and worked for its being better understood, the news business generally dismissed it out of hand.

The few critics from within the field have also been shrugged off. Only one of these, A. J. Liebling, was much known to outsiders; his irregular press critiques in the *New Yorker* were done with such style that few targets ever found it prudent to fight back. Instead he was treated with increasing condescension over the years, finally to the point where he was patronizingly indulged as good-old-Joe, the inimitable termagant without whom journalism really would be incomplete. Other able critics from within, such as Ben Bagdikian, simply never reached the elite audience of outsiders whose opinions were of importance to journalists and their bosses.

In contrast, since the mid-1960s Italian journalists have produced in steadily increasing numbers lively, sometimes scholarly, analyses of the fundamental problems of that country's media that have been widely read and discussed. References to them appear throughout this book.

I once asked an old friend, a news executive on the *Washington Post*, his opinion of a book by a political scientist dealing with relationships between political reporters and government officials.

"I suppose it's good; he's done his homework, and all that," he replied. "The trouble is—he just doesn't *know*, does he?" He tried to think of another way to say it and gave up. "I mean, he just doesn't *know*."

That is a variant on the attitude that so often infuriates those who complain to journalists about unfairness or incompleteness in the stories those journalists have written; the reply is usually not apology, or explanation, or even defense, but instead a taciturn indication that there is no point to discussing the matter because the complainant would not understand in any case.

This comes down, it seems to me, to a feeling on the part of the profession that journalists not only have a special status in law, but a competence so special that advice from other quarters is irrelevant at best and dangerous if heeded. There are persuasive arguments against that attitude, but one great argument for it; when the members of both the business and the profession of journalism believe that, it is unlikely that in their work they will reflect any values other than their own.

In Italy there are some signs of change that could be the beginning of a growing independence rooted in the sense of professional commitment. One example was discussed earlier, that of the staff of *Avanti!* requesting the replacement of a direttore responsabile whose chief interest was in party affairs with one devoted to journalism. The rise of Piero Ottone and Arrigo Levi, both more journalist than public figure, to the editorships of

Corriere and *La Stampa* has also been noted; and, although other factors also were involved, the revolt at *Corriere* against the appointment of Franco Di Bella contained an element of professional concern.

Evidence can also be found in the appearance, in the late 1970s, of examples of what is referred to in Italian journalism as *auto-gestione,* publications whose operations are directed by employees, generally a cooperative of journalists and printers. The idea had been around Italian journalism since shortly after the Second World War; the occupation authorities, in their efforts to reestablish a free press in the country, specifically offered to assist cooperatives made up of journalists to acquire papers, but there were no takers.

In the mid-1970s *Gazzetta del Popolo* of Turin had a period of auto-gestione which, despite its brevity, had broad implications. *Gazzetta del Popolo* actually was founded almost twenty years before its illustrious competitor, *La Stampa,* although in modern times it has been consistently overshadowed by Agnelli's paper. In the 1960s and early 1970s *Gazzetta* served as an official mouthpiece of the Piedmont Christian Democrats; the party officially owned only about 5 percent of the stock, but the paper clearly was the voice of the party. A staff member told this writer that a proof of the front page of each day's paper was submitted to the regional DC secretary for approval before the press run started. With a circulation somewhere around 30 percent of *La Stampa, Gazzetta* had heavy deficits for years.

In 1974, 95 percent of the stock in the paper was acquired by a company headed by an Italian, Alberto Caprotti, but owned largely by a Swiss concern. The Christian Democrats continued to own their 5 percent, and a substantial advertising guarantee from Cefis's advertising agency, SPI, provided some financial help. Something more drastic was required, however, and Caprotti provided it by eliminating *Gazzetta*'s bureaus in New York, London, and Brussels, and reducing the Rome bureau from six staff members to two, in addition to firing the special correspondents. These were sensible moves, in theory, and it is possible the staff might have supported them in light of the paper's desperate financial condition. Caprotti ordered them all without consultation with the staff, however, and they rebelled. After a few weeks the new owner stopped all negotiations and simply closed the paper down.

It did not cease publication, however, but reappeared almost immediately as an enterprise of a new cooperative of printers, journalists, and FNSI, the journalists' trade union. For a bit less than a year this group remained in control, although they never formally took possession. They simply got the paper out.

There probably are a good many differing versions of what went on during that period. My source was a young staff member named Ezio Mauro, whose name I knew because he was a part-time correspondent for a national news magazine, *Panorama*.[19] He viewed those months as demanding but exciting. The cooperative was made up of both printers and journalists. Salaries were determined by simply dividing the amount of money available equally among the group; in no case did a journalist get more than the minimum, which at that time was about $430 per month for journalists with less than ten years' seniority and about $65 a month more for those beyond that experience level. There were times, according to Mauro, when there was not enough income for minimums and people simply took what they could get.

Nor was there an editor, in the conventional sense, or, for that matter, a managing editor, although members of the staff bore those titles. Rather there was a meeting at noon each day of the newsroom staff around the scarred, ancient conference table and all hands pitched in to decide what stories should be carried and at what length. They were demanding sessions.

"It's not easy," Mauro said, "to be free."

One of the first things that disappeared was partisan politics. All the major parties were represented on the staff, including the Communists, but there was immediate, undebated agreement that political bias was too subtle a commodity to take seriously.

I mentioned to Mauro the case of *Il Messaggero*, and the constant examination of headlines and lead paragraphs. That kind of thing did not happen at *Gazzetta del Popolo*, he said. Then, after more thought, he came up with one case, that of the report of the bombing of a Turin-Rome express train with the loss of several lives.

"The headline in the first edition referred to a 'Fascist bombing,'" he said. "We changed that because there was no proof of its being a Fascist bomb, although everybody knew it was."

The daily newshandling routine was complicated by the loss of all foreign correspondents, part-time correspondents (stringers) who reported from around the province, and a sharp reduction in the Rome bureau—changes that reduced costs, but that skewed the patterned functioning that is characteristic of journalism. Nor was there an in-house contract, although Mauro seemed not to have thought about it until I asked. Seized by the fervor of mutual work in a good cause, nobody worried about such things, apparently.

No newspaper can be run indefinitely on adrenalin and the spirit of good will. The daily scramble clearly became exhausting and nerves began to go raw. My discussion with Mauro took place only a few weeks after the paper had been sold to a new owner with whom the staff was sympathetic;

he was moving back toward more normal operations. While Mauro spoke with great pride of the days of the cooperative, he indicated no regret whatever at its passing. Neither *Gazzetta del Popolo* nor *Il Telegrafo* of Leghorn, which underwent a similar metamorphosis when its owner tried to close it down, provides a model for better Italian journalism. They may suggest, however, a growing interest in professionalism and a declining one in the political man.

Most of this analysis of the Italian press has been critical. Italian newspapers mean very little to most Italians, or to the way the Italian polity functions, or to the quality of Italian life; their chief importance is in their service as a channel of political communication. Italian magazines are popular and stronger financially, at least some of them, but like contemporary magazines everywhere, they serve specialized and self-selected audiences whose members use what they read for reinforcement. Establishment Italian broadcasting is hopelessly politicized, and the pattern of development of the substantial private broadcasting system indicates that it will continue to be devoted almost entirely to entertainment. Government television is very well done, but its competence generally is a gloss upon emptiness.

But the important thing that journalism in the rest of the world, and particularly in the United States, can learn from Italian journalism is not from the product, but from the way the profession is practiced. Italian journalists have gone further in the direction of "reporter power" than those of any other country, although professionals in most European countries have been interested in the idea and have worked at it. It seems to me that American journalism can learn from the Italian experience, and that journalism as a profession in the United States would be more satisfying for the journalist and more effective for the industry if there were more staff involvement in policy making and newsroom administration.

(The phrase "reporter power" seems more a slogan than a name; so does another common version of the same idea, the "democratic newsroom." The use of either is certain to alienate all management and some journalists before serious discussion even begins. There is need for a term that is both dispassionate and descriptive. One occurs to this writer that meets that standard: the "collegial newsroom." There is no chance of its taking hold, of course; it would be misunderstood by those who associated it with higher education, and everybody, understanding or not, would find it stuffy. Perhaps an Italian could invent the word *lemondismo* after the great French daily that started it all.)

The first moves in Europe toward a bigger role for the professional staff in the affairs of the editorial enterprise did not go completely unnoticed in the United States. The American Newspaper Guild (ANG), the trade union that represents newspaper and magazine employees in this country, began informal examination of the idea in the 1960s. In 1972 the first contract incorporating reference to such a role was signed; as of 1981, it remained the only one. The contract was between the Newspaper Guild and the *Minneapolis Star* and *Minneapolis Tribune,* morning and afternoon publications of the same company. It established what has since come to be known in the guild as a "voice committee." This committee was made up of representatives of the newspaper's employees and its top management, and the contract stipulated its meeting at the request of either group and in no case less than once a month. The role of the committee was set out as advisory, and, while the contract required its consultation specifically in the appointment of new supervisory personnel, it also specified the lack of any veto power. Staff members at the *Star* and *Tribune* feel that management has taken the voice committee seriously, and that its influence has been felt. It has, however, no formal authority.

In this respect it closely resembles the provisions of the Italian national contract before the reform movement got underway. From this point forward in its campaign for a more important staff voice, however, the ANG will have to overcome weaknesses that the Italian union did not face. More than 90 percent of all Italian journalists belong to FNSI. While most major U.S. papers are operationally organized by the guild, there are outstanding exceptions, including the *Chicago Tribune,* the *Los Angeles Times,* and the *Wall Street Journal.* All told, the guild has contracts in 141 newspapers in the United States and Canada (there are more than 1,700 daily newspapers in the United States alone), and only about 50 of these are union shops.

In contrast, there is a single national contract in Italy and every paper, every journalist, is bound by its provisions. Guild contracts in the United States are negotiated one unit at a time, a process that permits what is sometimes called "whipsawing" on the part of either side in negotiations: one newspaper in a struck city may sign to get a competitive advantage, as did the *New York Post* in the strike of 1978, putting tremendous pressure on the other owners; or a chain ownership may come to terms with the guild in one city and then offer the same contract to the unorganized papers in the chain, providing all the benefits of unionization without drawbacks, such as payment of dues, to keep the union out.

The Newspaper Guild, although it cannot negotiate an industry-wide contract, is organized on an industrial rather than a craft base. In Italy, FNSI is made up of certified professionals who have gone through apprenticeship and various ceremonies that have obtained them admission to an exclusive club; they are like American plumbers and psychiatrists, a proud, homogenized elite that shares the same framework of discourse about professional concerns. A typical American Newspaper Guild unit, on the other hand, includes not only everybody connected with collecting or handling the news, but also typists, librarians, and those who spend their days taking classified ads over the telephone.

Certainly the most expeditious way to establish a larger role for staff is the one that seems least likely—directly by management. News executives would be the biggest barrier to such an action. Most newspaper publishers in the United States, like publishers everywhere, are primarily interested in profit, and therefore tend to accept whatever promises to improve the smooth operation of the business. The American editor and his management associates, however, come from a strongly authoritarian tradition. The role of unquestioned sayer of the last word is a part of his self-perception, and to be required to consult with those who work for him cuts away a piece of ego.

This resistance on the second level of management may well be enough to prevent the establishment from the top of the principle of more staff participation; the wide base of organization of the Newspaper Guild, which makes it difficult for the organization to draw upon the strength of a group held together by a sense of unique professional obligations and commitment, will probably impede whatever initiatives the guild may undertake in the future. Perhaps the most effective agent of such a change, if it is to come at all, would be the organizing—better, the coalescing, out of a pervasive sense of need—of a genuinely professional force. There are many reasons why journalism as a profession is not the same as medicine, which has produced the American Medical Association; or the law, with its American Bar Association. Furthermore, there are important reasons why the resemblance to those trades must not become too close. There is no blinking the fact, however, that those organizations and a few others like them have a kind of power in American society that has permitted their establishment not only of the rules under which they operate, but also the delineation of what the society may properly expect of them.

Much of the argument in the United States against a larger staff role in the newsroom has been directed at straw men. "You mean you want a committee to decide, with press time coming up, what stories to use?" On the face of it, that is an impractical idea; it has never been seriously proposed, in any country. The situation that most closely resembled it probably was at *Il Messaggero*. The practice only contributed to the precipitous drop in that paper's standing in Italian journalism.

Another specious argument is based on the assumption that newsroom management jobs would be filled by the vote of the staff; that individuals who wanted to be variously city editor or sports editor or chief of the editorial page would campaign like nascent aldermen among their colleagues. Nothing of the sort has happened in even the most extreme Italian examples of "democratic newsrooms," nor is there any indication of serious attempts to install it. In contract negotiations, FNSI has pressed for what would amount to a veto over management nominees, but it has had to settle for a requirement for "close collaboration." There has been considerable politicking in some editorial rooms for election to the Journalists Committee, but this would not be new to several U.S. editorial departments that have seen hot competition for officers' jobs in the guild unit.

From the systems already functioning and a certain amount of common sense it is possible to draw some attributes that make a substantial staff role workable.

In matters of policy, the voice committee device is a beginning. The most important element is constant involvement, rather than scheduled joint meetings that may have an air of confrontation about them. The number of American newspapers that hold daily planning meetings is increasing, and the group now includes most of the major dailies. The editor presides, flanked by other news administrators, including the editors of sections such as business, sports, foreign news, national news, the section called by whatever inoffensive replacement has been found for the one-time name "women's section," the editorial page, and the like. These are working sessions in which the only partisanship is based upon professional judgment, and an easy channel of communication could be established if some representative of the staff was always included.

There would also seem to be a need for some system that would provide presentation of the point of view of the staff when a substantial part of it is in disagreement with the editor or publisher. Italian in-house contracts, as we have seen, generally include a requirement that any official statement generated and approved by the staff must be published. Any attempt at such a provision in American journalism would be ill-advised, to say the least. There is a possibility that it violates the first amendment to the U.S. Constitution. In Italian journalism, furthermore, the effect of the provision has largely been mischievous, more often used as a symbolic show of force than as a statement of principle.

Other routes are available. The press ombudsman device, which provides an outlet for criticism of the newspaper, is an example, although it is still rare in this country. The best known has been the regular column by Charles Seib and others in the *Washington Post*. It generally has been concerned with criticism of the media, including particularly the *Post,* but it occasionally has served as a starting place for debate within the organization. Letters to the editor are another possibility; on at least one occasion, the *New York Times* has used this channel to air disagreements within its staff. An increasing number of U.S. newspapers have been establishing "op-ed" (opposite the editorial page) sections, and these could also serve.

The staff of any news operation, print or broadcast, also deserves a role in the selection of the people under whose direction they will be working. That does not mean a right to make the final decision, or even a right of veto. It does mean a careful and serious sounding-out of opinion within the full staff; the editor or publisher who does so will at least understand his or her problems better if an unpopular choice is made. This kind of consultation is common, although not standard procedure, in many business organizations. It is standard procedure to varying extents in college faculties, where promotions in rank, hiring, and the appointment of department heads and deans are matters of earnest and often protracted conferral.

The chief barrier to the development of a more collegial newsroom in this country is the common attitude of those second in command, cited earlier. There are few jobs outside the military anymore that are freighted with as much unquestionable authority as those of city editor, managing editor, and editor (to name them in ascending order) of a major newspaper. Furthermore, there is a strong tradition of their rejoicing in it, and to the point where they are feared, or at least disliked. That stereotype has been seen for years in movies and comic strips and more lately on television. (The stereotype includes a heart of gold beneath the prickly exterior.) But reality feeds on stereotypes; they become role models, some psychologists would say, and reinforce the natural tendency to be even more of what they think a city editor should be. In a good many cases the heart of gold is omitted.

It is a group accustomed to command, and its members—even those of soft demeanor—will fight sharing or diluting their power. If they accepted that idea, however, there might be eventual improvement in the workings of American journalism.

That obviously is a personal judgment, and I should point out first that it is set out in reference to effectiveness, not normative considerations. In most countries in which journalism has moved toward the collegial idea there has been a great deal of moralizing mixed with the organizing; most of all, not surprisingly, in Italy. The first line of argument is in terms of democracy versus autocrats, sharing instead of exploitation, the inherent moral superiority of the oppressed over those corrupted not only by their own authority, but also by the vaguely evil establishment that they represent.

Such arguments, it seems to me, regardless of the satisfaction that they might give their proponents, are at best irrelevant to the business of improving the journalist's trade. The most persuasive case to be made, at least in this country, is a practical one.

There is a good possibility, it seems to me, that a larger role in policy and administration would help keep the best journalists in the profession longer and keep them more committed to the newspaper or broadcasting station for which they work.

The great majority of those who become journalists are, as we have seen, from the middle and professional class; they do not enter for upward mobility. Once in the profession, they find it an extraordinarily structured bureaucracy that has an obliterating momentum of its own. Sizable numbers leave within the first five years. These represent no great loss, nor should they be of much concern to the industry; trial and error in selecting a job is an old tradition, particularly in mobile America.

The best ones persevere and in many cases move up very quickly. They often acquire major responsibilities before they are thirty. And then, somewhere around forty, some begin to move out of the profession. Not all the movers physically vacate the premises; they simply settle into the system, often with both mind and conscience stored in a leak-proof container and carefully set aside. Others quit the profession and start looking elsewhere.

Among these, it is clear, are some of the most promising journalists of their generation. They are people who might be, or perhaps have been, Pulitzer prize winners or top-flight editors or broadcast journalists with audiences of millions. Everyone who has been around journalism for very long knows dozens of them. That includes journalism teachers, who get letters from them, inquiring about teaching jobs. They represent a lost investment for their employers and an even worse loss to the profession.

Most of them, I am convinced, quit primarily for a reason that was summed up by one of them who was well into a fine career at the *New York Times* at the age of forty. He was assistant editor of one of the paper's most important news sections. Since I was teaching in the journalism department in which he had studied, I was particularly interested in him—and particularly startled when he wrote me saying he wanted to get out.

When we talked about it later I asked him why. He obviously had thought about it a good deal. "Because I feel I don't have a damn thing to do with what the *New York Times is,"* he said.

There is no certainty that he would have stayed with the paper if he had been involved in the conference that made the decision to endorse

Richard Nixon instead of George McGovern in 1972 or his opinion solicited and carefully considered in the selection of a new managing editor. The fact that French and Italian journalists, once in the profession, almost never leave it proves little or nothing, since many other factors are clearly involved. Nevertheless there is evidence that indicates that the idea of more participation is worth assessing.

In the study made by John W. C. Johnstone and his colleagues, *The News People,* careful attention was given to the 38 percent who were not committed to remaining in their jobs. A small percentage of the sample planned to retire, but most were young, in the twenty-five to thirty-four age group. The researchers pointed out that "after the age of thirty-five most newsmen who plan to enter other fields of employment have already done so." Most of these simply hoped to find better jobs elsewhere in the media; some planned to get out altogether; but the 8.2 percent who were undecided interest the researchers most.

> This group constitutes an enigma, for it contains newsmen who clearly are among the most highly trained and among the most successful in the cohort. Undecideds are heavily overrepresented with college graduates, with advanced degree holders, and with graduates from elite colleges and universities. Moreover, average earnings in this group are high—almost $2,000 above the median for the age group—and more than a quarter (25.7 percent) work for nationally recognized news organizations. By all objective criteria, this group represents an elite among younger newsmen. Why, then, should these persons be so indecisive about remaining in the field? While a definitive answer to this question cannot be offered, [the data] suggest one explanation: namely, that these newsmen experience a considerable gap between their professional ideals and their opportunities to pursue these ideals in their work. . . . Undecideds are by far the most strongly committed to participant professional values, yet they also are the group least likely to report a high level of editorial autonomy. . . . It is not unlikely that newsmen oriented to this style of doing journalism either do experience more editorial constraints or *at least feel they do.*

Johnstone comes to the conclusion "that many of the best trained, best situated, and perhaps most skilled young newsmen in the field today are at least potential dropouts from the news media."[20]

All this sounds remarkably like a description of journalists who want to leave the *New York Times* or the National Broadcasting Company (NBC) News or the *Bloomington Herald-Telephone*—because they feel they have nothing to do with what those news enterprises *are.*

It is far from certain that a more collegial newsroom would increase the chances of their remaining. Considering the responsibility that both the profession and the rest of society assigns journalists, however, it seems an idea worth trying.

Into the 1980s: An Update

This book is based upon the premise that by the beginning of the 1980s an identifiable and definable era in Italian journalism had ended, and that, in great part because of the reform movement, some characteristics of both the profession and the industry were permanently altered. The fact that a writer decides that something is an "era" and that it is over does not, however, mean that the principal actors or the institutions in which they functioned have disappeared. This afterword, written in early 1982, is an update that will, of course, be in turn out of date by the time it is in print.

There were references earlier in this study to a trend toward more professionalization, less politicization, and therefore less factionalism in the Italian newspaper press. This was visible to some extent in the election of 1976 (see p. 170); the national election of 1979 demonstrated it clearly. An analysis of major dailies for that campaign indicated sharply fewer partisan campaign stories and more attention to happenings that seemed to threaten national unity, particularly the activities of terrorist groups.[1] The kidnapping and killing of Aldo Moro in the spring of 1978 jarred Italian journalists as had no other event since the end of the Second World War, and a growth of concern for national stability became visible. The Italian journalists' view of the world had become more serious.

The Legacy of *La Riforma*

The role of Journalists Committees had settled into what seems to be a stable pattern by the end of the decade; they were almost invisible during the 1979 campaign, with the exception of a confrontation at *La Stampa* of Turin about carrying advertising from, and news stories about, the MSI-DN. The Journalists Committee lost. The importance of party identification among committee members has also diminished. In conversations in late 1979 I heard this repeatedly; the old activists in once lively shops either had settled down or become bored. At *Il Giorno,* for years marked by noisy (although ineffective) agitation, a three-man Journalists Committee made up entirely of Communists was replaced in the voting of late

1979 by one made up of a mainline Socialist, a Christian Democrat from that party's conservative wing, and a Radical. "Party affiliation," a member of the new committee told me, "was simply a coincidence—in both cases."

This general decompression has not meant that the profession and the industry in Italy are back where they were before the reform movement began. Some of the original objectives are now achieved and automatically written into the national contract or codified in law (as an example of the latter, public disclosure of ownership and yearly balance sheets). As of 1980, most efforts by the organized profession were related to the hiring and firing of editors and the general political line of the newspapers; FNSI, the trade union, which installed new leadership in the early 1980s, was concentrating its activities on influencing the shape of the press subsidy bill.

Press Subsidies
That bill had not yet made it through the Italian Parliament at the end of 1981; most of the delay has been due to what is sometimes called "fine tuning" by American politicians. There has never been serious partisan opposition, as indicated earlier, and the general assumption is that passage is only a matter of time.

The Papers
Meanwhile the economic situation of publishers, with almost all properties in the hands of oligopolies interested largely in profit, remains difficult. From the early days of the Rizzoli empire there had been rumors of its financial shakiness, and in 1981–82 the enterprise began to come apart. *Corriere della Sera,* the flagship, began to lose circulation heavily, apparently because of the involvement of its editor and chief financial officer in the P2 scandal, which will be discussed later. In an attempt to settle some of its enormous debt, the corporation sold some of its properties (including all its television interests), closed down some, and put *Corriere* up for sale. No sale had been negotiated as late as the summer of 1982.

Party papers continued to decline, and the most important and strongest of the group was caught in a bizarre misadventure that diminished its stature and shattered its staff. In March of 1982 *L'Unità* carried a document that apparently proved that the Christian Democrats had paid the Red Brigades two million dollars as ransom for one of its officials; the document was a fabrication, passed to a trusting female reporter by her lover. The resulting scandal damaged not only *L'Unità* but the PCI, with echoes throughout the government.

Two of the national giornali d'informazione frequently discussed in the preceding pages were less important at the beginning of the 1980s than they had been a decade earlier. Circulation and advertising in *Il Giorno* and *Il Messaggero* did not decline sharply, but their influence did. This was not so much due to their own faults—although *Il Giorno* did somehow seem to lose character after Afeltra arrived, and *Il Messaggero* after Perrone departed—as to the rise of powerful competitors in their own home towns.

In Rome, Eugenio Scalfari's *La Repubblica* by 1980 had established itself as the country's most important political daily. Scalfari, a Socialist at odds with the mainstream faction led by Bettino Craxi, had made his paper into an important platform for leading politicians. In February, 1978, Aldo Moro, president of the Christian Democrats, called Scalfari to his office; in the interview that followed he opened the door for a rapprochement with the Communists. In other interviews, PCI leaders, including Enrico Berlinguer, responded in conciliatory terms, easing the way to the "governments by abstention" of Andreotti and Giovanni Spadolini that followed. That role, combined with the impression of integrity drawn from Scalfari's independence from conventional party rhetoric and a straightforward treatment of nonpolitical news, gave *La Repubblica* increasing prestige in contrast to an *Il Messaggero* that seemed not to know what it wanted to be and an *Il Tempo* that was the voice of a time long gone and an increasingly isolated social class.

The old dailies also lost some circulation, although not as much as expected by many, to the Roman edition of *Corriere della Sera*. Estimates from dependable industry sources were that *Corriere* had settled down to around twenty-five thousand copies daily, although it claimed seventy thousand.

Some reasons for the decline in prestige of *Il Giorno* were set out earlier (p. 159). In addition to these, the considerable success of Montanelli's *Il Giornale Nuovo* had an effect. *Il Giornale* probably took few readers away from *Il Giorno;* the erosion was more complex than that. For a good many years *Il Giorno* was the Milanese opposition to *Corriere,* and that role automatically gave it a certain cachet. As a counter to a more left-oriented *Corriere,* Montanelli's paper provided a more sharply defined opposition. *Il Giorno* has floundered in between, lacking both *Corriere*'s massive traditional prestige and the provocative personality of *Il Giornale.* Since 1979 *Il Giorno* has been for sale, but meanwhile ENI has continued to cover its deficits, the largest of any single daily in the country's newspaper history.

Once removed from the *scala mobile* ("consumer price index"), the price of individual copies of Italian newspapers had soared to 400 lire at the end of 1981 (and raising the real cost, even with persistent inflation;

with the lire at 1,200 to the dollar, an Italian daily at that point cost about thirty-three cents).

As a part of the concern with profitability, replacement editors increasingly were chosen on the basis of professional acceptability. The era of Spadolini, Ronchey, and Levi clearly was over; even Ottone, who followed Spadolini at *Corriere,* seemed a man of broad dimensions compared with Franco Di Bella, who succeeded him (see pp. 46–48). Di Bella was forced out in 1981, and his replacement, Alberto Cavallari, had a long history of concern for professional values. By the end of 1981, the only Italian newspaper editor who could be regarded as a major national figure was the elderly Indro Montanelli.

Di Bella was one of many casualties of the P2 scandal in the spring of 1981. The term *P2* was the designation of a secret Masonic lodge. (The P stands for *propaganda,* which in standard Italian has no pejorative connotation, simply referring to organized activity to sell an idea or doctrine.) Freemasonry is not illegal in Italy, but lodges must be registered; P2 was not. The scandal developed when the list of P2 members, for reasons irrelevant here, appeared in print. That in itself was uncommon in Italian journalism, and the presence of hundreds of names of major financiers, government officials, politicians, and other members of the country's functional elite provided powerful reinforcement for the traditional endemic suspicions about conspiracies. Only a few journalists were involved, but Di Bella was one of them. His was part of a pattern of ties to *Corriere* in the scandal. A financier named Roberto Calvi was preparing to buy, on behalf of the Banco Ambrosiana, 45 percent of the stock of Rizzoli, whose *Corriere della Sera* enterprises made up a major portion of the conglomerate. Two days after that news broke, the membership list for P2 appeared; Calvi was on it, and two days later he was arrested and charged with involvement in previous suspect financial activities. A total of four *Corriere* journalists—in addition to Di Bella, two regular staff members, and a collaboratore—were on the list of P2 members. Di Bella resigned after what amounted to a vote of censure by the staff; he was replaced by Alberto Cavallari.

Private Broadcasting
This medium to this point has increasingly taken on a commercial character, and with that development an increasing crystallization into chains. It has been predicted that within a few years the surviving *private* (nongovernment broadcasters) will be grouped into two or three networks.[2] This might be affected by regulatory legislation passed by the Italian Parliament; such legislation has been under consideration since 1980. Like the legislation providing subsidies to the newspaper press, its move-

ment has been slow. Whatever regulations come out of the process will probably be rooted largely in commercial considerations. Although some of the first "free" stations were established for political purposes, that importance is lessening; it is worth noting that during the campaign of 1979, the Rusconi chain, with five television stations in Rome, not only carried no political news but refused political advertising. It captured almost 50 percent of the private television audience, although there were an estimated forty Roman stations at that point. A review of program guides at the time of this writing indicates that most of the programming on major stations consisted of such once popular American series as Kojak and CHiPs.

The Order of Journalists

This system continues to function much as it has since its official establishment in 1963, but it seems to have acquired a few more opponents, and more important ones, than at the time the bulk of the research of this book was carried out. Chief among these has been Paolo Murialdi, who was president of FNSI for the decade of the 1970s and who has indicated his opposition on several occasions. There have been no organized initiatives to disestablish it, however, and both entry into, and the practice of, the profession continue to be controlled by the 1963 law.

And Others

The story of *Occhio,* the attempt to create a popular daily written in simple language (see footnote, p. 214) seemed to be coming to an end in 1982. *Occhio* was a carefully constructed and pretested publication. In addition to its presumed fifteen-hundred-word vocabulary, its owners hired a well-known consultant to British television, in the attempt to make the paper as visually appealing as the small screen. It acquired generous advertising contracts for the first year, and its beginning circulation was about one hundred thousand.

Occhio began to decline almost immediately, however; the editor was replaced, and the paper altered to make it more resemble the British sensational tabloids. Nothing seems to have helped. There is general agreement among Italian journalists that its passing will be no perceptible loss.

Alessandro Perrone, owner and editor of *Il Messaggero* during most of the decade of the 1970s who, upon finally losing that paper, retreated to the direction of *Il Secolo XIX* in Genoa, died in 1981.

Finally, it should be noted that Giovanni Spadolini, Il Professore who was the editor of *Il Resto del Carlino* and *Corriere della Sera,* became the head of the Italian government in June of 1981. He was the first person to hold that post since the end of the Second World War who was not a member of the Christian Democratic party (he is a member of the centrist, anti-clerical Republican party), and the first to have a lifelong continuing professional involvement in journalism.

Notes

Introduction

1. Harold Isaacs, *Scratches on Our Minds* (New York: John Day, 1958).
2. *Panorama,* April 28, 1977.

Chapter 1

1. *Informatutto* (Milan: Reader's Digest, 1971), pp. 720–37.
2. Angelo Del Boca, *Giornali in crisi* (Turin: Casa Editrice Aeda, 1968), pp. 88–89.
3. Del Boca, *Giornali in crisi,* p. 90.
4. *Panorama,* November 18, 1971.
5. *Corriere dello Sport* (Rome); *La Gazetta dello Sport* (Milan); *Stadio* (Bologna); *Tuttosport* (Turin).
6. Enzo Forcella, "Millecinquecento lettori," *Tempo Presente,* November, 1959, pp. 452–58.
7. Joseph M. Jones, *The Fifteen Weeks* (New York: Harcourt, Brace, and World, 1964).
8. Personal interview, March 8, 1973.
9. Ignazio Weiss, *Il potere di carta: il giornalismo ieri e oggi,* Itinerari d'oggi no. 6 (Turin: Unione Typographico Editore Torinese, 1965), p. 163.
10. Tullio De Mauro, in *La stampa italiana del neocapitalismo,* ed. Valerio Castronovo and Nicola Tranfaglia, Storia della stampa italiana, vol. 3 (Bari: Editori Laterza, 1976), p. 497.
11. "Come valuta i quotidiani e come giudica i giornalisti," *Prima Comunicazione* 42 (1977):55.
12. Castronovo and Tranfaglia, *La stampa italiana del neocapitalismo,* p. 477.
13. Castronovo and Tranfaglia, *La stampa italiana del neocapitalismo,* p. 469. De Mauro also cites as words "displeasing to purists" a number of others that have long been in common usage: *attualità, concentrare, comunicare, evadere,* for example.
14. Quoted in Castronovo and Tranfaglia, *La stampa italiana del neocapitalismo,* p. 478.
15. Giovanni Spadolini, "La stampa libere ieri, oggi e domani," *Nuova Antologia,* no. 2006 (1968):147–61.
16. *Informatutto,* 1971, p. 584.

17. *Informatutto,* 1971, p. 584.
18. Arrigo Levi, *Televisione all'italiana* (Milan: ETAS KOMPASS, 1969), p. 79.
19. *Panorama,* January 18, 1977.
20. *Washington Post,* July 25, 1976.
21. *Prima Comunicazione* (1977). Details of this research, including other findings, are discussed in chapter 9.

Chapter 2

1. *Il Giornale Nuovo,* June 25, 1974.
2. Renzo Di Rienzo in *L'Espresso,* November 13, 1977.
3. Personal interview, June 20, 1977.
4. Lino Januzzi, "Rapporto sui giornalisti-spia," *Tempo,* September 19, 1975.
5. Giovanni Spadolini, "La stampa libera, ieri, oggi e domani," *Nuova Antologia,* no. 2006 (1968):147–61.
6. Personal interview, April 22, 1975.
7. Alberto Ronchey, *Accadde in Italia 1968–1977* (Milan: Aldo Garzanti editore, 1977), p. 125.
8. Ronchey, *Accadde in Italia 1968–1977,* p. 124.
9. *Washington Post,* July 31, 1977.
10. *Washington Post,* August 16, 1977.
11. *Contratto nazionale di lavoro giornalistico,* January 1977–December 1978, p. 38 (official text).
12. *Code du travail,* art. L. 761-7, sec. 3; appears as appendix in official text of *Convention collective nationale de travail des journalistes,* p. 22.
13. Giampaolo Pansa, *Comprati e venduti* (Milan: Bompiani, 1977), p. 65.
14. Pansa, *Comprati e venduti,* p. 66.
15. Pansa, *Comprati e venduti,* p. 36.
16. *Panorama,* November 1, 1977.
17. *Corriere della Sera,* September 29, 1977.
18. Giampaolo Cresci, quoted in *Panorama,* November 1, 1977.

Chapter 3

1. Gay Talese, *The Kingdom and the Power* (New York: World Publishing Company, 1969), pp. 273–74.
2. *Il Regolamento* [Bylaws], *L'Ordinamento della professione di giornalista,* art. 44.
3. These figures were supplied by the central office of the Order of Journalists in 1977.
4. *Avanti!,* May 28, 1972.
5. *Rassegna,* no. 5 (May, 1972).
6. Angiolo Berti and Leonardo Azzarita, with Antonio Pandiscia and

Antonio Viali, eds, *L'Ordine dei giornalisti: ricostruzioni storico-giuridiche*, Studi e dibattiti sul giornalismo (Rome: L'Ordine dei giornalisti, 1974).

7. *L'Ordine dei giornalisti*, p. 127.

8. Official English translation from *Constitutional Administration in Italy* (Rome: Presidency of the Council of Ministers, 1976), pp. 143–44. Several detailed modifications of article 21 have been incorporated in later legislation—to cover new media, for example—but none of substance.

9. For a more complete account, see Paolo Murialdi, *La stampa italiana del dopoguerra 1943–1972*, Tempi nuovi no. 62 (Bari: Laterza, 1974), pp. 150–60.

10. *L'Ordine dei giornalisti*, p. 251.

11. *L'Ordine dei giornalisti*, pp. 244–45.

12. *L'Ordine dei giornalisti*, p. 151.

13. *Panorama*, September 20, 1980.

14. *Panorama*, July 24, 1975.

15. *Panorama*, April 20, 1976.

Chapter 4

1. *Agenda del giornalista 1976* (Rome: Centro di Documentazione Giornalistica, 1976), p. 455. Reprint of *Contratto nazionale di lavoro giornalistico*, 1976–1977 contract, art. 19.

2. *Contratto nazionale di lavoro giornalistico* 1977–1978, art. 23, p. 30.

3. Figures based on 1975–1976 contract, with amounts calculated at L850=$1.00.

4. "I funzionari della stampa," *Il Mondo*, August 23, 1960.

Chapter 5

1. Enrico Mattei, quoted in Ferruccio Borio, C. Granata, and S. Ronchetti, *Giornali nella tempesta* (Turin: Edizioni EDA, 1975), p. 95.

2. Paolo Murialdi, *La stampa italiana del dopoguerra 1943–1972*, Tempo nuovi no. 62 (Bari: Laterza, 1974), pp. 161–63. Murialdi is bitter because journalists were encouraged, including through offers of financial assistance, to get into ownership; none did.

3. Castronovo and Tranfaglia, *La stampa italiana del neocapitalismo*, p. 520.

4. Conversation with author, Turin, June 14, 1977.

5. Pansa, *Comprati e venduti*, pp. 23–24.

6. *Corriere della Sera*, February 25, 1972.

7. Quoted in Pansa, *Comprati e venduti*, p. 122.

8. As of 1975; from Castronovo and Tranfaglia, *La stampa italiana del neocapitalismo*, pp. 554, 557, 577. The figures are those claimed by the papers, and clearly are somewhat inflated.

9. Borio, Granata, and Ronchetti, *Giornali nella tempesta*, p. 249.

10. Borio, Granata, and Ronchetti, *Giornali nella tempesta*, p. 250.

11. Castronovo and Tranfaglia, *La stampa italiana del neocapitalismo*, p. 42.

12. Pansa, *Comprati e venduti*, p. 170.

13. Pansa, *Comprati e venduti*, p. 90.
14. *Panorama*, July 10, 1975.
15. Pansa, *Comprati e venduti*, chap. 10.
16. All figures from Pansa, *Comprati e venduti*, pp. 316–17.
17. Castronovo and Tranfaglia, *La stampa italiana del neocapitalismo*, p. 14.
18. *Panorama*, February 17, 1976.
19. Castronovo and Tranfaglia, *La stampa italiana del neocapitalismo*, app. pp. 514–82.
20. *Panorama*, February 17, 1976.

Chapter 6

1. Del Boca, *Giornali in crisi*, p. 175.
2. Quoted in Pansa, *Comprati e venduti*, p. 17.
3. Castronovo and Tranfaglia, *La stampa italiana del neocapitalismo*, pp. 17–18.
4. Quoted in Castronovo and Tranfaglia, *La stampa italiana del neocapitalismo*, p. 8.
5. Murialdi, *La stampa italiana*, pp. 244–46.
6. Murialdi, *La stampa italiana*, p. 245.
7. Murialdi, *La stampa italiana*, pp. 245–46. Murialdi does not provide figures for coverage of the Communists in *Corriere della Sera*.
8. Murialdi, *La stampa italiana*, pp. 529–53.
9. Castronovo and Tranfaglia, *La stampa italiana del neocapitalismo*, p. 19.
10. "Stampa Democratica," March 4, 1970.
11. Murialdi, *La stampa italiana*, p. 559.
12. Borio, Granata, and Ronchetti, *Giornali nella tempesta*, p. 251.
13. Borio, Granata, and Ronchetti, *Giornali nella tempesta*, p. 253.
14. Borio, Granata, and Ronchetti, *Giornali nella tempesta*, p. 290.
15. Borio, Granata, and Ronchetti, *Giornali nella tempesta*, p. 291.
16. Paolo Barile and Enzo Cheli, *La stampa quotidiana tra crisi e riforma: problemi giuridici e organizzativi* (Bologna: Società editrice Il Mulino, 1976), p. 443 n. 31.

Chapter 7

1. Guglielmo Rospigliosi, letter to the author, August 25, 1975.
2. *Il Tempo*, July 5, 1973.
3. Conversation with Felice La Rocca, January 13, 1970.
4. Personal interview, April 22, 1975.
5. Quoted in Pansa, *Comprati e venduti*, p. 69.
6. *La Stampa*, March 2, 1966.
7. *Paese Sera*, October 29, 1977.
8. Quoted in Pansa, *Comprati e venduti*, p. 276.
9. Pansa, *Comprati e venduti*, p. 250.

10. *Panorama,* June 3, 1975.
11. Interview, June 14, 1977.
12. Enrico Mattei; he does not name the paper, but it is clear from the context that he is talking about *La Stampa.*
13. *Corriere della Sera,* June 6, 1976.
14. Quoted in *Corriere della Sera,* June 16, 1976.
15. Pansa, *Comprati e venduti,* p. 160.
16. Quoted in Pansa, *Comprati e venduti,* p. 157.
17. *Il Resto del Carlino,* May 5, 1974.
18. Quoted in Pansa, *Comprati e venduti,* p. 107.
19. Quoted in Pansa, *Comprati e venduti,* p. 109.
20. Quoted in Pansa, *Comprati e venduti,* p. 109–10.
21. Quoted in Pansa, *Comprati e venduti,* p. 133.
22. Pansa, *Comprati e venduti,* p. 283.
23. Pansa, *Comprati e venduti,* p. 160.
24. Pansa, *Comprati e venduti,* p. 172.
25. Pansa, *Comprati e venduti,* p. 264.
26. *Panorama,* November 23, 1976.
27. *La Stampa,* June 16, 1976.
28. *Il Messaggero,* March 20, 1976.

Chapter 8

1. As the title for chapter 8, p. 277, *Comprati e venduti.*
2. Source: *Elezione politiche del 20 giugno 1976 resultati* (Rome: Ministry of the Interior, 1976). There are slight variations among even official sources on exact party percentages; for example, between these figures and those of the *Annuario statistico italiano, 1977.*
3. By the magazine *Prima Comunicazione,* quoted in Pansa, *Comprati e venduti,* p. 308.
4. Quoted in Pansa, *Comprati e venduti,* p. 309.
5. Pansa, *Comprati e venduti,* p. 330.
6. See "A Note on Sources" for specific titles.
7. Letter to author, May 9, 1977.
8. Pansa, *Comprati e venduti,* pp. 318–19.
9. *Oxford English Dictionary,* 1971 microfilm ed., s.v. "prudence."
10. According to the *Dizionario Garzanti della lingua italiana* (Milan: Aldo Garzanti editore, 1974), p. 641.
11. Pansa, *Comprati e venduti,* p. 52.
12. Pansa, *Comprati e venduti,* p. 52.

Chapter 9

1. John W. C. Johnstone, Edward J. Slawski, William W. Bowman, *The News People: A Sociological Portrait of American Journalists and Their Work* (Urbana: University of Illinois Press, 1976).

2. Jeremy Tunstall, *Journalists at Work: Special Correspondents: Their News Organizations, News Sources, and Competitor Colleagues,* Communications and Society Series, no. 1 (Beverly Hills, Calif.: Sage Publications, 1971).
3. "Come valuta i quotadiani e come giudica i giornalisti i lettore italiano," *Prima Comunicazione,* no. 42 (1977):67.
4. "Il profilo dei giornalisti," *Prima Comunicazione,* no. 42 (1977): 71.
5. Tunstall, *Journalists at Work,* p. 96.
6. Mariapia Gianotti and Claudio Castellani, "Sopratutto figli di papà," *Prima Comunicazione,* no. 40 (1977):68.
7. "Il profilo dei giornalisti," p. 71.
8. Tunstall, *Journalists at Work,* p. 31.
9. Tunstall, *Journalists at Work,* pp. 250–54.
10. Johnstone, Slawski, and Bowman, *The News People,* p. 142.
11. "Il profilo dei giornalisti," p. 70.
12. "Il profilo dei giornalisti," p. 71.
13. "Il profilo dei giornalisti," p. 71.
14. Johnstone, Slawski, and Bowman, *The News People,* p. 117.
15. Gianotti and Castellani, "Sopratutto figli di papà," pp. 67–73.
16. *Detroit Free Press,* October 6, 1978.
17. "Come valuta i quotadiani e come giudica i giornalisti il lettore italiano," *Prima Comunicazione,* no. 42 (1977):60.
18. Fred G. Bonfils of the *Denver Post.*
19. Conversation in Turin, June 15, 1977.
20. Johnstone, Slawski, and Bowman, *The News People,* pp. 147–48, emphasis added.

Into the 1980's: An Update

1. See William E. Porter, "The Mass Media in the Italian Elections of 1979," in *Italy at the Polls, 1979,* ed. Howard R. Penniman (Washington, D.C.: American Enterprise Institute, 1981), pp. 254–61.
2. By, among others, Gianni Fusato of the International Communications Agency office in Milan, who has made continuing studies of the development of private broadcasting.

A Note on Sources

The brief bibliography that follows is a listing of books that contributed directly to this study. Three were used extensively: Angelo Del Boca's *Giornali in crisi,* so far as I can determine the first data-based, analytical survey of the Italian press; Paolo Murialdi's *La stampa italiana del dopoguerra 1943–1972,* a rich, thoughtful analysis of the development of the Italian press as a part of Italian society during the indicated period; and Giampaolo Pansa's *Comprati e venduti,* a bright, gossipy chronicle of financiers, publishers, and editors during the 1970s. Pansa is particularly good on the reform period, and any reader of citations will observe that I leaned upon him considerably.

Two magazines also provided a continuing resource. *Panorama* is a weekly Italian newsmagazine resembling *Newsweek,* which covers the mass media in detail, including occasional overview articles updating the current state of various media industries. It is widely available in the United States. *Prima Comunicazione,* source of the Italian survey material in chapter 9, is a monthly magazine that critiques and reports Italian media in detail, particularly the printed press. It is one of the best magazines anywhere about journalism; better, in my judgment, than any single U.S. publication concerned with the field. Magazines come and go even more frequently in Italy than in this country, but as of this writing it still is being published.

A great many books touching on the media and the profession in Italy are not listed here because they are peripheral to the concerns of this study. The point has been made earlier that Italian journalists, over the past two decades, have become increasingly visible *personaggi* ("celebrities"); not only do many of them write their memoirs, but they also write books of personal commentary on life, and art, and dozens of other large topics. There is a trace of relevance in many of them, largely because of the sometimes-unintended insights they offer into the writers' minds, but they are too many to mention here.

Barile, Paolo, and Cheli, Enzo, eds. *La stampa quotadiana tra crisi e riforma: problemi giuridici e organizzativi.* Bologna: Società editrice Il Mulino, 1976.

Berti, Angiolo, and Azzarita, Leonardo; with Pandiscia, Antonio, and Viali, Antonio. *L'Ordine dei giornalisti: ricostruzioni storico-giuridiche.* Studi e dibattiti sul giornalismo. Rome: L'Ordine dei giornalisti, 1974.

Bocca, Giorgio. *Vita di giornalista: i segreti del mestiere raccontati da uno che viene dalla gavetta.* I Giornalibri, no. 3. Bari: Editori Laterza, 1979.

Borio, Ferruccio, with Granata, C., and Ronchetti, S. *Giornali nella tempesta.* Turin: Edizioni EDA, 1975.

Carcano, Giancarlo. *L'affare Rizzoli: editoria, banche e potere.* Dissensi no. 90. Bari: De Denato editore, 1978.

Castronovo, Valerio, and Tranfaglia, Nicola. *La stampa italiana del neocapitalismo.* Storia della stampa italiana, vol. 5. Bari: Editori Laterza, 1976.

———. *La stampa italiana nell'età liberale.* Storia della stampa italiana, vol. 3. Bari: Editori Laterza, 1979. [N.B.: volumes in this series have not been published in numerical sequence.]

De Gregorio, Domenico. *Teoria e storia della comunicazione sociale, parte prima: teoria generale ed evoluzione storica.* Roma: Edizione Bizzarri, 1975.

Del Boca, Angelo. *Giornali in crisi.* Turin: Casa Editrice Aeda, 1968.

Fattorello, Francesco. *Il giornalismo italiano.* Udine: Casa Editrice Idea, 1941.

Johnstone, John W. C.; Slawski, Edward J.; and Bowman, William W. *The News People: A Sociological Portrait of American Journalists and Their Work.* Urbana: University of Illinois Press, 1976.

Levi, Arrigo. *Televisione all'italiana.* Milan: ETAS KOMPASS, 1969.

Morganti, Piero. *Come si diventa giornalista?* Serie Struzzi Società no. 201. Turin: Giulio Einaudi editore, 1979.

Murialdi, Paolo. *Come si legge un giornale.* Universale Laterza no. 309. Bari: Editori Laterza, 1975.

———. *La stampa italiana del dopoguerra 1943–1972.* Tempi nuovi no. 62. Bari: Editori Laterza, 1974.

Palumbo, Marcello. *Il giornalista in europa.* Quaderni professionali no. 1. Rome: Editrice Europea, 1968.

Pansa, Giampaolo. *Comprati e venduti.* Milan: Bompiani, 1977.

Penniman, Howard R. *Italy at the Polls: The Parliamentary Elections of 1976.* Washington, D.C.: American Enterprise Institute for Public Policy Research, 1977.

———. *Italy at the Polls, 1979: A Study of the Parliamentary Elections.* Washington, D.C.: American Enterprise Institute for Public Policy Research, 1981.

Radius, Emilio. *Cinquant'anni di giornalismo.* Milan: Guido Miano Editore, 1969.

Silj, Alessandro. *Brigate rosse—stato: Lo scontro spettacolo nella regia della stampa quotadiana.* Florence: Vallechi, 1978.

Tunstall, Jeremy. *Journalists at Work: Specialist Correspondents: Their News Organizations, News Sources, and Competitor Colleagues.* Communication and Society series, no. 1. Beverly Hills, Calif.: Sage Publications, 1971.

Weiss, Ignazio. *Il potere di carta: il giornalismo ieri e oggi.* Itinerari d'oggi no. 6. Turin: Unione Typographico Editore Torinese, 1965.

Index

Abortion, 101, 124
"Above All, Daddy's Boys," 189
Advertising, 12, 106, 109, 162
Advertising, political, 153, 172, 210, 214
Advertising agencies, 106–7
Afeltra, Gaetano, 46, 147, 155, 159, 182
Against the Family (magazine), 74
Agenzia Generale Italiana Petrolio. See AGIP
Agenzia Nazionale Stampa Associata. See L'ANSA
Agnelli, Gianni (nephew), 97–99, 136–37
Agnelli, Giovanni (uncle), 96
Agnelli, Susanna, 97
Agnelli, Umberto, 97
Agnelli family, 44, 63, 96–97
AGIP (*Agenzia Generale Italiana Petrolio*), 104
Ajello, Aldo, 102
Albertini, Luigi, 96
"Album, the," 62. *See also* Registry of journalists
Alfa Romeo, 164–65
Almirante, Giorgio, 49
"Americanization," 12
American journalists, 91, 157–58, 202, 207; and party affiliation, 42, 158; public view of, 196, 198; on the reform movement, 145
American Newspaper Guild, 80, 202–4
American Society of Newspaper Editors, 198

Anaconda Copper, 95
Andreotti, Giulio, 45–47, 49, 73
Andreotti government, 8, 45
Angeli, Vanni, 58
Annabella (magazine), 154–55
Antelope Cobbler, 185
Apprentices, ix, 51, 54, 66; and salaries, 52, 85
Arena, L', 141–43
Arrests of journalists, 74–78
Articolo di fondo. See Editorials
Arts, 41
Assembly, 133–34, 136–37, 141, 143, 148–49
Associated Press, 88
Associazione della stampa periodica italiana, 61
Avanti!, 59–60, 114, 117, 199
Azzarita, Leonardo, 68

Bagdikian, Ben, 199
Banca dell'Agricoltura, bombing of, 125
Bank of Naples, 177
Baraghini, Marcello, 74, 77
Barzini, Luigi, Jr., 11, 30 n, 129, 145; and *Il Messaggero* editorship, 102, 131; as president of regional association, 80, 129
BBC (British Broadcasting Corporation), 20–21, 40, 107
Bechelloni, Giovanni, 122
Bella figura, la, 17, 25–27
Berger, Meyer (Mike), 53
Berlinguer, Enrico, 49, 164, 212
Bernstein, Carl, 31, 127

225

Betti, Marco, 34–35, 92
Beuve-Méry, Hubert, 119–20
Biennale of Venice, 38
"Black funds" (*fondi neri*), 161
Bo, Carlo, 12
Bombings, 1, 76, 121, 125–26
Bonuses, 84
Borio, Ferruccio, 102, 122
Bribes, 29–34
British Broadcasting Corporation. *See* BBC
Broadcasting, 20–21. *See also* Private broadcasting
Broun, Heywood, 80
Bustarelle, 30, 33. *See also* Bribes

Calvi, Roberto, 213
Caprotti, Alberto, 200
Carli, Guido, 41
Carnevali, Renzo, 150–51, 164
Caroli, Giuseppe, 85–86
Carter, Jimmy, 151
Castellani, Claudio, 188, 193
Castronovo, Valerio, 122, 179
Catholic church. *See* Roman Catholic church
Cattin, Carlo Donat, 129
Cavallari, Alberto, 213
Cefis, Eugenio, 44–45, 110, 163–64, 183; on buying newspapers, 94, 184; and Montedison, 105, 107, 133, 183–84
Censorship, 20, 64, 153
Center-left government, 45
Ceschia, Luciano, 130–31
Chamber of Deputies, 68, 76, 86, 124
Chicago Daily News, 158
Chicago Sun-Times, 158
Chicago Tribune, 100, 203
Christian Democrats (DC), 21, 36, 58, 124–26, 177, 200; on abortion, 123–24; and attacks on papers, 163; and coalition with Communists, 64; and divorce bill, 132, 155; and finances, 37–38, 133; and journalists' attitudes, 123, 131; and "opening to the left," 45, 117; and party loyalty, 40, 47; and relations with editors, 46–48, 101, 132; support for, 125, 172–73
Circulation of magazines, 19
Circulation of newspapers, 100, 106, 113–14, 175, 200, 211–212; and copies per thousand, 4, 18
Collegial newsroom, 202, 206, 209
Colombo, Furio, 130
Comic strips, 12, 113
Comitato di redazione. See Journalists Committees
Commissione Unica, 62–63, 66, 70
Committee for Freedom of the Press and for the Fight against Repression, 128
Communist party (PCI), 16, 36–41, 156, 210–12
Communists, 58, 129, 137, 142, 212
"Completeness of news," 125, 130, 140, 146, 164
Concessionàrio. See Advertising agencies
Conglomerates, 41, 103–6. *See also* AGIP, EGAM, ENI, IRI, and Montedison
Congress, U.S., 40, 48, 111
Constitutional Assembly, 63–64
Constitutional Court, 22, 68–69, 75
Consulta, 144, 160
Consultants, 34
Contract, national, 52, 79, 139, 203; of 1971, 130, 139–40; and political direction, 43–44; provisions of, 81–89; and style, journalistic, 167, 181
Contratto nazionale di lavoro giornalistico. See Contract, national
Contributors (*collaboratori*), 28
Cooperative publications, 156, 202
Copy editing, 14, 27–28, 143, 166–67
Corriere della Sera, 4, 8–9, 76, 125,

146, 151–52; changes in, 174–75; Di Bella as editor of, 48, 148–49, 182, 213; and divorce referendum, 155; and in-house contract, 82, 136–38; Missiroli as editor of, 80, 101, 130; and Montanelli, 43–44, 97, 137; Ottone as editor of, 28, 97, 137, 213; and ownership, 95–97, 105, 121, 137, 211; and profits and losses, 108, 137; Spadolini as editor of, 32, 44–45, 86–87, 96, 214–15; and staff pressures, 153–54, 158, 164; style of, 118

Corruption, 30, 35, 194; government and business and, 30, 73, 105, 123, 125–27, 161; Lockheed and, 29–30, 161, 185

Cossiga, Francesco, 171–72

Cost of living index, 6, 85, 212

Craxi, Bettino, 47, 212

Crespi, Benigno, 95

Crespi, Giulia Maria, 97, 137

Crespi family, 45, 96–97, 121

Critics, artistic, corruption of. *See* Corruption

Croce, Benedetto, 147

Cronaca nera, 56

Curzi, Alessandro, 77

Daily Worker, 116

Daley, Richard, 158

DC. *See* Christian Democrats

De Gasperi, Alcide, 123–24

De Gaulle, Charles, 40

Del Boca, Angelo, 4, 6, 129–30

De Lorenzo, Giovanni, 126–27

De Martino, Francesco, 46, 102, 163–64

Democratic Journalists Movement, 128

Democratic newsroom, 4, 119, 177, 205

Demoskopea, 172, 188

Departmental editor, ix, 138, 204–5

De Sanctis, Francesco, 15

Detroit Free Press, 109, 110

Di Bella, Franco, 46, 48, 148–49, 182, 213

Direttore responsabile, viii, ix. *See also Responsabile*

Disciplinary action, 71, 75

Discounts, 90. *See also Tessera*

Distribution of newspapers, 6, 9, 114

Divorce law, 132, 155–57

DOXA, 172

Economic development, Italian, 17, 32

Editore puro, 95, 97, 103

Editorials, 9, 170, 174

EGAM (*Ente Autonomo Gestione per le Aziende Minerarie Mettalurgiche*), 105

Einaudi, Luigi, 67, 148

Election, regional, 161

Election of 1953, 124

Election of 1979, 210

Election of 1976, 121, 153, 169–73, 176

Elections, 36, 152

ENI (*L'Ente Nazionale Idrocarburi*), 44, 104–5, 108, 133, 147, 162

Ente Autonomo Gestione per le Aziende Minerarie Metallurgiche. See EGAM

Ente Nazionale Idrocarburi, L'. See ENI

Esame di cultura generale, p. 51. *See also* Examination for the Order

Espresso, L', 115, 126, 163

EVN (Eurovision), 20

Examination for the Order, 52, 54–59

Examining commission, 57–58

Fallaci, Oriana, xi

Falvo, Adriano, 130

Fanfani, Amintore, 46–47, 73–74, 99, 132, 157, 161–62

Fascist regime, 51, 61–62, 66, 95–96, 100, 122, 156

Fascists, 76, 126–27, 133, 151, 153

Federation of Italian Newspaper Publishers. *See* FIEG
Federazione Nazionale della Stampa Italiana. See FNSI
Federstampa. See FNSI
Feltrinelli, Giangiacomo, 33
Feminists, Roman, 7, 22
Fenu, Giovanni, 166
FIAT, 94–95, 98–99
Fidora, Etrio, 74
FIEG (Federation of Italian Newspaper Publishers), 52
Field, Marshall, IV, 158
Fiengo, Raffaele, 178
Films, 39, 122. See also *Bella figura, la*
Financial relationships, 41, 47, 103–6, 184–85, 211, 213
Financial reporting, 35
First Amendment, 72, 205
"Flimsies," 31
FNSI (National Federation of the Italian Press), 52, 62, 79, 112, 124, 128–31, 139, 181, 203; criticism of, 91–92; and protest or arrest, 75, 77; and Salerno meeting, 127
Forcella, Enzo, 10, 17, 60, 128, 130
Foreign correspondents, 28, 109, 182
Forlani, Arnoldo, 46, 49
Fortini, Franco, 28
Fossati, Luigi, 182
Franco government, 98
Free and Responsible Press, A, (Hutchins), 198
Freedom of information, 68, 146
Freedom of Information Act, 146
Freedom of the press, 63, 65–67, 72, 146, 161, 165
Free expression, 63–64, 67, 77
"Free radio," 22–23. See also Private broadcasting
French contract (*code du travail*), 43
Fumagalli plot, 76

Gallup organization, 172, 197
Garimberti, Paolo, 88

Gazzetta del Popolo, 200
Ghirelli, Antonio, 148
Gianotti, Mariapia, 188, 193
Gilbert, Sari, 38
Giolitti, Giovanni, 32–33
Giornale, Nuovo, Il, 44, 108, 110, 176, 180, 212. See also Montanelli, Indro
Giornale dell'Emilia, 156
Giornali d'informazione, 8, 100, 105, 212
Giorno, Il, 8–9, 44–45, 52, 95 n, 152, 212; and divorce referendum, 155, 162; and ownership of, 104–5, 133; profits and losses of, 108, 162, 183; and staff relations, 132, 144, 159
"Girlie magazines," 22
Girotti, Raffaele, 46
Globo, Il, 105
Gonella, Guido, 149–50
Gorresio, Vittorio, 63–65, 80, 92, 99, 143
Government controls, 103
Government role in journalism, 72–73
Gramsci, Antonio, 16
Grisolia, M. Cristina, 122

Headlines, 133, 149–50, 164, 177, 201; on divorce bill, 155; in election campaigns, 72, 125, 170–71, 173; staff role in, 128, 138, 151–52, 158
Hearst, William Randolph, 73, 95, 183
Holidays, 2, 83–84
Hutchins, Robert M., 198

Individualists, Italians as, 24–25
Informazione, 145–46. See also "Completeness of news"
Ingrao, Pietro, 49
In-house contracts, 3, 81–82, 125, 147, 205; and journalistic style, 27, 167; provisions of, 131–36, 138–40, 148

International Herald-Tribune, 152
Interviews, personal, x–xii, 1, 3, 33–34, 119–21
Investigative reporting, 31
IRI (*Istituto per la Ricostruzione Industriale*), 104, 107
Isaacs, Harold, x
Isman, Fabio, 74, 77
Istituto Nazionale di Previdenza dei Giornalisti Italiani "Giovanni Amendola." See Medical insurance and pensions
Istituto per la Ricostruzione Industriale. See IRI
Italian Newspaper Publishers Federation, 81
Italian Press Officers Association, 34
Italian Secret Service. *See* SID
Izvestia, 116

Jacks, Allan, 88
Job security, 91
Job titles, Italian, viii–ix
Johnstone, John W. C., 187, 208
Journalistic style, 13–15, 159–60, 166–67; of *Corriere della Sera,* 118, 137, 174; of *Il Giornale Nuovo,* 28–29, 176
Journalist-politician, 48–49
Journalists Committees, 82, 134, 140, 144, 147, 167; and divorce referendum, 156; duties of, ix–x, 3–4, 138, 143; inactivity of, 141–42, 169, 210–11; and Milanese reformers, 128; and role in newsroom, 73, 143, 153–54, 157, 161–64, 167–68, 172

Knight, John S., 95
Krause, Petra, 152

Labor costs, 110. *See also* Overstaffing
La Malfa, Ugo, 49, 102
Language, Italian, 13–17, 216 n 13
L'ANSA (*Agenzia Nazionale Stampa Associata*), 78, 142
Lauro, Achille, 177

Lavoro, Il, 165
Law number, 69, 68–72
Leone, Giovanni, 45–46, 49, 73, 171
Levi, Arrigo, 20, 159, 170, 213; as editor of *La Stampa,* 97–98, 142–43, 153; professionalism of, 30, 182, 199–200
Liberals, 21, 45
Liebling, A. J., 199
Lippman, Walter, 11
Literacy rates, 13–14
Lockheed bribery scandal, 29, 170, 185
London Times, 27, 118
Longo, Luigi, 49
Los Angeles Times, 203
Luce, Henry, 95, 198
Luzzatti, Luigi, 61

McCormick, Robert, 73, 95
Magazines, 19
Makno, 197
Managing editor, ix
Manchester Guardian, 27
Mancini, Giacomo, 46
Manifesto, Il, 116, 185
Manzini, Luigi, 119
Martin, Graham, 31
Marxist-Leninist Party of Italy, 7
Mattei, Enrico (industrialist), 44, 104
Mattei, Enrico (journalist), 65, 143
Mattino, Il, 177, 184
Mauro, Ezio, 201
Mazzoni, Orazio, 177–78
Medical insurance and pensions, 60, 90
Messaggero, Il, 8, 11, 100, 110, 125, 144; and divorce referendum, 132, 155; and election eve interviews; and in-house contract, 82, 134–36; Missiroli as editor of, 101; ownership of, 105, 133; Perrone as editor of, 45, 95–96, 102, 159, 212; profits and losses of, 108

Messaggerro Publishing Company, Il, 134
Miceli, Vito, 32
Military coup attempt, 126–27
Minneapolis Star, 204
Minneapolis Tribune, 203
Ministry of Justice, 62, 70–71
Missiroli, Mario, 80, 96, 130
Modesti, Girolamo, 155–56
Monarchist party, 172, 177
Mondadori, 46
Monde, Le, 119, 147
Mondo, Il, 124, 147, 148
Montanelli, Indro, 80, 110, 142; and Cefis, 105, 108; and *Corriere,* 28, 43, 46, 97, 137
Montedison, 104–5, 134, 161–62, 164
Monti, Attilio, 44, 156
Moratti, Angelo, 97, 137
Moravia, Alberto, 14
Moro, Aldo, 73, 131, 210, 212
Morozzo della Rocca, Frederico, 153
Movimento Sociale Italiano. See MSI
Movimento Sociale Italiano–Destra Nazionale, 172
Mozzoni, Giulia Maria Crespi. *See* Crespi, Giulia Maria
MSI (Movimento Sociale Italiano), 31, 45, 115
Murialdi, Paolo, 80–81, 91, 124, 194; on the reform movement, 121, 130, 150, 179–80
Mussolini, Benito, 51, 61, 63, 96, 122, 166

National council of the Order, 70–71
National Federation of the Italian Press. *See* FNSI
National school of journalism, 66
Nazione, La, 156
Nenni, Pietro, 125
Networks, radio, 21–22
News analysis, 11
Newspaper circulation. *See* Circulation of newspapers

Newspaper Preservation Act, 111
Newspapers: and elitism, 17–18; establishment of (1979), 7; format of, 9–12; and names, 8 n, 18; per copy cost of, 6–7, 137, 212
News services, 32, 78, 142. See also *individual services*
News sources, 68–69, 126
Newsstands, 6
New York Journal-American, 101
New York Post, 203
New York Times, 46, 52–54, 100, 118, 120, 206–7
Nixon, Richard, 73

Occhio, 214
Office Radiodiffusion-Televisione Francaise, L', 40
Official Gazette, 55
Official Secrets Act, 77
Oltremare, 32
Ombudsman, 205
"1,500 Readers—Confessions of a Political Journalist," 10, 17
"Opening to the left," 45, 117
Ora, L', 74, 77
Order of Journalists, viii, x, 102, 112, 130; criticism of, 128, 214; history of, 61–68; professional examinations for, 54–60; and protest of arrests, 75–77. See also *Rassegna*
Oriane, Mario, 145
Orlando, Vittorio Emanuele, 124
Ottobre, 7
Ottone, Piero, 28, 46–48, 86, 178, 213; professionalism of, 97, 159, 199; and staff relationships, 138, 150, 154, 164–65, 182
Overstaffing, 104, 109–110, 114

Paese Sera, 100
Pajetta, Giancarlo, 171
Palermo meeting, 63–65
Pannella, Marco, 115
Panorama (magazine), 74, 115, 185; on Ottone, 46–47, 150; on Rizzoli, 177, 185

Pansa, Giampaolo, 99, 150, 169, 177, 185
Parliament, 37, 83, 102, 155, 176; commissions of, 111, 170; and Order of Journalists, 48–49, 51, 66; and RAI, 21, 151; and subsidies, 41, 111–12, 211
Partito Comunista Italiano (PCI). *See* Communist party
Partito Democratico di Unità Proletario, 116
Partito Socialista Italiano (PSI). *See* Socialist party and Socialists
Party headquarters, 36
Party loyalties, 41
Party papers, 112, 114–16, 126, 165–66, 193, 211
Party politics, 36–37, 40–42, 115
Pastone romano, 10–11, 137
PCI. *See* Communist party
Pella, Giuseppe, 125
Penal code, 75
Perrone, Alessandro, 138, 214; as editor of *Il Messaggero,* 101, 131, 133, 163
Perrone family, 44, 95–96, 101
Perrone, Mario, 100
Perrone, Pio, 100
Piccoli, Flaminio, 46–47
Pietra, Italo, 44–45, 74, 134, 147, 163–64
Pike, Otis, 32
Political leaders, 49
Politicization, 123, 160, 173–74, 202; and American journalists, 41–42, 50; of institutional structure, 35–41
Polls, 172, 197
Popolo, Il, 114, 117, 163, 173
Portugal, 2, 150
Praticante. See Apprentices
Pravda, 116
Prestigio (magazine), 120
Prima Comunicazione (magazine), 188
Private broadcasting, 23, 121, 202, 213–14. *See also* "Free radio"

Problemi dell'informazione magazine, 180
Professionalism, 42, 122, 128, 182–83, 195–96, 199. *See also* Levi, Arrigo; Ottone, Piero
Professional orders, 60–61, 67
Professionisti, 49, 61, 68, 81
Profits and losses, 103, 114, 136–37, 168, 180–81, 212; 1977 figures for, 108
Prova di idoneità professionale, 54. *See also* Examination for the Order
PSI. *See* Socialist party and Socialists
P2 scandal, 48 n, 211, 213
Pubblicisti, 49, 61, 68
Public relations, 34, 120, 183
Publishers' organization. *See* FIEG
Pulitzer, Joseph, 95

Qaddafi, Muammar al-, 94, 98
Quotidiano Donna, 7

Radical party, 115
Radicalautomobilisticodivorzista, 16, 163
Radio libere. See "Free radio"
Radiotelevisione Italiana. See RAI
RAI (*Radiotelevisione Italiana*), 19–23, 40, 107, 121, 151, 174–75
Rassegna, 59–60
Readership, 5, 10, 13–17, 19, 23. *See also* Journalistic style
Redattore, ix
Red Brigades, 69, 211
Reform, 4, 92; decline of, 170–75; and RAI, 21, 22; some reasons for, 23, 130, 140
Reform movement, 129, 143, 150; accomplishments of, vii, 93, 211; American journalists on, 145; beginnings of, 96, 122–23, 128–29, 149; decline in, 174, 178–83, 194
Regional councils, 69–71, 76
Registry of journalists, 62, 66, 68, 92. *See also Commissione Unica*

"Reporter power," 119, 142, 147, 202
Reporter's rights, 158
Repubblica, La, 46, 115, 212
Republica, 150
Republican party and Republicans, 21, 45
Responsabile, 132, 166, 199; definition and duties of, viii–ix, 73–74, 98
Resto del Carlino, Il, 8, 18, 32, 155–56, 182, 214
Retirement pay, 90
Riforma, La, 140. *See* Reform; Reform movement
Roman Catholic church, 36, 123–24, 155–57, 183
Ronchey, Alberto, 15, 48, 87, 97, 213
Rosenthal, A. M., 52, 54
Rossellini, Roberto, 39
Rothschild, 94
Rumor, Mariano, 171
Rusconi, Edilio, 101, 107–8, 131, 133, 161
Russo, Alfio, 96
Rizzoli, Angelo, 94, 177, 184; and financial relationships, 105–6, 184, 211; and ownership of *Corriere,* 46–47, 97, 138, 211

Salaries, 1–2, 80–81, 85–87, 114, 190–91
Salerno meeting, 127–28, 130–31
Salvatorelli, Luigi, 61
Salvemini, Gaetano, 148
Saragat, Giuseppe, 49, 127
Sassano, Marco, 59–60
Scalfari, Eugenio, 212
Scelba, Mario, 125
Secolo XIX, Il, 97, 100, 103, 138, 214
Secolo D'Italia, Il, 114–15
Secret Service, Italian. *See* SID
Securities and Exchange Commission hearings, 115 n
Segni, Antonio, 68

Segretario di redazione, ix
Seib, Charles, 205
Sensini, Alberto, 182
Servisio Informazione Difesa. See SID
Settimana corta. See Short week
Settimianale, Il (magazine), 149
Severance pay, 2, 43, 88, 111
Sexuality in mass media, 22
Short week, 82–83
SID (*Servisio Informazione Difesa*), 31–32, 76
Silone, Ignazio, 14
Sinistra, La, 7
SIPRA (*Società Italiana per la Pubblicità*), 107–8
Social Democrats, 36, 45, 117
Socialist party (PSI) and Socialists, 21, 58, 117, 137, 160; and election of 1976, 38, 117, 171; and support for Perrone on *Il Messaggero,* 132
Società Italiana per la Pubblicità. See SIPRA
Soviet Union, 98
Spadolini, Giovanni, 45, 49, 86, 118, 213–15; and bribes, 32, 33; as editor of *Corriere della Sera,* 44–45, 96, 174–75
"Special list," viii
Sport newspapers, 216 n 5
Stampa, La, 8, 30–31, 87, 125; and divorce referendum, 155; editors of, 45, 97, 142; profits and losses of, 108
Stampa italiana del dopoguerra, La (Murialdi), 179
Stampa italiana del neocapitalismo (Castronovo and Tranfaglia), 179
Sterling, Claire, 152
Stracquadanio, Raffaele, 133–34
Strikes, 78, 119, 133–34, 153, 159, 165
Student movements, 120, 123, 129, 151
Subsidies, 37–40, 78, 90, 107, 111, 184, 211

Sulzberger, Arthur Ochs, 95
Surveys, 23, 87, 188–94, 208
Sweden, 111
Swindle law, 124–25

Talese, Gay, 52
Telegiornale 1, 2 (TG1, TG2), 21, 151
Telegrafo, Il, 202
Telemalta, 94, 175
Tempo (magazine), 31–32, 34
Tempo, Il, 58, 105, 141, 153
Tempo Presente (magazine), 10
Terza pagina, la. See Third page
Tessera, 61–62
Test of professional competence. See Examination for the Order
Third page (*la terza pagina*), 11–12
Tito, Michele, 177
Togliatti, Palmiro, 16, 125
Torchia, Giorgio, 32
Trade Union (Italian Journalists'). See FNSI
Training (on the job), 53–54. See also Apprentices
Tranfaglia, Nicola, 179
Tunstall, Jeremy, 188. See also Surveys

Unione Petrolifera, 161
Unità, L', 5, 9, 39, 112–13, 165
United Press International. See UPI
United States Information Service, 118
UPI (United Press International), 88

Vacation, 2, 83–84
Vatican. See Roman Catholic church
Velinari, 31
Vittorelli, Paolo, 166
Voce Repubblicana, La, 129
Voice committee, 203, 205
Voting, 36

Wallace, DeWitt, 95
Wall Street Journal, 27, 203
Washington Post, 23, 38, 127, 152, 199, 205
Women journalists, xi, 154–55
Woodward, Robert, 31, 127
Working hours, 81, 82
Workers Movement for Socialism, 7

Zaccagnini, Benigno, 171
Zanetti, Armando, 64
Zicari, Giorgio, 76